Social Security Law in Switzerland

Social Security Law in Switzerland

Second Edition

Thomas Gächter
Dania Tremp

This book was originally published as a monograph in the International Encyclopaedia of Laws/Social Security Law.

Founding Editor: Roger Blanpain
General Editor: Frank Hendrickx
Volume Editor: Willy van Eeckhoutte

Stämpfli Publishers

Wolters Kluwer

Published by:
Kluwer Law International B.V.
PO Box 316
2400 AH Alphen aan den Rijn
The Netherlands
E-mail: international-sales@wolterskluwer.com
Website: lrus.wolterskluwer.com

Sold and distributed in North, Central and South America by:
Wolters Kluwer Legal & Regulatory U.S.
7201 McKinney Circle
Frederick, MD 21704
United States of America
Email: customer.service@wolterskluwer.com

Sold and Distributed in Switzerland by:
Stämpfli Publishers Ltd.
Wölflistr. 1, P.O. Box 5662
CH-3001 Berne
Switzerland
E-mail: verlag@staempfli.com
Phone: +41 31 300 66 44
Website: www.staempfliverlag.com

Sold and distributed in all other countries by:
Air Business Subscriptions
Rockwood House
Haywards Heath
West Sussex
RH16 3DH
United Kingdom
Email: international-customerservice@wolterskluwer.com

Printed on acid-free paper

ISBN 978-94-035-1774-2 (Kluwer)
ISBN 978-3-7272-2182-8 (Stämpfli)

e-Book: ISBN 978-94-035-1792-6
web-PDF: ISBN 978-94-035-1840-4

Printed in the United Kingdom.

The Authors

Prof Dr iur. Thomas Gächter holds the chair of Constitutional Law, Administrative Law and Social Security Law in the Faculty of Law at the University of Zurich, Switzerland (since 2006). He is at the same time Visiting Professor for Social Security Law and Health Law at the University of Lucerne, Switzerland. After university education at the Universities of Zurich and Louvain (Belgium), he graduated in Zurich and worked as a research assistant at the chair of Prof Dr Alfred Kölz (University of Zurich). In his practical work he was clerk of the justice at the Court of Administrative Law in Zurich. In 2002, he obtained a doctoral degree at the University of Zurich and was in the same year appointed as a private lecturer (*Privatdozent*) at the same university. From 2004 to 2006, he was associate professor at the University of Lucerne (Social Security Law) and research professor of the Swiss National Fund with a project on the Fundaments of Swiss Social Security Law at the University of Zurich. He teaches Constitutional Law, Administrative Law, Social Security Law and Health Law. He is author of a standard textbook in health law, as well as other publications in this field. He works on different projects in health law, social security law and administrative law.

Dr iur. Dania Tremp, lawyer, studied Law with a concentration in European law in the Faculty of Law at the University of Freiburg in Üechtland (Switzerland). She graduated with the Licentiate. Between 2005 and 2006 she did a variety of internships at court, in the administration and at law firms. In January 2007, after passing the bar examination, she was awarded the license to practice law by the Canton of Grisons. From January 2007 to December 2010 she worked as a research assistant for Professor Thomas Gächter in his capacity as chair of Constitutional Law, Administrative Law and Social Security Law at the University of Zurich. Her dissertation, which was accepted by the University of Zurich in 2010, was written on the subject of living organ donations. In addition to this topic, she has researched and published in the fields of constitutional law, administrative law, social security law and health law. Since January 2011 she has been working in the health administration of the Canton of Zurich.

The Authors

Table of Contents

Table of Contents

Table of Contents

List of Abbreviations

AHV	Old-Age and Survivors' Insurance Scheme (*Alters- und Hinterlassenenversicherung*)
AHVG	Federal Law on Old-Age and Survivors' Insurance (*Bundesgesetz vom 20. Dezember 1946 über die Alters- und Hinterlassenenversicherung, SR 831.10*)
AHVV	Ordinance on the Old-Age and Survivors' Insurance (*Verordnung vom 31. Oktober 1947 über die Alters- und Hinterlassenenversicherung, SR 831.101*)
AIG	Federal Law on Foreign Nationals and Integration (*Bundesgesetz vom 16. Dezember 2005 über die Ausländerinnen und Ausländer und über die Integration, Ausländer- und Integrationsgesetz, SR 142.20*)
ALV	Unemployment Insurance Scheme (*Arbeitslosenversicherung*)
ArG	Federal Law on the Protection of Work (*Bundesgesetz vom 13. März 1964 über die Arbeit in Industrie, Gewerbe und Handel, SR 822.11*)
AsylG	Federal Asylum Law (*Asylgesetz vom 26. Juni 1998, SR 142.31*)
ATSG	Federal Law on the General Section of the Social Insurance Law (*Bundesgesetz vom 6. Oktober 2000 über den Allgemeinen Teil des Sozialversicherungsrechts, SR 830.1*)
ATSV	Ordinance on the General Section of Social Insurance Law (*Verordnung vom 11. September 2002 über den Allgemeinen Teil des Sozialversicherungsrechts, SR 830.11*)
AVIG	Federal Law on the Unemployment Insurance (*Bundesgesetz vom 25. Juni 1982 über die obligatorische Arbeitslosenversicherung und die Insolvenzentschädigung, Arbeitslosenversicherungsgesetz, SR 837.0*)
AVIV	Unemployment Insurance Ordinance (*Verordnung vom 31. August 1983 über die obligatorische Arbeitslosenversicherung und die Insolvenzentschädigung, Arbeitslosenversicherungsverordnung, SR 837.02*)

List of Abbreviations

BAG	Federal Office of Public Health (*Bundesamt für Gesundheit*)
BGE	Ruling of the Federal Court
BGG	Federal Law on the Supreme Court (*Bundesgesetz vom 17. Juni 2005 über das Bundesgericht, Bundesgerichtsgesetz, SR 173.110*)
BSDA	Federal Law on Social Assistance and Loans to Swiss Nationals Abroad (*Bundesgesetz vom 21. März 1973 über Sozialhilfe und Darlehen an Schweizer Staatsangehörige im Ausland, SR 852.1*)
BSV	Federal Office of Social Insurance (*Bundesamt für Sozialversicherungen*)
BV	Federal Constitution of the Swiss Confederation (*Bundesverfassung der Schweizerischen Eidgenossenschaft vom 18. April 1999, SR 101*)
BVG	Federal Law on the Occupational Old-Age, Survivors' and Disability Provision (*Bundesgesetz vom 25. Juni 1982 über die berufliche Alters-, Hinterlassenen- und Invalidenvorsorge, SR 831.40*)
BVV 1	Ordinance on Supervision of Pension Funds (*Verordnung vom 10. und 22. Juni 2011 über die Aufsicht in der beruflichen Vorsorge, SR 831.435.1*)
BVV 2	Ordinance on the Occupational Old-Age, Survivors' and Disability (*Verordnung vom 18. April 1984 über die berufliche Alters-, Hinterlassenen- und Invalidenvorsorge, SR 831.441.1*)
BVV 3	Ordinance on Tax-Deductible Contributions to Accredited Forms of Provision (*Verordnung vom 13. November 1985 über die steuerliche Abzugsberechtigung für Beiträge an anerkannte Vorsorgeformen, SR 831.461.3*)
cf.	Confer (compare, consult)
CHF	Swiss Francs
e.g.	*Exempli Gratia* (For Example)
EC	European Community
ECHR	European Convention on the Protection of Human Rights and Fundamental Freedoms, dated 4 November 1950
ECJ	Court of Justice of the European Communities
EDI	Federal Department of Home Affairs (*Eidgenössisches Departement des Innern*)
EEA	European Economic Area
EEC	European Economic Community
EFB	Income Exemptions (*Einkommensfreibeträge*)
EFTA	European Free Trade Association

ELG	Federal Law on Supplementary Benefits to the Old-Age, Survivors' and Disability Insurance (*Bundesgesetz vom 6. Oktober 2006 über Ergänzungsleistungen zur Alters-, Hinterlassenen- und Invalidenversicherung, SR 831.30*)
ELV	Ordinance on Supplementary Benefits to the Old-Age, Survivors' and Disability Insurance (*Verordnung vom 15. Januar 1971 über die Ergänzungsleistungen zur Alters-, Hinterlassenen- und Invalidenversicherung, SR 831.301*)
EOG	Federal Law on Income Replacement for People Performing Military and Other Forms of Service and in Cases of Maternity (*Bundesgesetz vom 25. September 1952 über die Erwerbsersatzordnung für Dienstleistende und bei Mutterschaft, Erwerbsersatzgesetz, SR 834.1*)
EOV	Ordinance to the Law on Income Replacement (*Verordnung vom 24. November 2004 zum Erwerbsersatzgesetz, SR 834.11*)
et seq.	*Et Sequens/Sequentes* (and the following one/ones)
etc.	Et Cetera
EU	European Union
EU-15	European Union, fifteen Member States
EU-27	European Union, twenty-seven Member States
FamZG	Federal Law on the Family Allowances (*Bundesgesetz vom 24. März 2006 über die Familienzulagen, Familienzulagengesetz, SR 836.2*)
FamZV	Ordinance on Family Allowances (*Verordnung vom 31. Oktober 2007 über die Familienzulagen, Familienzulagenverordnung, SR 836.21*)
FINMA	Swiss Financial Market Supervisory Authority (*Eidgenössische Finanzmarktaufsicht*)
FLG	Federal Law on Family Allowances in Agriculture (*Bundesgesetz vom 20. Juni 1952 über die Familienzulagen in der Landwirtschaft, SR 836.1*)
FLV	Ordinance on Family Allowances in Agriculture (*Verordnung vom 11. November 1952 über die Familienzulagen in der Landwirtschaft, SR 836.11*)
FZA	Agreement on the Free Movement of People between Switzerland and the EC and its Member States (*Abkommen vom 21. Juni 1999 zwischen der Schweizerischen Eidgenossenschaft einerseits und der Europäischen Gemeinschaft und ihren Mitgliedstaaten andererseits über die Freizügigkeit, Freizügigkeitsabkommen, SR 0.142.112.681*)

List of Abbreviations

FZG	Federal Law on the Free Movement of People within the Scope of the Occupational Old-Age, Survivors' and Disability Provision (*Bundesgesetz vom 17. Dezember 1993 über die Freizügigkeit in der beruflichen Alters-, Hinterlassenen- und Invalidenvorsorge, Freizügigkeitsgesetz, SR 831.42*)
FZV	Ordinance on the Free Movement of People within the Scope of the Occupational Old-Age, Survivors' and Disability Provision (*Verordnung vom 3. Oktober 1994 über die Freizügigkeit in der beruflichen Alters-, Hinterlassenen- und Invalidenvorsorge, Freizügigkeitsverordnung, SR 831.425*)
i.e.	*Id Est* (that is/in other words)
ILO	International Labour Organization
IV	Disability Insurance Scheme (*Invalidenversicherung*)
IVG	Federal Law on Disability Insurance (*Bundesgesetz vom 19. Juni 1959 über die Invalidenversicherung, SR 831.20*)
IVV	Ordinance on the Disability Insurance (*Verordnung vom 17. Januar 1961 über die Invalidenversicherung, SR 831.201*)
IZU	Integration Allowances (*Integrationszulagen*)
KLV	Health Care Benefits Ordinance (*Verordnung des EDI vom 29. September 1995 über Leistungen in der obligatorischen Krankenpflegeversicherung, Krankenpflege-Leistungsverordnung, SR 832.112.31*)
KUVG	(Former) Federal Law on Health and Accident Insurance (*Kranken- und Unfallversicherungsgesetz*)
KVG	Federal Law on Health Insurance (*Bundesgesetz vom 18. März 1994 über die Krankenversicherung, SR 832.10*)
KVV	Health Insurance Ordinance (*Verordnung vom 27. Juni 1995 über die Krankenversicherung, SR 832.102*)
MVG	Federal Law on Military Insurance (*Bundesgesetz vom 19. Juni 1992 über die Militärversicherung, SR 833.1*)
MVV	Military Insurance Ordinance (*Verordnung vom 10. November 1993 über die Militärversicherung, SR 833.11*)
No.	Numero (Number)
OR	Federal Law on the Swiss Code of Obligations (*Bundesgesetz vom 30. März 1911 betreffend die Ergänzung des Schweizerischen Zivilgesetzbuches, Fünfter Teil: Obligationenrecht, SR 220*)
RAV	Regional Job Placement Centres (*regionale Arbeitsvermittlungszentren*)
SBB	Swiss Federal Railways (*Schweizerische Bundesbahnen*)
SECO	State Secretariat for Economic Affairs (*Staatssekretariat für Wirtschaft*)

SIL	Situational Benefits (*situationsbedingte Leistungen*)
SKOS	Swiss Conference on Social Welfare (*Schweizerische Konferenz für Sozialhilfe*)
SR	Classified Compilation of the Federal Legislation (*Systematische Sammlung des Bundesrechts*)
Suva	Swiss Accident Insurance Fund (*Schweizerische Unfallversicherungsanstalt*)
TARMED	Tarif Medical
UN	United Nations
UN Covenant I	International Covenant on Economic, Social and Cultural Rights, signed on 16 December 1966
UV	Accident Insurance Programme (*Unfallversicherung*)
UVG	Federal Law on the Accident Insurance (*Bundesgesetz vom 20. März 1981 über die Unfallversicherung, SR 832.20*)
UVV	Ordinance on the Accident Insurance (*Verordnung vom 20. Dezember 1982 über die Unfallversicherung, SR 832.202*)
VAG	Federal Insurance Supervision Law (*Bundesgesetz vom 17. Dezember 2004 betreffend die Aufsicht über Versicherungsunternehmen, Versicherungsaufsichtsgesetz, SR 961.01*)
VORA	Regulations on the Balancing of Risk in the Health Insurance Programme (*Verordnung vom 12. April 1995 über den Risikoausgleich in der Krankenversicherung, SR 832.112.1*)
VUV	Ordinance on the Prevention of Accidents and Occupational Diseases (*Verordnung vom 19. Dezember 1983 über die Verhütung von Unfallen und Berufskrankheiten, Verordnung über die Unfallverhütung, SR 832.30*)
VVG	Federal Law on the Insurance Contract (*Bundesgesetz vom 2. April 1908 über den Versicherungsvertrag, Versicherungsvertragsgesetz, SR 221.229.1*)
VwVG	Federal Law on the Administrative Procedure (*Bundesgesetz vom 20. Dezember 1968 über das Verwaltungsverfahren, Verwaltungsverfahrensgesetz, SR 172.021*)
ZGB	Federal Law on the Swiss Civil Code (*Schweizerisches Zivilgesetzbuch vom 10. Dezember 1907, SR 210*)
ZUG	Federal Law on the Legal Responsibility for the Support of the Needy (*Bundesgesetz über die Zuständigkeit für die Unterstützung Bedürftiger)*

List of Abbreviations

General Introduction

§1. General Background

I. Geography and Cultural Composition

1. Switzerland is a landlocked country in the heart of Western Europe, surrounded by Germany, Austria, Liechtenstein, Italy and France. It has a surface area of 41,285 square kilometres and its border measures 1,858 kilometres in circumference. Switzerland is divided into 26 cantons and 2,222 municipalities (January 2018). The country has 8,492,956 inhabitants (March 2018), with an average of 206 inhabitants per square kilometre. In comparison to other European countries, Switzerland is very densely populated. The population is concentrated largely in the urban regions in the midlands between Lake Geneva and Lake Constance. The more rural areas and peripheral regions are less populated.

2. Switzerland's population is not united by a single language. Traditionally, the four languages of the country are German, French, Italian and Romansh. German is spoken by 62.8% of the population, primarily in north-eastern and central Switzerland as well as in parts of Valais Canton. The French-speaking Swiss make up 22.9% of the population, and they live in the western part of the country. In Tessin and in certain regions of Grisons, Italian (8.2%) and – only in Grisons – Romansh (0.5%) are spoken, while 23.2% of the population either speaks another language or an additional main language (2016).

3. The various population groups living in Switzerland are marked by great diversity. At the end of March 2018, 2,132,650 foreign nationals were living in the country. The foreign portion of the permanent resident population is comparatively high at 25.11%. Only Liechtenstein and Luxembourg have higher percentages in Europe. A total of 83.7% of the foreign resident population comes from Europe (2016). Almost two-thirds of foreigners (66%) hail from one of the twenty-eight European Union countries (EU-28) or from countries with membership in the European Free Trade Association (EFTA).

II. Political System

A. *Federalism*

4. Switzerland consists of a total of twenty-six federal states (cantons) that differ widely in terms of their respective sizes and populations. Basically all cantons enjoy equal rights. Only six of the cantons have half of a canton-vote in Swiss plebiscites in which a federalist majority is required. These cantons are also only allowed to elect one – as opposed to two – members to the Council of States (the second house of parliament). The cantons are historically evolved polities that have pronounced autonomy in terms of law making, enforcement and organization.

B. *Governmental System*

5. The following key features of the Swiss political system are important to understanding some characteristics of Swiss legislation:

- The people can assume an oppositional role by dint of their direct democratic rights.
- The government is elected by parliament for a fixed term; the government may not be voted out of office preterm.
- The government may not dissolve parliament.
- There is collective government: decisions are made by a body whose members have equal rights.
- There is no head of state; the Federal President is merely the '*primus inter pares*' in the government.
- There is multiparty government (the concordance system).

C. *Importance of Direct Democracy*

6. The Swiss political system is strongly characterized by the people's direct democratic rights of participation. The people have extensive rights of participation at all levels of government. At the federal level there is the optional referendum on laws, the compulsory constitutional referendum, the referendum on treaties and the constitutional initiative. There is a possibility of initiating laws almost everywhere at the cantonal level. Moreover, cantonal governments are directly elected by the people.

7. The optional referendum on laws, existing since 1874, has had a special influence on the political system. The system is generally designated as concordance democracy, consensual democracy or referendum democracy. Common to all three of these terms is the stress they place on the importance of consensus and compromise for the Swiss style of government. In contrast to the parliamentary system, this is a political system in which governmental power is apportioned among the most important political currents, and parliament and government are controlled by the people through special referendums. The opposition role is thus assumed by the people together with individual parties. The system presupposes a certain stability and, above, all the presence of political determination to take collective action.

8. As a consequence of these highly developed referendum rights, the government and legislature are forced to draft bills with majority appeal so that they can survive any possible referendum. The result is that the legislative process becomes a search for a political compromise that can eventually withstand a referendum. This in turn strengthens the importance of the 'legislative process by consultation', by which interested groups can participate in the federal government's shaping of opinion and in the decision-making process. Corresponding political positions carry great weight, particularly when the participants in the legislative process by consultation (especially cantons, political parties and pressure groups) are so big and financially powerful that they are in a position to mount a referendum campaign.

9. And it is particularly in social security policy, which is dominated by various pressure groups, that the possibility of a referendum plays a decisive role in the political opinion-making process. The constant 'threat of intervention' by a referendum weakens the political system's ability to renew itself. By contrast, the popular initiative frequently functions as an agent of innovation, as an engine of the political system. But this happens less by way of direct acceptance of such initiatives through the people than through their indirect impact, as officials and parties are forced to develop direct or indirect counterproposals to the reform initiatives.

10. In the last decades a wide variety of popular social security initiatives have been launched, their object being the expansion, dismantling or reshaping of individual security systems. But in some cases these were retracted because parliament presented a counterproposal that was accepted by the initiative committee.

11. At the same time, various interest groups have repeatedly seized upon the instrument of the referendum to revise social security law. Most of these referendums have been rejected by the Swiss population, even when they would have resulted in a dismantling of the social system.

D. Parliament and Government

12. The Swiss Federal Constitution of 1874 as well as its successor of 1999 both stress the democratic principle by providing for the people's aforementioned direct rights of participation and by placing the parliament above a government only indirectly legitimized by the national elections. Furthermore, the Constitution establishes a relatively weak judiciary in comparison with other countries such as Germany.

13. The parliament, that is, the Federal Assembly, consists of two chambers. The National Council is the 'People's Parliament' and is composed of 200 members. The individual cantons form the electoral districts, and the number of seats is proportional to their population. The second chamber is the Council of States and has forty-six members. It is on an equal legal footing with the National Council in all essential matters. Every canton elects two members to the Council of States, but the six cantons possessing only half of a vote have merely a single seat in the chamber. Through its essentially equal distribution of seats, the Council of States strongly underscores the Swiss state's federalist element.

14. The government consists of seven ministers who are each elected by the united Federal Assembly for a period of four years and who constitute a council whose members are placed on an equal footing. Until the succeeding ministerial elections, parliament has no political means of forcing the council or one of the government ministers to resign. The ministers, who are usually chosen from the parliamentary ranks, must forfeit their seat in parliament following their election. But the separation between the executive and legislative branches of government is not as strict as in countries such as the United States, since the ministers can personally champion their bills in parliament and in the various commissions with great effectiveness.

E. Relationship with the European Union

15. Switzerland is not a member of the European Union (EU). The slim majority that decided to reject Switzerland's entrance into the European Economic Area (EEA) in 1992 led to an enduring political paralysis of Switzerland's European policy. Switzerland's relationship with the EU is essentially regulated by a series of bilateral treaties that have partially integrated Switzerland into the European market. This bilateral path has large support among the Swiss electorate. Accession to the EU is presently not on the political agenda.

16. Of particular importance is Switzerland's agreement with the EU and its Member States on the free movement of people, which has been in effect since 2002. This agreement guarantees citizens of an EU Member State free access to the Swiss job market and Swiss citizens unrestricted access to the European job market.

17. An important development in social security law has been the adoption of the body of coordinating European social law along with the Agreement on the Free Movement of People. Thanks to the agreement, Switzerland has become part of the European system. The Regulation 883/2004 and its implementing provisions have been valid for Switzerland since April 2012 (*see also* paragraphs 42 seq. below).

§2. HISTORICAL BACKGROUND

I. First Phase (Circa 1900)

18. With the rise of industrialization and liberal economic freedoms in the second half of the nineteenth century, the social nexus that had once provided a certain degree of social security was dissolved. The debate on who should be responsible for covering basic needs – the individual, the family, the employer, cooperative organizations or the state – increased in intensity. Liberal humanism, the Christian social ethic, and, in particular, the strength of the workers' movement provided a foundation for the development of the social welfare state.

19. Influenced by Otto von Bismarck, who had created a relatively self-contained state social security system for workers shortly before in the German Empire, the Swiss federal government was assigned a constitutional mandate in 1890 to establish health and accident insurance. The so-called Lex Forrer envisioned a well-coordinated system of health, accident and military insurance, but in the popular vote on 20 May 1900 the proposal failed due to the resistance of the groups that had an interest in preserving the existing health insurance schemes. In place of the failed bill, and after adoption of the uncontested Military Insurance Law in 1901, health and accident insurance took on fundamentally different forms in the Health and Accident Insurance Law (*Kranken- und Unfallversicherungsgesetz, KUVG*) of 1911: the existing health insurance funds were the sole providers of coverage in the health insurance programme, and the Suva Luzern (*Schweizerische Unfallversicherungsanstalt* (Swiss Accident Insurance Fund, Lucerne)) was the sole provider in the accident insurance scheme. This basic legislative decision had important long-term consequences: from this point on, when the social insurance system was expanded, consideration was given to the already existing private insurance entities and the system was not structured according to an overall plan. Swiss social security law was distinguished by a two-track structure, gaps and incoherence – at least until enactment of the Federal Law on the General Section of Social Insurance Law (*Bundesgesetz über den Allgemeinen Teil des Sozialversicherungsrechts, ATSG*) on 1 January 2003.

II. Second Phase (After the Second World War)

20. Influenced by the 1942 Beveridge Plan in England, which provided for a fallback system that covered the entire English population, the Swiss old-age and survivors' insurance scheme (*Alters- und Hinterlassenenversicherung, AHV*) was established in 1942 with the goal of protecting Switzerland's entire resident and working population against the consequences of aging or death of family providers. In the sequel, additional branches of social security were created and considerably expanded in terms of coverage. In response to the increasing migration of working populations, social insurance agreements were concluded with more than thirty states.

III. Third Phase (Around 2000)

21. After the individual social security laws were adapted to new social and legal development (equality of men and women, changes in family structure, etc.), the coordination of the fragmented legislation grew more important. Under the ATSG, which was passed on 6 October 2000 and went into effect in 2003, terms and institutes were uniformly defined, procedures were harmonized, and benefits were coordinated for all branches of social security (insofar as the individual laws declared the ATSG to be applicable, which was not the case with the Federal Law on the Occupational Old-Age, Survivors' and Disability Provision (*Bundesgesetz über die berufliche Alters-, Hinterlassenen- und Invalidenvorsorge, BVG*)). At the European level, the Agreement on the Free Movement of People, which Switzerland concluded on 21 June 1999 with the European Community (EC) and its Member States and which went into effect on 1 June 2002, coordinated the social security systems of the contracting states so that working people and their family members would not be disadvantaged in terms of social security when they moved from and to other states within the European internal market.

22. For the insured population, the most important step taken by legislators over the last two decades was the transformation of health insurance into a compulsory insurance scheme with a high level of benefits for all members of society in 1994/1996. The introduction of maternity insurance (including a maternity daily allowance) on 1 July 2005 was also of socio-political significance. As a result of this scheme, a binding constitutional mandate was finally carried out after a period of almost sixty years. Finally, the Federal Law on Family Allowances (*Bundesgesetz über die Familienzulagen, FamZG*), which aligns the various types and amounts of family allowances available in Switzerland, went into effect on 1 January 2009.

23. Another important development was the fifth revision of the Disability Insurance Law (*Bundesgesetz über die Invalidenversicherung, IVG*), which went into effect on 1 January 2008. The bill marked an important turning point in the Swiss social insurance system, since it was the first amendment of the law that sought to substantially contain, not expand, benefits. It was followed by the sixth revision of the same law, which had similar goals and strengthened the instruments for the reintegration of disabled people (2012).

24. Finally, the fourth revision of the Unemployment Insurance Law (*Arbeitslosenversicherungsgesetz, AVIG*) was put into effect on 1 April 2011 in order to restore financial balance to the unemployment insurance scheme (*Arbeitslosenversicherung, ALV*). This scheme was set up to provide support for around 100,000 unemployed people each year, but initial estimates were too optimistic and a large deficit was run up over the years. Higher contributions and reduced benefits have been introduced to reduce the mountain of debt.

IV. Formative Factors in the Development of Social Insurance Law

25. Social security systems more closely reflect prevailing political currents and the special features of a state than other legal structures. A look at the history of Swiss social insurance programmes shows a number of striking constants that left their mark on and continue to shape the socio-political discourse:

- Federalism (particularly as concerns implementation of processes and controversial political issues, e.g., the extent to which premiums can be reduced in the compulsory health insurance programme).
- (Semi-)direct democracy (popular initiatives: the opportunity to focus attention on pressing socio-political issues; and legislative referendums: the requirement that proposals be carefully formulated and balanced so that they can overcome the hurdles of legislative referendums).
- Liberalism and the (relatively) liberal stance of all Swiss political parties (aversion to compulsory insurance; aversion to centralized state solutions).

26. Of all these factors, it is the semi-direct democracy in Switzerland that has had the most profound impact on developments in comparison with other countries around the world. It is noteworthy that countries in which the population has a direct say in decisions on expanding or restructuring social welfare institutions (i.e., through referendums or popular initiatives) are characterized by more modest social security systems. In Switzerland, the majority has regularly voted down proposals for a comprehensive expansion of the social security system (e.g., Lex Forrer and Lex Schulthess (the first proposal for old-age and survivors' insurance in 1931); and the substantially scaled-down insurance scheme for a maternity daily allowance, which was not introduced until 2005, after several failed attempts).

§3. Sources of Social Security Law

I. General

27. The body of source material for social insurance law is complex. The norms that are required to resolve legal issues must often be sought at different levels of legislation and in different laws. Numerous regulations are elaborate and based on case law.

II. Legislation

A. Federal Constitution

28. Due to the efforts to create social insurance norms under public law, Switzerland's social insurance programmes – including those implemented by private bodies – are subject to the constitutional principles that are applicable to all state actions. These include the principles of constitutional action (Article 5, Swiss Federal Constitution (*Bundesverfassung, BV*)), fundamental rights (Articles 7–28, 35 et seq., BV) and the general procedural guarantees (Article 29, BV). By the same token, the social insurance courts are required to adhere to court procedural guarantees (Article 30, BV). Furthermore, Article 41 of the new Federal Constitution defines social goals. The legislative mandates (rules on jurisdiction) that are necessary for the individual branches of social insurance under the federal system can be found in Article 59, paragraphs 4 and 5, of the BV; Article 61, paragraphs 4 and 5, of the BV; and Articles 111–117 of the BV. In addition, the Constitution provides a foundation for the constitutionally compliant interpretations needed to apply social insurance law.

B. Federal Laws

29. There is often talk of the 'branches' of social insurance in conjunction with the various subsystems of social insurance law. Although many of these branches are closely related (e.g., various aspects of the AHV and the disability insurance scheme (*Invalidenversicherung, IV*)), most are based on an independent normative suborder.

30. This suborder (e.g., accident, health or unemployment insurance) is, in turn, normally based on a single (formal) federal law, which reflects the period in which the law was drafted. Family allowances law is regulated by two federal laws: the Law on Family Allowances in Agriculture (*Bundesgesetz über die Familienzulagen in der Landwirtschaft, FLG*) and the FamZG – though the latter is supplemented by cantonal regulations. By contrast, the occupational pension system, which is a special case in many ways, draws on important aspects of labour law from the Code of Obligations (*Obligationenrecht, OR*) and trust law from the Swiss Civil Code (*Zivilgesetzbuch, ZGB*) – in addition to its reliance on the BVG and the Law on the Free Movement of People within the Scope of the Occupational Old-Age, Survivors' and Disability Provision (*Freizügigkeitsgesetz, FZG*).

31. Social insurance law is essentially based on the following formal federal laws:

- Federal Law on the General Section of the Social Insurance Law, dated 6 October 2000 (*Bundesgesetz über den Allgemeinen Teil des Sozialversicherungsrechts, ATSG, SR 830.1*).
- Federal Law on Old-Age and Survivors' Insurance, dated 20 December 1946 (*Bundesgesetz über die Alters- und Hinterlassenenversicherung, AHVG, SR 831.10*).
- Federal Law on Disability Insurance, dated 19 June 1959 (*Bundesgesetz über die Invalidenversicherung, IVG, SR 831.20*).
- Federal Law on Supplementary Benefits to the Old-Age, Survivors' and Disability Insurance, dated 6 October 2006 (*Bundesgesetz über Ergänzungsleistungen zur Alters-, Hinterlassenen- und Invalidenversicherung, ELG, SR 831.30*).

- Federal Law on the Occupational Old-Age, Survivors' and Disability Provision, dated 25 June 1982 (*Bundesgesetz über die berufliche Alters-, Hinterlassenen- und Invalidenvorsorge, BVG, SR 831.40*).
- Federal Law on the Free Movement of People within the Scope of the Occupational Old-Age, Survivors' and Disability Provision, dated 17 December 1993 (*Freizügigkeitsgesetz, FZG, SR 831.42*).
- Federal Health Insurance Law, dated 18 March 1994 (*Bundesgesetz über die Krankenversicherung, KVG, SR 832.10*).
- Federal Accident Insurance Law, dated 20 March 1981 (*Bundesgesetz über die Unfallversicherung, UVG, SR 832.20*).
- Federal Military Insurance Law, dated 19 June 1992 (*Bundesgesetz über die Militärversicherung, MVG, SR 833.1*).
- Federal Law on Income Replacement for People Performing Military and Other Forms of Service and in Cases of Maternity, dated 25 September 1952 (*Erwerbsersatzgesetz, EOG, SR 834.1*).
- Federal Law on Family Allowances in Agriculture, dated 20 June 1952 (*Bundesgesetz über die Familienzulagen in der Landwirtschaft, FLG, SR 836.1*).
- Federal Family Allowance Law, dated 24 March 2006 (*Familienzulagengesetz, FamZG, SR 836.2*).
- Federal Law on the Unemployment Insurance (and Bankruptcy Compensation), dated 25 June 1982 (*Arbeitslosenversicherungsgesetz, AVIG, SR 837.0*).

32. In addition to the basic laws listed above, federal procedural laws play an important role in social insurance law. Article 55 of the ATSG states that, in the administrative procedure governing social insurance law, issues which are not exhaustively regulated in Articles 27–54 of the ATSG or in the individual laws themselves are subject to the Federal Administrative Procedure Law (*Verwaltungsverfahrensgesetz, VwVG, SR 172.021*). Furthermore, the Federal Supreme Court Law (*Bundesgerichtsgesetz, BGG, SR. 173.110*) provides a foundation for appealing social insurance law rulings before the Federal Supreme Court (Article 62, paragraph 1, ATSG).

33. The ATSG, which went into effect on 1 January 2003, coordinates federal social insurance law by defining the principles, concepts and important institutes of social insurance law, establishing a uniform procedure for social insurance, regulating the administration of justice, harmonizing benefits and structuring the recourse that can be sought from third parties by the social insurance programmes (Article 1, ATSG).

34. The provisions of the ATSG are applicable to the social insurance programmes that are regulated by federal law – if and to the extent that the laws governing these branches of social insurance make this stipulation (Article 2, ATSG). Contrary to what might be expected, the ATSG does not have a higher status but is placed on an equal footing with the other social insurance laws. Each law begins with a provision (Article 1) addressing whether and to what extent the norms of ATSG apply. Within the individual laws, the individual norms of the ATSG are declared to be applicable or inapplicable on a case-by-case basis.

35. Due to the structure of the occupational pension system, which is primarily governed by private law, the BVG and the FZG do not generally make reference to ATSG provisions – in other words, it is only in a narrowly defined field that direct links are made to the ATSG. In terms of coordination, it is regrettable that the occupational pension system is not regulated by the ATSG, but this is the result of a deliberate political decision. Because of this restriction, which runs counter to the framers' original intentions, the legislative project bore the official working title 'ATSG light' during its key drafting phase.

C. Cantonal Law

36. The introduction of the FamZG on 1 January 2009 sharply restricted one of the last large fields of cantonal social insurance legislation. Although the FamZG continues to allow the cantons a degree of freedom when structuring family allowances, key specifications are made by federal law. Nevertheless, the ELG has accorded the cantons a number of options for defining the supplementary benefits and the KVG gives them the competence for reducing health insurance premiums. Such norms form the basis of cantonal social insurance law.

37. Cantonal procedure law applies to various fields, particularly to the cantonal procedure governing social insurance jurisdiction. It must be noted, though, that this procedure is predefined by federal specifications (*see also* Article 61, ATSG).

D. International Law

38. In the area of United Nations (UN) convention law, a particularly important agreement for Swiss social insurance law is the International Covenant on Economic, Social and Cultural Rights, signed on 16 December 1966 (UN Covenant I, SR 0.103.1). A number of its mandates serve as guidelines for the development of social insurance law.

39. Of the numerous agreements that have been promoted by the International Labour Organization (ILO) and ratified by Switzerland, the documents of greatest interest are Convention No. 102 on Minimal Standards of Social Security (SR 0.831.102), Convention No. 128 on Invalidity, Old Age and Survivors' Benefits (SR 0.831.105), Convention No. 159 on Vocational Rehabilitation and Employment of Disabled Persons (SR 0.822.725.9), Convention No. 168 on Employment Promotion and Protection against Unemployment (SR 0.822.726.8), and Convention No. 173 on the Protection of Workers' Claims in the Event of the Employer's Insolvency (SR 0.822.727.3).

40. The Convention on the Protection of Human Rights and Fundamental Freedoms, dated 4 November 1950 (ECHR, SR 0.101), has had a profound influence on Swiss procedural law.

41. The European Code of Social Security, dated 16 April 1964 (SR 0.831.104), largely corresponds to ILO Convention No. 102 on Minimal Standards of Social Security. Despite repeated attempts, Switzerland has so far failed to ratify the European Social Charter due to political opposition.

42. Freedom of movement (a person's right to reside and work in other states together with his family members) is undermined if switching from the social insurance system of one state to that of another brings disadvantages. In order to guarantee this basic freedom, the EU possesses a highly developed system for coordinating social security structures. In the sectoral agreements – particularly the Agreement on the Free Movement of People between Switzerland and the EC and its Member States (*Freizügigkeitsabkommen, FZA, SR. 0.142.112.681*), which was signed on 21 June 1999 and went into effect on 1 June 2002 – Switzerland has committed to observing Regulation (EEC) No. 1408/71 of the Council, dated 14 June 1971, applying social security systems to employees, self-employed people and their family members who migrate within the community(SR 0.831.109.268.1); and employing the corresponding Implementation Regulation (EEC) No. 574/72. This has made Switzerland part of the European internal market. Even now, over fifteen years after the FZA went into effect, the adoption of EU law, including the dynamic, integration-friendly rulings of the Court of Justice of the European Communities (ECJ), poses a great challenge for Swiss jurists. As of April 2012, the new European rules (Regulation (EC) No. 883/2004 of the European Parliament and of the Council of 29 April 2004 on the coordination of social security systems, SR 0.831.109.268.1; Regulation (EC) No. 987/2009 of the European Parliament and of the Council of 16 September 2009 laying down the procedure for implementing Regulation (EC) No. 883/2004 on the coordination of social security systems, SR 0.831.109.268.11) are also applicable in the relation between Switzerland and the EU and its Member States.

43. Switzerland has signed social security agreements with more than forty states. These agreements regulate issues that are similar to those in the aforementioned EU regulations. However, in contrast to EU coordination law, the agreements are confined to a few branches of social insurance. In addition, there is no dynamic development in this area comparable to that in relations with the EU, since the agreements were not created with a view towards integration with other states. The Swiss-EU Agreement on the Free Movement of People and the EFTA-Agreement with Iceland, Liechtenstein and Norway (SR 0.632.31) – which has been adapted accordingly – largely replace bilateral social insurance agreements in their areas of application.

III. Regulations

A. *Ordinances*

44. As a rule, the aforementioned laws are defined more precisely in numerous ordinances that are issued by the Federal Council. The most important of these regulations incorporate the name of the respective law, e.g., the Ordinance on the Old-Age and Survivors' Insurance (*Verordnung über die Alters- und Hinterlassenenversicherung, AHVV*), the Ordinance on the Disability Insurance (*Verordnung über die Invalidenversicherung, IVV*) and the Ordinance on the Accident Insurance (*Verordnung über die Unfallversicherung, UVV*). But it is important to note that the remaining body of law governing ordinances is of enormous importance, too.

45. Furthermore, the subdelegated ordinances issued by the responsible federal department, such as the Health Care Benefits Ordinance (*Krankenpflege-Leistungsverordnung, KLV*), have a high degree of practical relevance. Regulations are of extraordinary importance in social insurance law. Key issues are often regulated at this level of legislation.

B. *Administrative Orders/Circular Orders*

46. To ensure the consistent and equitable legally compliant implementation of rules in the predominantly decentralized social insurance system, the supervisory authorities (the Federal Social Insurance Office, the Federal Health Office, and the State Secretariat for Economic Affairs (*Staatssekretariat für Wirtschaft, SECO*)) issue and publish a variety of administrative orders (guidelines, administrative regulations, directives, circular orders). These orders are not legal sources as such, but internal instructions for the implementation bodies. Although they are binding for these bodies, they are not binding for the insured people or courts. However, they are of *eminent practical importance* since the courts pay heed to these orders if they contain a persuasive interpretation of the law.

C. *The Law Governing Social Insurers*

47. Certain social insurance laws give the social insurance programmes a degree of freedom in shaping legal relationships. For example, the occupational pension funds are allowed to issue their own bodies of regulations governing occupational pensions that go beyond legal minimums. Interpretations of these regulations must consider the principles of the respective branches of social insurance and the minimum constitutional requirements.

IV. Adjudication

48. As in all areas of the law, rulings by high courts provide guidance and direction. Central concepts of social insurance law often require more precise definition (e.g., disability, reasonableness, adequate causality). Furthermore, despite the high level of detail in many individual regulations, there often remain gaps or contradictions in these regulations that must be clarified in practice. But it has also been shown that the system of laws derived from court decisions becomes less important if administrative orders and circulars exist. In such cases, the courts tend to adopt the solution of the administrative authority if laws and ordinances contain no other solution.

V. Labour Agreements

49. Minimum wages are sometimes negotiated in the collective agreements signed by trade unions and employers' organizations or by trade unions and a single employer. In principle, though, these agreements apply only to the employers and employees who are members of the trade unions and organizations that have signed them.

50. With the exception of the *Allgemeinverbindlicherklärung*, a declaration that makes collective agreements binding for all workers in a certain profession or branch of industry, there is no legal mechanism for extending these agreements' scope of application.

51. The impact of these agreements is much more limited in Switzerland than in other states in which the provisions of collective agreements form one of the most important pillars of the social security system. However, a few new points have been negotiated in recent collective agreements (e.g., the regulation and financing of early retirement in the construction industry by unions and the employers' associations).

Part I. The Institutions

Introduction

52. The fragmented structure of the Swiss social insurance system is a reflection of its formative factors. Many organizational features are difficult to understand without knowledge of their historical background.

53. A sound knowledge of the organizational structures and administrative processes is also highly important for legal practice. This knowledge is needed to determine what (procedural) rules are applicable, what legal action and legal remedies are available, and what scope of action is granted to the different insurance providers and implementation offices.

54. The decentralized implementation process, distributed across various insurance providers and administrative units, is a prominent feature of Swiss social insurance law. This extensive decentralization is a result of the highly developed Swiss form of *federalism*, which, at a minimum, leaves the execution of federal laws to the cantons. In contrast to other areas, though, the cantons are given little freedom to actually shape federal social insurance law. Furthermore, the decentralized implementation process has resulted in the necessity to supervise the various administrative units, which, in turn, must be carried out by additional, higher-level federal offices.

55. The insurance providers have very different legal forms. The spectrum runs from public institutions to various private organizational forms (corporations, foundations and cooperatives) that are charged with administering social insurance. The private forms include the 'other' registered accident insurers detailed in Article 68 of the UVG, private health insurance funds under Article 12 of the KVG, and private occupational pension funds under Article 48, paragraph 2, of the BVG.

56. There is no consistent definition of the commonly used term 'insurance provider' (*Versicherungsträger*). Usually this term refers to the entity that bears the main burden of administering a branch of insurance (e.g., the compensation funds in the AHV, the health insurance funds in the health insurance programme, and the Swiss Accident Insurance Fund (*Schweizerische Unfallversicherungsanstalt, Suva*) and other accident insurers in the accident insurance scheme).

57. The administrative units affiliated with an insurance provider (e.g., the compensation fund's branch offices) are called implementation offices (*Durchführungsstellen*). But the implementation offices or bodies are often not directly affiliated with an insurance provider. One example is the regional job placement centres (*Regionale Arbeitsvermittlungszentren, RAV*) in the ALV, which are set up not by the unemployment insurance funds, but by the cantons.

58. The insurance provider carries the risk only if it is responsible for the financial stability of the programme. This is the case if it sets insurance rates (subject to the approval of the supervisory authority). For example, it is the licensed insurers – not the compensation funds – that carry the risk in the Swiss Accident Insurance Fund, since the federal government, not the funds, sets the rates.

Chapter 1. Public Institutions

§1. Ministerial Departments

59. Under Swiss law, the ministries or departments no longer centrally implement social insurance law. Until 2005, a federal office directly administered military insurance, but now, due to a revision of the law, the Suva has taken over this task.

60. Due to the large number and diversity of the participating implementation bodies, the decentralized execution of social insurance law must be supervised by the federal government and the cantons. The supervisory authorities ensure the consistent application of laws and the proper performance of tasks.

61. Reflecting the multifaceted organization of implementation processes in the Swiss social insurance programmes, there is no central oversight in the hands of a single office.

62. The most important supervisory bodies are:

- The Federal Social Insurance Office (*Bundesamt für Sozialversicherungen, BSV*) for the following branches of insurance: old-age and survivors' insurance, disability insurance, supplementary benefits, the compensation scheme for lost income, as well as the occupational pension system (only for the Substitute Occupational Benefit Institution and the Guarantee Fund, for national and international pension funds, as well as for the pension funds of Swiss Federal Railways (*Schweizerische Bundesbahnen, SBB*), the National Bank, the Suva and the federal government pension fund (PUBLICA); Article 61, paragraph 2, and Article 63, paragraph 1, BVG, Article 3, paragraph 1, BVV 1).
- The Federal Office of Public Health (*Bundesamt für Gesundheit, BAG*) for accident and health insurance.
- The SECO for unemployment insurance.
- The cantons for the supervision of those funds in the occupational pension system that are not subject to federal oversight (Article 61, paragraph 1, BVG).
- The Swiss Financial Market Supervisory Authority (*Eidgenössische Finanzmarktaufsicht, FINMA*) for certain areas in the following three branches of insurance: the occupational pension system (Article 3, paragraph 4, BVV 1), the health insurance programme (supplementary insurance policies under the Insurance Contract Law (*Versicherungsvertragsgesetz, VVG*); Article 21, paragraph 2, KVG and Article 24, paragraph 2, KVV) and the accident insurance scheme (Article 68, paragraph 1a, UVG and Article 104, paragraph 3, UVV – though oversight by the FINMA is coordinated with that by the BAG (Article 104, paragraph 4, UVV)).

63. Oversight of the federal social insurance schemes is essentially the responsibility of the Swiss Federal Council (Article 76, ATSG, Article 64, BVG), but the council has delegated this authority to the Federal Department of Home Affairs (*Eidgenössisches Departement des Innern, EDI*).

64. All supervisory bodies act of their own motion. If third parties call the supervisory bodies' attention to problems or abuses, they must clarify and, if needed, remedy them.

65. The general orders issued by the supervisory bodies (circular orders, directives, etc.) are the most important preventative instrument of supervision. They are intended to guarantee consistent implementation processes at all implementation offices in Switzerland.

66. Furthermore, under various laws, the insurance providers are required to submit their regulations or statutes to the supervisory authorities for approval. This also serves the purpose of preventive oversight.

67. If a supervisory authority determines that the law has been violated, it may take punitive measures. In addition to warning and imposing conditions on the offices that have acted wrongfully, it may issue orders to settle individual cases. There is no uniform catalogue of measures in the various laws and regulations, but with respect to all their measures, the supervisory bodies must observe the principle of proportionality.

§2. Other Public Institutions

68. The individual branches of social insurance are run by different administrative bodies; organizational forms often differ considerably as well.

69. The public bodies in the Swiss system include independent public institutions such as both the Suva (Article 61, UVG) and the compensation agencies of the old-age and survivors' insurance scheme of the federation and the cantons (*Ausgleichskassen*; Articles 61 et seq., AHVG); dependent public institutions such as the unemployment insurance agencies (Article 77, paragraph 2, AVIG); independent public foundations such as the BVG Guarantee Fund (Articles 56 et seq., BVG) and the compensation fund of the old-age and survivors' insurance scheme (Article 107, paragraph 1, AHVG); as well as dependent foundations such as the compensation agencies of the ALV (Article 84, paragraph 1, AVIG). The public bodies established by private individuals are a special organizational form within the system and include the employers' compensation funds (Article 53, AHVG), the parity compensation funds (Article 54, AHVG) and the trade association funds in the ALV (Article 78, paragraph 1, AVIG).

70. The various branches of social insurance are mainly administered by the following public administrative bodies:

- Old-age and survivors' insurance: the compensation agencies of the federal government; cantonal compensation agencies; trade association compensation agencies; central compensation office.
- Disability insurance: disability insurance offices; compensation agencies of the AHV.
- Supplementary benefits: cantonal implementation office (in most cases the cantonal compensation agencies of the AHV).
- Occupational pensions: private and public pension funds that have no right to issue administrative decisions; Guarantee Fund, Substitute Occupational Benefit Institution.
- Accident insurance: the Suva, compensatory fund (*Ersatzkasse*), private insurance companies.
- Military insurance: administered by the Suva.
- Compensation scheme for lost income: implementation by the bodies of the AHV (cantonal or federal compensation agencies of the AHV, trade association compensation agencies).
- Family allowances in the agricultural sector: administration of child benefits by the cantonal compensation agencies of the AHV.
- Unemployment insurance: public compensation agencies of the ALV of the cantons, compensation agencies of the AHV; compensation office.

Chapter 2. Position and Authority of the Public Institutions

§1. The Compensation Agencies

71. The compensation agencies are involved in executing no fewer than six or seven federal social insurance laws. These are, in addition to old-age and survivors' insurance, disability insurance, compensation for lost income, unemployment insurance and family allowances, the compensation agencies are also allowed to take part (voluntarily) in administering accident insurance (collection of premiums; Article 93, paragraph 6, UVG and Article 118, paragraph 2, UVV). Moreover, the cantons often entrust the compensation agencies with implementing the law on supplementary benefits related to old-age, survivors' and disability insurance – the 'seventh branch' of the system. In some cantons, the compensation agencies also perform tasks related to premium reductions in the health insurance programme.

72. The tasks performed by the compensation agencies in the AHV include registering the people required to pay contributions, determining and collecting their contributions, as well as setting and providing benefits. They have similar responsibilities in the fields of disability insurance, compensation for lost income and family allowances in the agricultural sector. Despite this concentration of responsibilities in the hands of the compensation agencies, other important branches of the compulsory social insurance system (health insurance, accident insurance, occupational pensions) have been assigned to insurance providers that are quite different by nature. A certain concentration of implementation processes has resulted from the above-mentioned administration of military insurance by the Suva.

73. Although in terms of their specific function the compensation agencies primarily carry out the tasks listed in Article 63, paragraph 1, of the AHVG, they were conceived from the start with growth in mind. They can be assigned other responsibilities through legislation – as has occurred in the case of most of the affiliated branches mentioned at the start of this chapter. Similarly, under Article 63, paragraph 4, of the AHVG, they can be assigned, subject to approval by the Swiss Federal Council, further responsibilities by the cantons and the founding associations, particularly related to insurance coverage for soldiers and families.

74. However, it is impermissible, based on the law, to simply assign all tasks to the compensation agencies. The purpose of the examples listed in Article 63, paragraph 4, of the AHVG is probably best described by Binswanger when he writes of social insurance and 'related fields'. His comment makes clear that the areas transferred to the agencies must be closely linked to the field of social insurance without actually being a form of social insurance themselves.

75. There are three types of compensation agencies:

- The *trade association compensation agencies* are established by the trade associations in which employers and the self-employed are organized. The regulations of these agencies must be approved by the Federal Social Insurance Office for them to become legal entities. Once they have this approval, the agencies are independent public institutions and have official authority and the right to issue binding administrative decisions. The compensation agencies' highest body is their board of directors, which consists of representatives of the founding association and possibly representatives of employee organizations. This board appoints a director to manage the compensation agency. The members of the founding association – i.e., employers and self-employed people together with their staff – are affiliated with the trade association compensation agencies and have various participatory options.

- Every canton is required to establish a *cantonal compensation agency* as an independent public institution that is separate from the cantonal administration. Since the cantonal compensation agencies have an office in almost every municipality, they are easily accessible to the citizenry. In addition, they check whether all people in the canton who are required to pay contributions are registered. The largest group of people insured in the cantonal compensation agency consists of cantonal and municipal civil servants.
- Finally, the *federal government* administers two additional compensation agencies: the Swiss Compensation Fund for the staff of the federal administration, the Swiss courts and offices of the federal government; and the Swiss Compensation Office, which runs the voluntary AHV. Both compensation funds are public institutions of the federal government.

§2. Central Compensation Office

76. The central compensation office is headquartered in Geneva. Simply put, it is the central accounting and records office for the entire AHV. It also serves as the office for the scheme's compensation fund. It ensures that the individual compensation agencies transfer the balances from invoicing to the compensation fund of the AHV and that reimbursements are made from this fund to the individual compensation agencies.

§3. Compensation Fund of the AHV

77. The compensation fund is a public institution with a legal personality (Articles 107 et seq. AHVG). It has an administrative council whose eleven members are appointed by the Swiss Federal Council. The compensation fund is responsible for managing the assets of the AHV. Furthermore, it manages the assets of the IV, the compensation scheme for lost income, and the family allowances for the agricultural sector.

§4. Disability Insurance Offices

78. The offices of the IV are the actual administrative bodies of disability insurance. They are set up as independent authorities by every canton (Article 54, IVG).

It is also possible for several cantons to establish such offices collectively, but this has never happened. These offices have to be set up as independent institutions by the cantons.

79. Under Article 57, paragraph 1, of the IVG, the main responsibilities of these offices include registering people at an early stage; determining, supervising and carrying out early intervention measures; clarifying insurance-related requirements; clarifying the capacity of insured people to become integrated into working life; providing career counselling and job placement services; determining and supervising integration measures and providing the support needed by insured people during such measures; evaluating disabilities and need for assistance; issuing administrative decisions on the benefits of disability insurance; and, finally, performing public relations work.

80. In order to perform these tasks efficiently and professionally, the disability insurance offices must have the necessary services at their disposal (Article 59, paragraph 1, IVG). Since 1 January 2005, they have been assisted by interdisciplinary regional medical services (*regionale ärztliche Dienste*), whose job is to check medical eligibility requirements (Article 59, paragraph 2 and 2*bis*, IVG). A variety of disciplines are represented in the regional medical services, including general and internal medicine, orthopaedics, rheumatology, paediatrics and psychiatry (Article 48, IVV). The regional medical services fall under the direct oversight of the Federal Social Insurance Office, but are independent with respect to their medical decisions in particular cases (Article 59, paragraph 2, sentence 3, IVG and Article 50, IVV).

81. The disability insurance offices administer the insurance scheme in cooperation with the bodies of the AHV, particularly the compensation funds. Above all, the compensation funds are required to help clarify insurance-related requirements, set pensions and daily allowances, and pay pensions, daily allowances and attendance allowances. The compensation funds also collect contributions.

§5. The Cantonal Unemployment Insurance Agencies

82. The unemployment insurance agencies are the most important providers of unemployment insurance. Apart from these agencies there are between eight and ten further implementation offices responsible for administering unemployment insurance.

83. Each canton has a public unemployment insurance agency that must be established as a dependent public institution (Article 77, AVIG). Private agencies may be also established and are treated in Chapter 3.

84. The tasks performed by the agencies include clarifying eligibility for claims, suspending eligibility, providing benefits, administering working capital and submitting a periodical invoice to the compensation office.

85. The compensation agencies in the AHV collect the unemployment insurance contributions together with other contributions shared equally by employers and employees. They remit these contributions to the central compensation office, which in turn transfers the amounts to the unemployment insurance compensation fund.

§6. The Unemployment Insurance Compensation Fund and Office

86. The compensation fund is a legally dependent fund with its own accounting (Article 84, paragraph 1, AVIG). As in the AHV, the compensation fund in the ALV is administered by a compensation office run by the SECO.

§7. The Swiss Accident Insurance Fund (Suva)

87. In contrast to the systems discussed above, the providers of accident insurance have financial autonomy – that is, they charge premiums based on their own rates and provide benefits on their own account. There is no redistribution of funds with other insurers.

88. The Suva, founded in 1918 and headquartered in Lucerne, is a public institution with a legal personality that is subject to federal oversight by the BAG. Its basic organizational structures are described in Articles 61 et seq. of the UVG and it has considerable autonomy. The Suva runs agencies throughout Switzerland (Article 65, UVG).

89. The Suva has a partial monopoly on accident insurance, since all the 'other' insurers are allowed only to operate in fields that it does not control (*see also* Article 68, paragraph 1, UVG).

90. The delimitation of the Suva's area of operations is especially important since it has a monopoly on this area that excludes the other insurers. There are frequent disputes on the scope of this monopoly. In simplified terms, the companies and administrations that are compulsorily insured by the Suva are those that face a great or serious risk of accidents (e.g., industrial companies) or those for which coverage seems appropriate for other reasons (e.g., simpler procedures or better conditions for the insured companies). This latter group includes, for example, training workshops, workshops for the disabled and agencies that provide temporary workers. The types of companies listed in Article 66, paragraph 1, of the UVG are discussed in greater detail in the relevant regulations (Articles 73 et seq., UVV). Presently around 2,000,000 people are insured in the Suva.

91. The coexistence of the Suva and private insurers in the social accident insurance scheme has also been shaped by considerations grounded in economic constitutional law. When the UVG was framed, the Suva's monopoly was restricted to certain companies that face an especially high risk of accidents (Article 66, UVG and Articles 73 et seq., UVV). The remaining companies are allowed to freely choose private accident insurance providers (Articles 68 et seq., UVG), which compete with each other (*see* Chapter 3).

Chapter 3. Private Institutions

92. The private institutions that administer social insurance can be found in the ALV, among the registered accident insurance providers, the health insurance funds and the funds in the occupational pension system.

§1. The 'Other' Accident Insurers

93. People who are subject to compulsory accident insurance and for whom the Suva is not responsible are insured by what the provisions of the UVG refer to as 'other' providers. These providers are required to register in a public register maintained by the BAG.

94. These other insurance providers are listed exhaustively in the UVG and include private insurance institutions subject to the Insurance Supervision Law (*Versicherungsaufsichtsgesetz, VAG*); public accident insurance funds; and health insurance funds in the sense of the KVG. With the exception of the public accident insurance funds, the other providers in the accident insurance scheme are governed by private law. Since the public accident insurance funds are of little importance in practice, the other providers of accident insurance will be treated here.

95. Although these accident insurance providers are not governed by public law, they have a right to issue administrative decisions in cases dictated by law. In other words, private legal entities are awarded a public right to issue binding decisions.

96. The entity behind these other providers is the compensatory fund (*Ersatzkasse*) that they have set up (Article 72, paragraph 1, UVG). The insurers are required to transfer to this fund a portion of the revenue they earn from accident insurance premiums. This portion is calculated in such a way that the fund is able to pay all expenditures not covered by direct revenues and set aside sufficient reserves (Article 72, paragraph 2, UVG). The compensatory fund provides coverage for all insured people who are subject to compulsory accident insurance but whose employer, in violation of his duties, has failed to sign up with an accident insurance provider. The fund not only provides statutory benefits to these insured people but also collects substitute premiums from the negligent employer. In cases where the employer repeatedly and culpably violates his duty, these premiums may amount to ten times the actually owed premium. Moreover, the fund assumes the costs of the statutory benefits owed by one of the 'other' providers that have gone bankrupt (Article 73, paragraph 1, UVG).

97. The BAG has oversight over implementation – with the exception of the insurance providers governed by the VVG, which are organized by the FINMA.

§2. Health Insurance Funds

98. Under Article 12, paragraph 1, of the KVG, health insurance funds are private or public legal entities that do not pursue commercial aims, are primarily responsible for providing social health insurance and are recognized by the EDI.

99. Since commercial aims are ruled out, the only possible legal forms for these funds are those of association, foundation, cooperative, corporation with a non-commercial purpose and legal entity under cantonal public law (Article 12, paragraph 1, KVV). Most health insurance providers are established under private law and are therefore discussed in this chapter.

100. The approved insurers include health insurance funds as well as private insurance companies subject to the Insurance Supervision Law (Article 11, KVG). In 1990, 246 approved health insurers existed in Switzerland; in 2018, only 58. They vary greatly in size: the smallest funds have just a few hundred members, the largest around 850,000.

101. The health insurance providers perform public tasks and have a right to issue binding administrative decisions in their sphere of activity.

102. The health insurers are permitted to reinsure the benefits they provide under the KVG. The reinsurers require the approval of the EDI; (Article 14, KVG).

§3. Common Institutions of the Health Insurance Providers

103. The 'Common Institution under the Federal Health Insurance Law' is a foundation run by health insurance providers. It primarily serves the interests of those insured people whose insurance provider has gone bankrupt (Article 18, paragraph 2, KVG), providing them with statutory benefits (reimbursement claims, payment of health care provider fees).

104. In addition, the institution performs numerous tasks requiring central implementation, including those related to international commitments (Article 95a, KVG and Article 19, KVV) and the balancing of risks among health insurance providers (Article 105, paragraph 3, KVG; Regulations on the Balancing of Risk in the Health Insurance Programme, dated 12 April 1995 (*Verordnung über den Risikoausgleich in der Krankenversicherung, VORA*); SR 832.112.1).

§4. Private Unemployment Insurance Agencies

105. These private funds are set up by national, regional and cantonal trade unions and employers' organizations and must be authorized by the compensation office of the ALV.

106. The private agencies may limit their activities to a certain field or to a certain group of people or professions (Article 78, AVIG).

§5. Pension Funds in the Occupational Pension System

107. There are a large number of private pension funds in the occupational pension system.

108. Since the occupational pension system is essentially a funded system, it is highly important that the accrued assets are preserved. It is absolutely essential that the pension assets be transferred to an independent legal entity, which in most cases is a foundation. There are a number of other regulations that protect against the loss of pension assets, particularly the regulations dealing with the investment of foundation money with the employer.

109. The law mainly prescribes the possible legal forms of the registered pension funds for these entities (foundation, public institution; Article 48, paragraph 2, BVG). The funds are required to appoint an auditing agency bring in an approved expert on occupational pensions for certain reviews and ensure that employers and employees participate in administering the fund on an equal basis (Article 51, BVG). By far the most common organizational form is that of foundation. Cooperative pension funds are of little importance in practice. There continue to exist numerous public pension funds in Switzerland.

110. When the BVG was drafted, more than 18,000 pension funds existed in Switzerland. More than 80% of all employees already took part in a staff pension scheme. The prevailing view in the parliamentary consultations at the time was that achievements in the area of occupational pensions should be preserved, expanded and strengthened within the scope of a compulsory scheme. The legislators' declared goal was to enable the existing pension funds to meld organically with the new BVG occupational pension system. The idea of integrating existing structures into the newly created system can be described as a basic organizational principle of the occupational pension system and as one of the main causes of its extremely complex organizational structures.

111. One important consequence of this concept of integration is the rather extensive organizational autonomy of the pension funds in comparison to the autonomy accorded other social insurance providers (Article 49, paragraph 1, BVG). Even so, the private pension funds lack the authority to issue binding administrative decisions.

112. Pension funds that aim to take part in administering the obligatory occupational pension scheme must register with the supervisory authority and fulfil the related requirements (Article 48, paragraph 1, BVG). Around 1,440 of the existing

1,713 pension funds are currently registered (2016). This means that, compared to other social insurance programmes, the occupational pension system has by far the largest number of insurance providers.

113. Employers who are unable or do not want to establish their own pension funds (e.g., because they do not have enough employees or costs are considered too high) may join multi-employer or collective funds (*Gemeinschaftsstiftungen or Sammelstiftungen*) by entering into an affiliation contract (*Anschlussvertrag*). Multi-employer funds are pension funds in which a single fund is maintained with its own regulations for every employer (also called a *Vorsorgewerk*, or, loosely, pension arrangement). Multi-employer funds are usually established by and closely associated with financial institutions, despite being legally independent entities. In collective funds, the conditions and organization are the same for all the employers who are members. They are usually founded by professional associations.

114. Although the majority of insured people today belong to a multi-employer or collective fund, occupational pension law contains only a few rules devoted to their special characteristics. Often it is unclear whether these pension funds meet all the basic organizational decisions of the BVG. These problems have been recognized and are the subject of ongoing and completed revision work.

115. The Substitute Occupational Benefit Institution (*Auffangeinrichtung*) provided for in the BVG is a pension fund that serves as the 'sag wagon' of the occupational pension system. It takes in people who for certain reasons have not joined other pension funds (e.g., employers have failed to meet their duty to join a fund); who want to insure themselves voluntarily (Articles 44 et seq., BVG); who are not permitted to join another pension fund (recipients of a daily allowance from the ALV); or who do not wish to join another pension fund (voluntary membership on the part of the employer in this fund).

§6. THE GUARANTEE FUND IN THE OCCUPATIONAL PENSION SYSTEM

116. The Guarantee Fund provided for in the BVG is a kind of legally dictated reinsurance scheme for everyone in the occupational pension system. If a pension fund goes bankrupt, it guarantees not only the statutory benefits, but also, to a limited extent, the additional benefits stipulated in the fund's regulations. In this sense, its tasks can be compared to those of the compensatory fund (*Ersatzkasse*) in the accident insurance scheme. Furthermore, to the extent stipulated by law, it pays subsidies to the pension funds that have an unfavourable age structure and also performs numerous other tasks. The Guarantee Fund is financed by the affiliated pension funds.

117. The Federal Social Insurance Office (BSV) has oversight of the Guarantee Fund.

Part II. Contribution and Financing

Introduction

§1. General Remarks

118. The social insurance schemes are funded through different sources. In all branches of social insurance, the most important cash inflows come from the contributions paid by the insured people (and their employees) and the public authorities. The latter's share can be quite substantial depending on the branch.

119. In addition, funds flow back to the insurance schemes from recourse claims and cost sharing and shifting, though this income is only of secondary importance compared to the two sources mentioned above. It is only in the accident insurance scheme that income from recourse claims plays a more substantial role, though even here it lags behind premium income.

120. Finally, all the insurance schemes that set aside various financial reserves usually generate investment income, which flows back into the schemes. This portion of revenues is important primarily for the funds in the occupational pension system since they often manage substantial assets.

§2. Financing Models

121. Various models are used to finance the Swiss social insurance schemes. The most important models are the pay-as-you-go method, the funded method and the terminal funding method (*Rentendeckungsverfahren*, also known as the pay-as-you-go system with an intensified accumulation of reserves (*Rentenwertumlageverfahren)*).

122. In the pure *pay-as-you-go* system, the insurance schemes must plan revenues in such a way that they are sufficient to cover current costs. In other words, current revenues defray current costs. Since it is impossible to precisely plan revenues and costs in social insurance systems, the pay-as-you-go system is usually supplemented by a system of fluctuation reserves (fluctuation reserve fund). This version of the pay-as-you-go system, supplemented by a reserve fund, can be found in the old-age and survivors', disability, compulsory health and ALVs. It is also used to finance temporary accident insurance benefits. Military insurance, whose costs are covered almost entirely by the federal government, is based on a pure pay-as-you-go system (Article 82, MVG), as are the family allowances in the agricultural sector. However, the family allowance programme does not set aside fluctuation reserves but relies on the public authorities to cover shortfalls (Article 18, paragraph 4, FLG).

123. Under the *funded method* (or qualifying funded method (*Kapitaldeckungsverfahren* or *Anwartschaftsdeckungsverfahren*)), the expected benefits are financed in advance for every insured person, which naturally leads to a significant accumulation of capital in the various insurance funds. The funded method is employed by the occupational pension system, primarily to cover the risk of old age.

124. The *terminal funding method* (or *pay-as-you-go system with an intensified accumulation of reserves*) is a variation of the funded method. Under this system, reserves (actuarial reserves for pensions) must be set aside when the pension is set and are used to finance the future pension benefits. These methods are employed in the Swiss social security system for pensions from the accident insurance scheme.

§3. Special Systems

125. The following section takes a closer look at the contribution requirements of employed, self-employed and non-employed people. It must be noted at the start, though that some branches of insurance are funded in special ways – that is to say, independent of employment status.

126. For example, the requirement to pay contributions in the health insurance programme does not depend on a person's employment status. Nor are the health insurance premiums based on financial strength (i.e., on income or some other benchmark for setting premiums). All insured people pay the same amount – the so-called single premium – regardless of age and gender. The primary purpose of the single premium is to ensure solidarity between the healthy and the sick. Health insurance providers calculate the single premium in such a way as to cover all the current costs of the fund – including reserves – in a pay-as-you-go system.

127. The *military insurance scheme*, which can be seen as a pension system for people who suffer damage to their health during or as a result of service, is largely a non-contributory system: only a small number of military insurance benefits are financed by the premiums from professionally insured people (Article 2, paragraph 1, MVG). The federal government assumes the remaining costs (Article 81 paragraph 1, MVG). This means that military insurance is financed almost entirely through taxes.

128. The *supplementary benefits* – which provide support for the first pillar of the system by helping achieve the central aims of benefits – are also financed exclusively through taxes. Five-eighths of funding for the annual supplementary benefits comes from the federal government and three-eighth from the cantons (Article 13,

ELG). By contrast, the costs of illness and disability that are covered by the supplementary benefits programme are assumed entirely by the cantons (Article 16, ELG).

129. A small portion of the *family allowances for the agricultural sector* is covered by contributions from agricultural employers (Article 18, paragraph 1, FLG). The remaining portion – as well as family allowances for self-employed farmers – is financed by the federal government and the cantons from tax revenues (Article 18, paragraph 4, and Article 19, FLG).

Chapter 1. Contribution Regulations for Employees

§1. Field of Application

I. Territorial Field of Application

130. Contributions must in principle be paid for all employees who work *in Switzerland*, but there are exceptions to this rule depending on the branch of social insurance.

131. For example, employed people are also insured in the old-age and survivors'/IV (and are liable for contributions) if they work abroad for the Swiss government, for an international organization or for an aid organization funded by the federal government (Article 1a, paragraph 1, letter c, AHVG; Article 1b, IVG). In addition, people who work abroad for an employer headquartered in Switzerland may continue to be members of these schemes (Article 1a, paragraph 3, letter a, AHVG; Article 1b, IVG).

II. Personal Field of Application

132. Under Article 10 of the ATSG, people are considered employees if they carry out work in dependent positions and receive a salary for this work on the basis of the applicable individual law.

133. With respect to the liability for contributions and the amount paid, it is immaterial whether the insured person is hired under private or public law. The same rules are used to set premiums for all employees, regardless of whether they work in the private or public sector.

134. There are special systems (i.e., pension systems for civil servants) only for a limited number of employee categories in Switzerland: as a rule, only for the highest-level officials known as *Magistrate* (members of government, chief justices, etc.). The remaining employees belong to the normal insurance systems, which greatly simplifies structures and promotes the openness of the various employment systems.

§2. Calculation of Contributions

I. Basis of Calculations

A. Old-Age and Survivors' Insurance, Disability Insurance, Compensation Scheme for Lost Income

135. The key reference parameter is the 'relevant salary' (*massgebender Lohn*). With respect to old-age and survivors' insurance, disability insurance and the compensation scheme for lost income, contributions by and for employees are calculated as percentages of their relevant salary. The relevant salary also includes cost-of-living and other fringe benefits, commissions, bonuses, in-kind benefits, paid vacation, paid holidays, as well as tips if tips are an important component of pay (Article 5, paragraph 2, AHVG).

136. Other components of the salary, as well as items not falling under this term, are described in detail in Articles 7 et seq. of the AHVV. The importance of the 'relevant salary' goes far beyond the scope of the AHVG, since most of the other systems make repeated reference to this parameter.

B. Accident Insurance Scheme

137. A person's insured income is used to calculate accident insurance premiums. Insured income is based on the relevant salary in the sense of the AHVG, though certain deviations are necessary for calculations (Articles 22 et seq., UVV). Under Article 18 of the ATSG, the Swiss Federal Council is responsible for setting the maximum insured income. This maximum amount must ensure that the entire earnings of at least 92%, but not more than 96%, of all insured people are fully insured. Since 1 January 2016, the maximum insured income has been set at CHF 148,200 per year (Article 22, paragraph 1, UVV).

C. Unemployment Insurance Scheme

138. As in the accident insurance scheme, unemployment insurance contributions are set on the basis of the insured income, with the insured income reflecting the relevant salary as defined in the AHVG. The maximum insured income is the same as in the accident insurance scheme (CHF 148,200 per year; Article 3, paragraphs 1 and 2, AVIG).

D. Occupational Pension System

139. The basis for determining the insured income is essentially the relevant salary as defined in the AHVG (Article 7, paragraph 2, BVG). A certain portion of this salary is compulsorily insured. This portion, known as the 'coordinated salary', is defined by an upper limit and the 'coordination deduction' (*see also* Article 8, paragraph 1, BVG). Prior to the first revision of the BVG in 2005, the lower limit of the compulsorily insured salary (minimum salary) was identical with the coordination deduction. Both amounts corresponded to the maximum simple old-age pension from the AHV. In other words, 'coordination' meant that the second pillar of the pension system only insured amounts not covered by old-age and survivors' insurance.

140. As a result of the first revision of the BVG, most of which gradually went into effect in 2005, this system was slightly modified. As (mainly political) compensation for the reduction of the conversion rate from 7.2% to 6.8% (Article 14, paragraph 2, BVG), the minimum salary for compulsory insurance was lowered by around 20% to CHF 21,060. As of 1 January 2015, the minimum salary has been raised to CHF 21,150 (Article 7, paragraph 1, BVG). However, the lower limit of the coordinated salary was reduced only by around 10% to the present CHF 24,675 (Article 8, paragraph 1, BVG). As a result, these two key amounts diverge.

141. In other words, if the minimum salary of CHF 21,150 is exceeded, the coordinated salary is determined by subtracting the coordination deduction from the salary. Since the coordination deduction is higher today than the minimum limit for compulsory insurance, the coordinated salary is always rounded up to CHF 3,525, in keeping with Article 8, paragraph 2, of the BVG. In concrete terms, this means that it makes no difference whether an employee earns CHF 22,000 or 26,000. In both cases the coordinated salary (i.e., the salary minus the coordination deduction) is less than CHF 3,525. As a result, due to Article 8, paragraph 2, of the BVG, the same amount must be (compulsorily) insured with the pension fund for both insured people.

E. Family Allowances

142. Contributions to the family allowance schemes described in the FamZG and the FLG are calculated as percentages of a person's income that is subject to old-age and survivors' insurance contributions.

II. Contribution Amount

A. Equal Contributions

143. Both employers and employees are required to pay contributions to old-age and survivors' insurance, disability insurance, the compensation scheme for lost income and unemployment insurance. These contributions are divided in half, which is why one speaks of equal or 'parity' contributions.

144. However, only the employer owes the contributions to the compensation fund. When making salary payments, he deducts the contributions 'at the source' and transfers them along with his own contributions (cf. Article 14, paragraph 1, AHVG).

145. Contributions to the occupational pension system are not strictly equal as just described since the exact shares are based on the regulations of the respective pension fund (Article 66, paragraph 1, BVG). Nevertheless, the employer's contribution must be at least equal to the contributions paid by his employees ('collective parity of contributions', Article 66, paragraph 1, sentence 2, BVG). The employer owes the pension fund both portions of the contribution and deducts the employee's portion from his salary (Article 66, paragraphs 2 and 3, BVG).

B. *Other Contributions*

146. The contributions for coverage against industrial accidents and occupational illnesses are assumed entirely by employers (Article 91, paragraph 1, UVG). The contributions for coverage against non-industrial accidents are paid entirely by employees (Article 91, paragraph 2, UVG). It must be noted, though, that the employer owes the entire contribution and deducts the employee's portion from his salary (Article 91, paragraph 3, UVG).

147. Under Article 18, paragraph 1, of the FLG, contributions to the programme for family allowances in the agricultural sector amount to 2% of the relevant salary and are paid by employers if the allowances are not financed by tax revenues – as is the case for family allowances for small farmers (Article 18, paragraph 4, FLG, Article 19, FLG). Employees are not liable for the premium. In the case of cantonal family allowances for all other employees, the same rule typically applies, though the cantons are free to use other financing models as well (Article 17, paragraph 2j, FamZG).

C. *Old-Age and Survivors' Insurance, Disability Insurance, Compensation Scheme for Lost Income*

148. All told, the contributions to old-age and survivors' insurance, disability insurance and the compensation scheme for lost income amount to 10.3% of the relevant salary; employers and employees both pay 5.15%:

- 8.4% for old-age and survivors' insurance (Article 5, paragraph 1, and Article 13, AHVG; each pay 4.2%);
- 1.4% for disability insurance (Article 3, paragraph 1, IVG);
- 0.5% for the compensations scheme for lost income (Article 27, paragraph 2, EOG; Article 36 of the Ordinance to the Law on Income Replacement (*Verordnung zum Erwerbsersatzgesetz, EOV*)).

149. One special feature of these systems is the (deliberate) decision not to impose a limit on the basis of contributions. As a result, there is also no upper limit on the amount of the contributions, meaning that high income earners pay a considerable amount as solidarity.

150. If the relevant salary does not exceed CHF 2,300 per employer in a calendar year, contributions to old-age and survivors' insurance are collected only at the insured person's request (Article 14, paragraph 5, AHVG and Article 34d, paragraph 1, AHVV). This exception does not apply to people employed in private households (Article 34d, paragraph 2, AHVV).

151. If contributions are not paid for old-age and survivors' insurance, they are not paid for disability insurance, the compensation scheme for lost income, unemployment insurance, family allowance programmes and accident insurance, since in all these social insurance schemes liability for contributions is based on the AHVG.

D. Accident Insurance Scheme

152. The premiums are structured into insurance rate groups by the insurance providers and set as per mille of the insured salary. They consist of a net premium reflecting risk and also include additional charges for administrative costs, the costs involved in preventing accidents and occupational illnesses, as well as the cost-of-living allowances not covered by interest income (Article 92, paragraph 1, UVG). In order to calculate premiums for industrial accident insurance, the insurance providers assign companies to different rate classes according to business type and operational conditions and arrange them in levels within the classes. Special consideration is given to the risk of accidents and the state of accident prevention (Article 92, paragraph 2, UVG). The rates are set by the insurance providers and are not specified by law.

E. Unemployment Insurance Scheme

153. Until late 2010, the contributions paid by the insured people and their employers were set at 2% of the yearly salary up to a limit of CHF 126,000. Contributions were not charged on the portion of the salary above this limit and neither was the salary insured. As the result of a revision of the AVIG that went into effect in April 2011, a contribution of 2.2% was charged on the annual salary up to CHF 126,000 and an additional 'solidarity percent' was charged on the portion of the salary between CHF 126,000 and CHF 315,000 – though salaries were still only insured up to CHF 126,000. In June 2013 the Swiss parliament decided to charge the 'solidarity percent' on the whole income higher than CHF 126,000. In January 2016, the threshold for the annual salary was raised to CHF 148,200, meaning that up to that amount, 2.2% is charged, and above that, 1%.

F. Occupational Pension System

154. The law does not specify the amount of the contributions paid by employees and their employers to the occupational pension system (e.g., as percentages of the insured salaries). Rates are defined in each pension fund's applicable regulations (Article 66, paragraph 1, BVG).

G. Family Allowances

155. Under the FamZG, the cantons are responsible for determining how family allowances are to be financed (Article 16, paragraph 1, FamZG). It is left to them to decide whether the contributions are to be paid by the employer alone or by both the employer and his employees. As a rule, the cantons require contributions to be assumed and transferred by the employer. The amount of the contributions is also set at the cantonal level, which is why there is no uniform rate for all of Switzerland. In 2015, the contributions varied between 1.1% and 3.1% of the insured salary.

156. The family allowances for agricultural workers are financed in part by their employers. Employers pay a contribution of 2% on all cash and in-kind wages subject to old-age and survivors' insurance. Two-thirds of the remaining funding comes from the federal government, one-third from the respective canton.

§3. Reductions and Exemptions

157. The contribution system for employees has a relatively simple structure in Switzerland. There are only a few exceptions to the liability for contributions and only a few reasons for reducing contributions.

158. One of the most important exceptions to the requirement to pay contributions is the *minimum income limit*: contributions to old-age and survivors' insurance are generally only imposed on that part of the relevant salary that exceeds the predefined amount of CHF 2,300 per employer in a calendar year (Article 14, paragraph 5, AHVG and Article 34d, paragraph 1, AHVV). Contributions are paid on amounts under this threshold only at the employee's request. This exception does not apply to people employed in private households and to those employed by dance and theatrical producers' orchestras, producers of sound and audiovisual media, radio and television stations, as well as by schools specializing all areas of the arts (*see also* Article 34d, paragraph 2, AHVV). Due to the relevant references in the applicable laws, this rule also applies to the IV and the compensation scheme for lost income.

159. People insured by the old-age and survivors' insurance scheme are generally required to pay contributions as long as they continue to work (Article 3, paragraph 1, AHVG). But women who have turned 64 and men who have turned 65 are granted an exemption from contributions: they are only required to pay contributions on that part of their income as employees that exceeds CHF 1,400 per month or CHF 16,800 per year for each employer (Article 6*quater*, paragraph 1, AHVV). Due to the relevant references in the applicable laws, this rule also applies to the IV and the compensation for lost income.

§4. Administration

I. Old-Age and Survivors' Insurance, Disability Insurance, Compensation Scheme for Lost Income

160. In order to facilitate the collection of contributions, the employer is required to report every new employee to the responsible compensation agency within one month after the employee begins work. As confirmation, the agency issues the employer an insurance certificate that he must hand over to the insured person. In addition to the name of the issuing compensation agency, this document contains the insured person's surname, given name, insurance number, date of birth and the name of the employer subject to payment.

161. Under the insured person's number, the compensation agency maintains an individual account of the earned income on which contributions are paid until the person becomes eligible for a pension.

162. When an employer hires workers, he must submit his new employees' old-age and survivors' insurance ID to his compensation agency if it does not contain the compensation agency's code. Then he must report the changed salary to the compensation agency, which will adapt the next invoice for advance payment accordingly. At the end of the year, the compensation agency provides a yearly statement listing every employee and his salary for the past year. Finally, the employer receives the final invoice on the basis of this data.

163. Once the insured person is registered with the AHV, notice is given to the IV, the compensation scheme for lost income and the ALV, and the employer must not establish contact with them himself.

II. Accident Insurance Scheme

164. Nevertheless, the employer must take out accident insurance for his employees. He is required to contact an insurance provider and conclude the required contract, provided he is not compulsorily connected with Suva.

III. Unemployment Insurance Scheme

165. The contributions to the unemployment scheme are also collected by the compensation agencies, together with the contributions to the old-age and survivors' insurance, the disability insurance and the compensation scheme for lost income.

IV. Occupational Pension System

166. The employer is also responsible for his employees' occupational pensions. In most cases, after consulting with the employees, an employer will meet this responsibility by entering into an affiliation contract (*Anschlussvertrag*) with an existing pension fund. But he may also establish a pension foundation for his own company. This must be registered with the authorities in order to manage the occupational pensions.

V. Family Allowances

167. The employer is also required to register with a family compensation agency (*Familienausgleichskasse*). He pays contributions to this agency and is reimbursed by it for any benefits he pays himself. In many cases the responsible compensation agency also serves as a family compensation fund, but the employer is free to join another fund that grants him more favourable conditions.

Chapter 2. Contributions for the Self-Employed

§1. Field of Application

I. Territorial Field of Application

168. Due to their work status, self-employed people are covered only by old-age and survivors' insurance, disability insurance and the compensation scheme for lost income. These programmes in principle insure only self-employed people who work in Switzerland. However, due to the coordinating body of European social law, self-employed people who work abroad may also be subject to compulsory Swiss insurance if this is provided for by the relevant rules relating to conflict of laws (*see*, for example, Articles 11 et seq., Regulation (EC) No. 883/2004).

169. By contrast, under health insurance law, compulsory coverage is essentially linked to residence in Switzerland, not to employment. But due to the coordinating provisions of European social law, the place of employment, not the place of residence, may be the key criterion.

170. In addition, when it comes to international coverage under health insurance law, an important role is played by the special rules for cross-border commuters, who are only granted a right of choice if this right is established in the FZA.

II. Personal Field of Application

171. Article 12 of the ATSG defines self-employed people as individuals who earn income from work that is not pay for work performed as employees. They work in their own name and for their own account. They have an independent position and bear the economic risks of their activity themselves.

172. A self-employed person can be simultaneously categorized as an employee if he earns relevant employment income (Article 12, paragraph 2, ATSG). A self-employed person's liability for contributions is not dependent on whether he works full or part-time in his self-employed activity.

§2. Basis for the Calculation of Contributions

I. Old-Age and Survivors' Insurance, Disability Insurance, Compensation Scheme for Lost Income

173. The whole income that self-employed individuals earn from their self-employed activity forms the basis for calculating old-age and survivors' insurance contributions. Under Article 9, paragraph 1, of the AHVG, income from self-employment is defined as all earned income that is not paid to an individual for work he does as an employee.

174. This definition is explained in greater detail in Article 17 of the AHVV, which also cites the law governing direct federal taxation. The items listed in Article 9, paragraph 2, of the AHVG are deducted from gross earnings.

175. Earned income is determined by the cantonal tax authorities and reported to the compensation agency (Article 9, paragraph 3, AHVG). The tax assessment is binding for the compensation agency, except when it is obviously incorrect. In other words, when the AHVG was framed, a deliberate decision was made not to create a separate assessment system.

176. Income from self-employment is also used as the basis for calculating contributions in the IV and the compensation scheme for lost income (Article 3, paragraph 1, IVG; Article 27, paragraph 2, EOG).

II. Family Allowances

177. *See* paragraphs 186 et seq.

III. Voluntary Accident Insurance

178. The premiums for voluntary insurance under the UVG (Articles 4 et seq., UVG) are calculated on the basis of the insured salary defined in Article 22, paragraph 1, of the UVV. The insured salary is written into the contract and can be adjusted annually (Article 138, sentence 1, UVV). Freedom of contract is subject to certain limitations, since the maximum insured income (CHF 148,200 as of 2018) is set as a maximum limit for the insured salary and half of this (one-third in the case of family members) is defined as a minimum limit (Article 138, sentence 2, UVV).

179. Supplementary accident insurance policies are subject to the different provisions of the VVG and are not part of social insurance.

IV. Voluntary Occupational Pensions

180. A self-employed person may voluntarily join an occupational pension fund if he is insured under the first pillar of insurance coverage (old-age and survivors' insurance). The basis for calculating contributions – i.e., the insured salary – is determined in accordance with the regulations of the respective pension fund.

V. Voluntary Insurance for a Daily Sick-Pay Allowance

181. In practice, under both the KVG and the VVG, the premiums for a (voluntary) insurance policy for a daily sick-pay allowance are based on the following factors: the amount of the insured daily allowance (which is set in the contract), the duration of the claim for an allowance, and the start of the claim. If eligibility arises later (e.g., only on the thirtieth day instead of the tenth day after onset of the incapacity to work), the premiums are lower.

§3. AMOUNT OF CONTRIBUTION

I. Old-Age and Survivors' Insurance, Disability Insurance, Compensation Scheme for Lost Income

182. Under Article 8, paragraph 1, of the AHVG, an old-age and survivors' insurance contribution of 7.8% is charged on income from self-employment. For disability insurance and the compensation scheme for lost income, self-employed people pay an additional 1.4% and 0.5% of their income, respectively. All together they pay 9.7% of their income as contributions to these three schemes.

183. In order to ease the burden on self-employed people living in modest circumstances, a decreasing scale of contributions is applied. If annual income amounts to at least CHF 9,400 but no more than CHF 56,400, the contribution of 7.8% is reduced as low as 4.2% (Article 8, paragraph 1, AHVG and Article 21, AHVV). If income amounts to CHF 9,300 or less per year, a minimum contribution of CHF 392 is charged per year (Article 8, paragraph 2, AHVG).

184. As in the AHV, a decreasing contribution scale is used in the IV and the compensation scheme for lost income (Article 3, paragraph 1, IVG and Article 27, paragraph 2, EOG).

185. If income from a part-time self-employed activity does not exceed CHF 2,300 per calendar year, contributions are paid only at the self-employed person's request (Article 8, paragraph 2, AHVG and Article 19, AHVV).

II. Family Allowances

186. Until late 2012, self-employed persons were not subject to the family allowance scheme in all of the cantons. From January 2013 onwards, they have been mandatory subject to the FamZG. They have to select a family compensation agency and have to pay contributions according to the legislation of the cantons. Contributions have to be paid on the income lower than CHF 148,200 (Article 16, paragraph 4, FamZG).

187. In the case of family allowances for self-employed farmers, alpine herdsmen and professional fishermen, two-thirds of the funding comes from the federal government and one-third from the cantons. The eligible people are not required to pay contributions.

III. Voluntary Accident Insurance

188. With respect to voluntary accident insurance, insurance providers may charge a net premium that covers both industrial and the non-industrial accident coverage. The premium must be set in such a way that voluntary insurance is self-supporting – that is, it may not be provided at the expense of the compulsory accident insurance scheme.

IV. (Voluntary) Occupational Pensions

189. No general statement can be made about the amount of the contributions for voluntary occupational pensions. They depend on the applicable regulations for each fund.

V. Voluntary Insurance for a Daily Sick-Pay Allowance

190. *See* paragraph 181.

§4. Reductions and Exemptions

191. Women who have turned 64 and men who have turned 65 only pay contributions for old-age and survivors' insurance, disability insurance and the compensation scheme for lost income on that portion of their self-employment income that exceeds CHF 16,800 per year (Article 6*quater*, paragraph 2, AHVV).

192. In principle, all self-employment income is subject to contributions, meaning there is no minimum limit for the liability for contributions. But if the self-employed activity is pursued only part-time and the associated income amounts to less than CHF 2,300 per year, contributions are paid only at the insured person's request (Article 8, paragraph 2, AHVG and Article 19, AHVV).

193. If the insured person cannot reasonably be expected to pay the required contributions, these contributions can be reduced to an appropriate degree for a definite or indefinite time in response to a justified request. But they may not amount to less than the minimum contribution (Article 11, paragraph 1, AHVG). If payment of the minimum contribution causes severe hardship for the compulsorily insured person, he can be exempted if a justified request is submitted and a public authority named by the canton of residence has been consulted. The canton of residence pays the minimum amount on behalf of the insured person (Article 11, paragraph 2, AHVG).

§5. ADMINISTRATION

I. Old-Age and Survivors' Insurance, Disability Insurance, Compensation Scheme for Lost Income

194. Self-employed people are required to register of their own accord with a cantonal compensation agency or a compensation agency run by a trade association. This agency then checks whether the person in question can really be defined as self-employed in the sense of the AHVG. If the definition applies, the self-employed person makes advance payments (provisional contributions) that are set by the compensation agency on the basis of his probable income in the current contribution year. As a rule, these contributions are paid on a quarterly basis. If the person's income changes substantially, he must inform the compensation agency. The final contributions are set on the basis of the person's tax assessment. The compensation agency computes the difference between the final contributions and the advance payments and then collects the outstanding amount from the insured person or returns excessive advance contributions.

II. Family Allowances

195. Furthermore, self-employed people are required to register of their own accord with a compensation agency for family allowances (*Familienausgleichskasse*).

III. Voluntary Occupational Pension Plans, Voluntary Accident Insurance Scheme, Voluntary Insurance for a Daily Sick-Pay Allowance

196. If a self-employed person wishes to insure himself voluntarily in the occupational pension system, he can do so with the occupational pension fund run by his trade or industry association. If this is impossible, he is eligible to join the Substitute Occupational Benefit Institution (*Auffangeinrichtung*) of the occupational pension system.

197. A self-employed person may take out voluntary accident insurance with the accident insurance provider that administers the compulsory accident insurance scheme.

198. For the voluntary insurance for a daily sick-pay allowance, a self-employed person can freely choose between a large range of companies offering this kind of insurance. Apart from the health insurers, private companies offer different solutions to cover the risk.

Chapter 3. Contribution Regulations for Non-employed People

§1. Field of Application

199. In the insurance programmes for all members of society – old-age and survivors' insurance, disability insurance, the compensation scheme for lost income and health insurance – there is also compulsory coverage for non-employed people.

200. Furthermore, if they meet the applicable conditions, they are eligible for the family allowances covered by the FamZG.

§2. Basis for Calculating Contributions

I. Old-Age and Survivors' Insurance, Disability Insurance, Compensation Scheme for Lost Income

201. Non-employed people pay contributions according to their social circumstances. Assets and pension income form the basis for calculating contributions (Article 28, paragraph 1, AHVV). However, pension income does not include pensions from the IV. In the case of married people, contributions for each are calculated on the basis of half the couple's assets and pension income (Article 28, paragraph 4, AHVV).

202. Non-employed students up to the age of 25, as well as insured people who are supported by public funds or by third parties, pay the minimum contribution (Article 10, paragraph 2, AHVG). Non-employed people who receive supplementary benefits related to old-age and survivors'/disability insurance also pay the minimum contribution (Article 28, paragraph 6, AHVV).

II. Health Insurance

203. So-called single premiums are charged in the health insurance programme (*see also* paragraphs 126, 299 et seq.).

III. Family Allowances

204. Family allowances for non-employed people are financed by the cantons. Under certain circumstances, though, the cantons may introduce a requirement to pay contributions (Article 20, FamZG). At the moment, five cantons require non-employed people to co-finance the family allowances for which they are eligible. The contributions range from 5% to 20% of the old-age and survivors' insurance contribution if this contribution exceeds the minimum contribution defined in Article 10 of the AHVG.

§3. Amount of Contributions

I. Old-Age and Survivors' Insurance, Disability Insurance, Compensation Scheme for Lost Income

205. Depending on the insured people's social circumstances, contributions range between CHF 392 and 19,600 per year (Article 28, AHVV).

Assets or Annual Pension Income Multiplied by 20		*Annual Contribution Francs*	*Amount for each Additional 50,000 Francs in Either Assets or Annual Pension Income Multiplied by 20*
less than	300,000	392	–
	300,000	420	84
	1,750,000	2,856	126
	8,400,000 and greater	19,600	–

206. The AHVG is applied analogously to the calculation of contributions in the IV and the compensation scheme for lost income (Article 3, paragraph 1, IVG; Article 27, paragraph 2, EOG). The contributions take the form of additional charges on the contributions for old-age and survivors' insurance (Article 3, paragraph 2, IVG; Article 26, EOG). The disability insurance contributions range from CHF 65 to 3,250 per year, and the contributions for the compensation scheme for lost income from CHF 21 to 1,050 per year (Article 3, paragraph 1*bis*, IVG; Article 27, paragraph 2, EOG).

207. Non-employed spouses of employed or self-employed insurees are subject to a special rule: their contributions are considered paid if their spouses have paid contributions equal to at least double the minimum contribution (Article 3, paragraph 3, AHVG).

II. Health Insurance

208. *See* paragraphs 126, 299 et seq.

III. Family Allowances

209. *See* paragraph 204.

§4. Reductions and Exemptions

I. Old-Age and Survivors' Insurance, Disability Insurance, Compensation Scheme for Lost Income

210. If the insured person cannot reasonably be expected to pay the required contributions, these contributions can be reduced to an appropriate degree for a definite or indefinite time in response to a justified request. But they may not amount to less than the minimum contribution (Article 11, paragraph 1, AHVG). If payment of the minimum contribution causes severe hardship for the compulsorily insured person, he can be exempted if a justified request is submitted and a public authority named by the canton of residence has been consulted. The canton of residence pays the minimum amount on behalf of the insured person (Article 11, paragraph 2, AHVG).

II. Health Insurance

211. The single premium may lead to an intolerable financial burden for financially disadvantaged insured people. This consideration gave rise to Article 65 of the KVG, which provides for state support in reducing premiums. The cantons have been charged with implementing premium reductions and have been given a great deal of autonomy to do so. The models vary widely between the cantons. Article 65, paragraph 1, of the KVG sets forth the guiding principle that the cantons must grant premium reductions to insured people 'in modest economic circumstances'.

212. Furthermore, since 1 January 2006, the cantons have been required to reduce premiums by at least 50% for children and young adults in 'lower- and middle-income groups' (Article 65, paragraph 1*bis*, KVG). It is left to the cantons to more precisely define general eligibility requirements, including relevant income and asset limits (*see also* Article 65, paragraph 3, KVG).

213. When the KVG was issued, a general (political) goal was for households to pay a maximum of 8% of taxable income on health insurance premiums. Today the limit for premium reductions is considerably higher. In 2017, around 37% of all households were supported by the state. The premium reductions are funded by contributions from the federal government and the cantons (Article 66, KVG).

§5. Administration

I. Old-Age and Survivors' Insurance, Disability Insurance, Compensation Scheme for Lost Income and Family Allowances

214. Non-employed people are generally registered with the compensation agency of the canton where they live. The cantonal compensation agency collects contributions from non-employed people and provides benefits.

II. Health Insurance

215. Non-employed people must insure themselves with a licensed health insurance provider. They may freely choose providers.

216. The premium reduction systems are organized differently in each canton. Procedures are not uniform. In some cantons, potentially eligible people must report to the responsible cantonal authorities of their own accord in order to claim premium reductions; in others, the reductions are paid to the insurance providers based on relevant tax data on the insured people.

Chapter 4. Other Contributions and Government Funding

§1. Introduction

217. In addition to the contributions of the insured people and their employers, the social insurance schemes in Switzerland are financed by contributions from public authorities, investment income, as well as other revenues (e.g., recourse claims, earnings from services, additional neutral revenues). The following data is based on the official statistics of social insurance in Switzerland. The actual edition of the statistics (2017) is based on the definitive data from 2014 to 2016.

218. For the most part, the social insurance schemes in Switzerland are funded through the contributions of the insured people and their employers. In 2006, 62.3% of social insurance revenues came from insured people and their employers (insured people: 33.6%; employers: 28.7%). By comparison, the total figure in the EU-15 was 58.9%, and the portion paid by the insured people – 20.6% – was considerably lower than in Switzerland. In 2006, the Swiss public authorities contributed 22.3% of social insurance funding (in EU-15: 38%), while 'other revenues' (investment income, recourse claims, etc.) amounted to 15.4% (EU-15: 3.2%).

219. In 2015, 76% of funding came from the contributions of the insured people and their employers. The public authorities' portion decreased to 14.5% and 'other revenues' to 9.6%.

220. All Branches of Social Insurance

Revenues in 2015	*in Million Swiss Francs*	*in %*
Contributions, insured people/ employers	132,398	75.91
Contributions, public authorities	25,274	14.49
– federal government	16,160	9.27
Investment income	16,143	9.26
Other revenues (recourse claims)	598	0.34
Total	**174,413**	**100**

§2. OLD-AGE AND SURVIVORS' INSURANCE SCHEME

221. AHV: Revenues

Revenues in 2016	*in Million Swiss Francs*	*in %*
Contributions, insured people/ employers	30,862	71.82
Contributions, public authorities	10,896	25.36
– federal government (tobacco tax)	2,131	4.96
– federal government (alcohol tax)	224	0.52
– federal government (VAT)	473	1.10
– federal government (general federal funds)	5,487	12.77
– VAT	2,307	5.37
– casino tax	274	0.64
Investment income	1,205	2.80
Other revenues (recourse claims)	6	0.01
Total	**42,969**	**100**

222. Ever since the new Swiss fiscal equalization scheme (*Finanzausgleich*) was introduced on 1 January 2008, the cantons no longer contribute to funding old-age and survivors' insurance. The federal government has since contributed 19.6% of the annual costs of the insurance programme (Article 103, paragraph 1, AHVG). The federal government provides this contribution in advance, from taxes on tobacco and alcohol (Article 104, paragraph 1, AHVG). The rest is covered by general funds (Article 104, paragraph 2, AHVG)).

223. The federal government also transfers casino tax revenue to the insurance scheme (Article 103, paragraph 2, AHVG). The casino tax has been in effect since 1 April 2000 and goes in its entirety to old-age and survivors' insurance.

224. Moreover, since 1999, 1% of the value added tax (VAT) has been charged to finance old-age and survivors' insurance. Around 83% of this revenue goes directly to the scheme, while 17% is credited on an ongoing basis to its reserves, which are set aside by the federal government.

§3. Disability Insurance Scheme

225. IV: Revenues

Revenues in 2016	*in Million Swiss Francs*	*in %*
Contributions, insured people/employers	5,171	51.59
Contributions, public authorities	4,667	46.59
– federal government	3,525	35.17
Investment income	131	1.31
Other revenues (recourse claims)	55	0.55
Total	**10,024**	**100**

226. The federal government contributes 37.7% of the annual costs of the insurance scheme (Article 78, paragraph 1, IVG). Article 104 of the AHVG (*see* above paragraph 93) is applied analogously (Article 78, paragraph 2, IVG).

227. In order to reduce the IV's deficit, VAT was temporarily increased from 7.6% to 8% from 1 January 2011 to 31 December 2017 (or from 2.4% to 2.5% and 3.6% to 3.8%).

§4. Compensation Scheme for Lost Income (Including Maternity Insurance)

228. Compensation Scheme for Lost Income: Revenues

Revenues in 2016	*in Million Swiss Francs*	*in %*
Contributions, insured people/employers	1,658	97.87
Contributions, public authorities	–	–
Investment income	-35	-2.07
Other revenues (recourse claims)	–	–
Total	**1,694**	**100**

§5. Supplementary Benefits

229. Supplementary Benefits: Revenues

Revenues in 2016	*in Million Swiss Francs*	*in %*
Contributions, insured people/employers	–	–
Contributions, public authorities	4,901	100
– federal government (general tax revenues)	1,465	29.89
– cantons	3,436	70.11
Investment income	–	–
Other revenues (recourse claims)	–	–
Total	**4,901**	**100**

230. Under Article 13, paragraph 1, of the ELG, the federal government provides five-eighths of the funding for the annual supplementary benefits, while the cantons provide three-eighths. Contributions by the federal government are financed through general funds if they cannot be taken from the reserves described in Article 111 of the AHVG (Article 13, paragraph 3, ELG).

§6. The Occupational Pension System

231. The Occupational Pension System: Revenues

Revenues in 2015	*in Million Swiss Francs*	*in %*
Contributions, insured people/employers	54,316	79.61
Contributions, public authorities	–	–
Investment income	13,796	20.22
Other revenues (earnings from services, etc.)	113	0.17
Total	**68,225**	**100**

§7. Health Insurance Programme

232. Health Insurance Programme: Revenues

Revenues in 2015	*in Million Swiss Francs*	*in %*
Contributions, insured people/employers	22,866	84.11
Contributions, public authorities	4,110	15.12
– federal government	2,244	8.25
– cantons	1,713	6.30
Investment income	154	0.57
Other revenues (other neutral expenditures and revenues, other operating revenues)	56	0.21
Total	**27,186**	**100**

233. In terms of financing, the health insurance programme must be self-supporting (Article 60, paragraph 1, KVG). The public authorities are responsible for funding premium reductions (Articles 65–66a, KVG).

§8. Accident Insurance Scheme

234. Accident Insurance Scheme: Revenues

Revenues in 2015	*in Million Swiss Francs*	*in %*
Contributions, insured people/employers	6,176	73.80
Contributions, public authorities	–	–
Investment income	1,946	23.25
Other revenues (recourse claims)	248	2.96
Total	**8,369**	**100**

§9. Unemployment Insurance Scheme

235. ALV: Revenues

Revenues in 2016	*in Million Swiss Francs*	*in %*
Contributions, insured people/ employers	6,937	91.22
Contributions, public authorities	657	8.64

Revenues in 2016	*in Million Swiss Francs*	*in %*
– federal government	481	6.32
– cantons	160	2.10
Investment income	5	0.06
Other revenues (recourse claims)	6	0.08
Total	**7,605**	**100**

236. The fourth revision of the AVIG, which took effect on 1 April 2011, aims to reduce the debt mounted by the ALV. Among other things, it includes a 1% solidarity premium on income between CHF 126,000 and 315,000. Half of the premium is paid by employees, the other half by employers. In June 2013 the Swiss parliament decided to charge the 'solidarity percent' on the whole income higher than CHF 126,000. In January 2016, the threshold for the annual salary was raised to CHF 148,200, meaning that up to that amount, 2.2% is charged, and above that, 1%.

§10. Family Allowances

237. Family Allowances: Revenues

Revenues in 2015	*in Million Swiss Francs*	*in %*
Contributions, employers	5,651	95.17
Contributions, public authorities	207	3.49
– federal government	65	1.09
– cantons	32	0.54
Investment income	–	–
Other revenues (recourse claims)	79	1.33
Total	**5,938**	**100**

Part III. Health Care

Introduction

238. The costs of medical care are assumed by the compulsory health insurance programme, by a private supplementary health insurance plan or by the patient himself insofar as the service costs are not in fact assumed by an insurance plan.

239. Because supplementary health insurance is not a social but rather a private form of insurance in the Swiss system, it will not be treated here. The following will focus solely on the compulsory health insurance programme based on the Federal Health Insurance Law (*Bundesgesetz über die Krankenversicherung, KVG*), which is part of the Swiss social insurance system.

240. The current KVG first went into effect in 1996 and has since undergone several revisions. Additional reforms, some of which are quite far-reaching, are presently under discussion as a result of rising costs in the health care system.

241. When the Swiss legislators passed the KVG, they sought to tackle two central issues. On the one hand, they wanted to strengthen solidarity among the insured and, on the other, to create an efficient system that guarantees high-quality service at an affordable rate for the entire resident population.

242. The health insurance programme has been conceived as a social insurance programme that provides the entire population with comprehensive coverage against the social risk of illness (*see* Article 41, paragraph 1b, and Article 41, paragraph 2, BV).

243. A primary objective was to strengthen solidarity between the sick and the healthy, and to this end the legislators took the following measures:

- Mandatory coverage was introduced for the entire country. The entire resident population is now not only entitled but obliged to join this community, which is based on the principle of mutual solidarity. No one is exempt.
- The insured may freely choose and switch between health insurance providers. Health insurers must accept every person seeking insurance – regardless of their health, age or gender. Reservations about providing insurance, waiting periods and other obstacles have been eliminated.

- The sick and the healthy essentially pay the same premiums ('single premium'). Insurers are in principle forbidden to tier insurance based on factors indicating a greater risk of illness, such as gender and age (with the exception of children and young adults, *see* Article 61, paragraph 3, KVG).
- A comprehensive legal list of benefits was created that is binding for health insurers. The benefits are the same for everyone insured by the programme.
- The economic situation of the insured plays no role in setting the single premium. The danger that the economically weak will be unable to pay their insurance premiums makes additional solidarity between the rich and poor necessary. The KVG provides for contributions from public authorities to reduce premiums when there is an economic need to do so (Articles 64 et seq., KVG).

244. In addition to strengthening solidarity, the legislators focused on containing costs, which can be achieved in two different, even contradictory, ways: through more competition or through greater state regulation. The framers of the law did not come down clearly on the side of either a free-market or a state-directed model, but instead created a system based on competition and regulation.

245. From the perspective of health economics, the health insurance market doubtless requires a certain degree of regulation. First, there is a danger that the sick will be shunned by insurers and become concentrated in the hands of a single insurer ('adverse selection'). Second, the existence of insurance in itself creates false incentives for the insured, leading them to use more services than they normally would if they were uninsured ('moral hazard').

246. The legislators have introduced a broad set of state regulations alongside the elements of competition, and the balance of power between the market and state is the subject of ongoing political debate.

247. As far as health insurers go, the KVG primarily relies on competition. Social health insurance is provided by a body of insurers whose numbers are not restricted by law. They compete for the business of the insured, who can freely choose and switch between them (full freedom of trade). This promotes competition, but the state intervenes in the market as a strong regulator by barring risk-based premiums and by legally defining the list of services covered by the programme.

248. As for the health care providers, the state mainly relies on the instruments of a planned economy. Although the insured may in principle freely choose their care providers (Article 41, KVG), the system is not based on true competition because the care providers' costs are borne by the insurers rather than the insured. In fact, the large number of care providers increases costs since demand from the insured expands with the greater supply (supply-driven market): the insured have neither a financial incentive nor the necessary knowledge to apply pressure to the care providers so that they will work more efficiently.

249. Insurers are not allowed to select the care providers with whom they cooperate ('obligation to contract'). It is the state and not the insurers that determine the care providers who are authorized to charge services to the social health insurance scheme. The cantons are even legally required to conduct demand-driven planning for hospitals and nursing homes (Article 39, KVG).

Chapter 1. Who Is Entitled to Health Care?

§1. Territorial Field of Application

250. Article 34 of the KVG introduces the principle of territoriality. Insurers may in principle only defray the costs of services provided in Switzerland. Nevertheless, Article 34, paragraph 2, KVG and Articles 36 et seq. of the Health Insurance Ordinance (*Verordnung über die Krankenversicherung, KVV*) provide for exceptions to this rule, particularly if, in case of illness or maternity, there are medical reasons for having services provided abroad. Medical reasons are deemed to exist if a service cannot be performed in Switzerland and in cases of emergency (Article 36, paragraphs 1 and 2, KVV). The assumption of costs is limited to two times the cost that would have been incurred in Switzerland (Article 36, paragraph 4, KVV).

251. The criterion of territoriality has increasingly been relaxed in recent years, not only by the FZA (*see also* Article 36, paragraph 5, KVV), but also by Article 36a of the KVV, within whose scope pilot projects can apply for permission to diverge from Article 34, paragraph 2, KVG.

252. The principle of assistance with in-kind benefits is applicable within the scope of the FZA. Accordingly, people insured in Switzerland are entitled to benefits in kind in EU/EFTA countries if they live or temporarily reside there. These benefits are not based on Swiss law but on the regulations and modalities of the individual EU/EFTA states. The same is true if a person insured in an EU/EFTA country resides in Switzerland.

§2. Personal Field of Application

253. The health insurance programme is a people's and not a class-based insurance. Coverage is basically compulsory for the entire resident population and not limited to certain groups (e.g., employees). One of the main criteria is a person's residence as defined under civil law, irrespective of nationality (Article 3, paragraph 1, KVG; Article 1, paragraph 1, KVV; Article 13, paragraph 1, ATSG). Under civil law, a person's legal residence is that place where he intends to reside permanently and that is at the centre of his or her vital interests.

254. Exceptions exist to this practice of linking insurance to a person's civil law residence. On the one hand, certain individuals domiciled in Switzerland are not required to participate in the compulsory insurance programme (Article 3, paragraphs 2 and 4, KVG). These individuals include people who already have adequate insurance coverage through another domestic or a foreign social insurance programme. On the other hand, some individuals are subject to the compulsory health insurance even though they are not domiciled in Switzerland (Article 3, paragraph 3, KVG), such as foreign nationals with a temporary residence permit. In this case, the decisive criteria are their place of work or their place of habitual residence (Article 3, paragraph 3a, KVG). Such exceptions are defined in detail in Articles 1–6 of the KVV.

255. The provisions in state treaties may also be applicable. For instance, within the scope of the FZA, which Switzerland signed with the EU/EFTA, the country of employment and family insurance are the relevant criteria for health insurance. According to the former principle, insurance coverage is essentially dependent on the place of work and not on the place of residence. According to the latter, non-employed family members must be covered by the insurance of the employed person. Since both principles are alien to the health insurance scheme in Switzerland, its legal framework had to be adapted accordingly. On the one hand, the legal obligation to be insured needed to be expanded to include, for example, people working in Switzerland but living in the EU/EFTA; on the other hand, this obligation needed to be restricted to exclude, for example, Swiss residents working in the EU/EFTA.

256. Compulsory health insurance takes the form of insurance for the individual: every individual insures himself; family members are not co-insured under the law.

257. Furthermore, the health insurance programme no longer allows collective insurance policies with which the insuree (e.g., an employer) insures several persons.

Chapter 2. Benefits

§1. Care Provided

258. Health insurance basically covers the costs associated with care of the sick. This generally includes all the medical measures necessary to diagnose and treat damage to a person's health, such as diagnostic and therapeutic services, the cost of analyses, pharmaceuticals and stays in a hospital or the cost of medical rehabilitation (*see* Article 25, KVG). Health insurance also covers services that cannot actually be described as care for the sick but that nevertheless trigger a similar need for benefits (prevention, maternity care, legal termination of pregnancies, rescue costs, etc.; *see* Article 25, paragraph 2g, Articles 26, 29 and 30, KVG).

259. The most important exception to insurance coverage is dental treatment, which is covered only on a very small scale – primarily when dental disease is related to a severe general illness sustained by the insured (Article 31, KVG).

260. In addition, insurance does not cover psychotherapeutic services that are not provided or ordered by a doctor (cf. Articles 2 et seq. of the KLV). This means that non-medical psychotherapists are currently not licensed care providers within the scope of the health insurance scheme.

§2. Amount of Benefit

261. Health insurance is based on the principle of cost reimbursement. This means that health insurers do not provide services themselves ('benefits in kind'), but only bear the costs of such services (Articles 24 and 42, KVG).

262. So, fundamentally speaking, health insurance assumes the total costs of the services provided. But only a partial amount is paid for non-hospital services, physician-prescribed spa treatments, and medically necessary transport and emergency medical costs (*see* Articles 7 et seq., Articles 25 et seq., KLV).

263. In normal cases, the system of Tiers garant is applied within the scope of the KVG. This means, on the one hand, that the insured person owes the health care provider a fee and, on the other, that they are entitled to reimbursement by their health insurer. A variation on this principle would be the insurer and the health care provider agreeing that remuneration should be paid directly by the insurer (system of Tiers payant). The KVG also provides for the system of Tiers payant for in-patient treatments, which are often very cost-intensive. This is why the insurer makes payment on that part of the remuneration to which it is liable (cf. Article 42, KVG).

264. Article 41, paragraph 1, of the KVG states that one has free choice in selecting those authorized health care providers that are suitable for treating a particular illness. This freedom of choice is valid for all of Switzerland.

265. But freedom of choice is greatly limited by the law in terms of the scale of charges. Health insurance basically only assumes the full costs if the insured person chooses a health care provider in their own vicinity, in which case a distinction is drawn between in-and out-patient care.

266. In out-patient treatment, the insurer assumes, at most, the costs according to prices that hold for the region where the insured person lives or works or those applicable in that person's vicinity (Article 41, paragraph 1, KVG).

267. For in-patient treatment, the insurer and the relevant canton assume, at most, the costs according to the prices that apply to treatment in an officially listed hospital (*Listenspital*) of the canton of residence (Article 41, paragraph 2, KVG). If the insured person chooses another health care provider, then he bears the financial risk that the provider has higher prices. In this case, the individual must make up the difference himself.

268. There are exceptions to this regulation concerning price differences. They apply in cases of emergency or if the required services are not offered by a health care provider in the canton of residence or work or in the vicinity (Article 41, paragraphs 2 and 3, KVG).

269. In order to prevent the insured from making excessive use of services covered by health insurance ('moral hazard'), the insured are required to pay a part of the costs themselves (Article 64, paragraph 1, KVG). The law provides for various forms of cost sharing, and a common feature to all is that they are not tiered according to the economic circumstances of the insured:

- Deductible (called a 'franchise'): This is the fixed annual sum the insured must pay before insurance kicks in (Article 64, paragraph 2a, KVG). It currently amounts to a minimum of CHF 300 per calendar year (Article 103, paragraph 1, KVV).
- Copayment: The insured are required to pay 10% of the costs exceeding the deductible (Article 64, paragraph 2b, KVG). This copayment is limited by law and currently capped at CHF 700 a year (Article 103, paragraph 2, KVV).
- Cost sharing in the event of a hospital stay: A patient's contribution to the costs of a hospital stay is currently set at CHF 15 per day (Article 64, paragraph 5, KVG in conjunction with Article 104, paragraph 1, KVV).

270. Cost sharing by children is subject to a number of restrictions. Children are not required to pay a deductible and they need only to pay half the highest permissible yearly copayment (Article 64, paragraph 4, KVG). Furthermore, they normally do not have to pay the daily contribution to the costs of a hospital stay (Article 104, paragraph 2a, KVV). If several children in a family are covered by the same insurer, their obligation to share costs is restricted even further (Article 64, paragraph 4, KVG).

271. Insurers are not permitted to impose any of the aforementioned forms of cost sharing in the case of maternity care (Article 64, paragraph 7, KVG; Article 104, paragraph 2c, KVV). This includes the deductible, copayments and contributions to the costs of a hospital stay.

§3. Determining Rates of Fees and Prices

272. The legal regulations on fees define the extent to which costs are assumed by health insurers. For care providers, these provisions – together with the list of services covered by health insurance – are the most important factor for calculating income.

273. The question of the amount of costs covered by the health insurance is only relevant to the legally defined standard services provided by licensed care providers who have not opted to work outside the system (i.e., those who stay out, *see* Article 44, paragraph 2, KVG). The insured basically have a right to full assumption of costs by health insurers.

274. The fee protection provisions in Article 44, paragraph 1, of the KVG generally state that care providers must adhere to the legally defined fees. For the services they provide, they only have the right to be paid according to the fee system and may not demand additional payment.

275. The setting of fees is based on the principle of freedom of contract. In most cases, fees are specified in agreements between insurers and care providers (Article 43, paragraph 4, KVG). Consequently, the two parties have a high level of autonomy when it comes to negotiating fees, even if the agreements ultimately need to be approved by the authorities (Article 46, paragraph 4, KVG).

276. In setting the fees, the general principles with regard to pricing are to be heeded. The goal is always to strive for health care that is suitable and of high quality at the most favourable cost. The services are to be compensated for both in terms of outlay and those providing them, and the fees must conform with the Constitution and the law, and they must be in harmony with the precept of cost-effectiveness.

277. The fee system forms the basis for calculating remuneration. The charges can be designated as individual services, as provided over a certain period of time or as flat rates (Article 43, paragraph 2, KVG). Essentially, the parties can freely choose between these variants, combine them, or create new types of fees.

278. If no agreement on rates is reached, the authorities (the responsible entity is the cantonal government where the health care provider is headquartered) officially lays down a substitute system of fees (Article 47, KVG).

I. Physicians and Dentists

279. Out-patient services are subject to a combination of time-based rates and individual service fees. This type of combined system is found in tarif medical (TARMED), the out-patient fee schedule applicable to all of Switzerland. Under TARMED, services are converted into so-called tax points (*Taxpunkte*), and the amount of money for each point is fixed in negotiations between insurers and care providers.

280. If the parties to the contract agree to a fee for an individual service, this must be based on an agreed nationwide and uniform fee structure. Certain variations are possible within the framework of the tax points, whose value is laid down in cantonal fee agreements in consideration of regional cost differences. Presently TARMED encompasses over 4,500 fee items, as all the possible services provided by physicians these days are listed. At present, however, TARMED does not apply in the form that was agreed on by the parties. Twice already has the Federal Council exercised its right to adjust the tariff when it was no longer deemed appropriate (Article 43, paragraph 5*bis*, KVG).

281. Care providers who do not wish to abide by the fee system may choose to work outside the system, but then they have no right to receive compensation on the basis of the KVG and they must inform any insured patients consulting them that their services are not covered by the health insurance programme. Only a few care providers have made use of this option.

II. Paramedical Auxiliaries

282. The principle of freedom of contract also holds for other health care providers such as midwives, physician-prescribed physiotherapists, ergotherapists, etc. These health care providers can also agree to compensation for the performed services within the framework of fee agreements with the insurers.

III. Hospitals

283. For out-patient treatments the parties to the fee – that is, the insurers and hospitals (or birth houses) – freely choose the type of fee and the allocation of costs in negotiations.

284. This freedom of choice does not hold in the sphere of in-patient treatments, including hospital stays and nursing. In this area, services are only paid for by means of flat rates (Article 49, KVG). Until the end of 2011, in-patient services in hospitals and nursing homes were generally charged at daily rates. Since 1 January 2012, payment is made in the form of a case-based lump sum and procedural rate that reflect the services performed and are based on uniform nationwide structures. The fee for the case-based lump sum and procedural rate is structured according to 'diagnosis-related groups' (DRG; 'SwissDRG'). Every hospital stay is categorized according to certain criteria such as the main and secondary diagnoses, treatments and degree of severity, and recompensed at a flat rate.

285. The fee structure of 'SwissDRG' has no fixed prices. These must be agreed on separately and there is no need – as in the case of TARMED – for them to be uniform. But legislators go on the assumption that the price differences will be equalized in time.

286. The case-based lump sum and procedural rate (DRG) are intended to ensure transparent and fair payment. In particular, the burden of payment should not be completely borne by the health care insurer but should be assumed on a legally defined minimum scale (55%) by the canton in which the insured person lives.

IV. Pharmaceuticals and Technical Aids

287. Analyses, pharmaceuticals, materials and technical aids are not subject to fee agreements. When defining these services, the federal government also sets their fee (Article 52, KVG; Articles 20 et seq., KLV). The principle of fee protection also applies in a basic way here: it is not permissible to place additional burdens on the insuree (Article 44, paragraph 1, sentence 1, KVG).

288. Only the materials and resources are expressly exempted from fee protection (Article 44, paragraph 1, sentence 2, KVG). This is the result of the particular structure of the relevant list. In terms of the individual service items, it contains only general product descriptions. The insuree can choose the specific product himself, but also bears the additional costs of more expensive products (*see* Article 24, paragraph 2, KLV).

§4. Budget Limitation

289. The costs of health care have been sharply rising for many years, which has led to an annual increase of 4% –10% in health insurance premiums. For some time now, legislators have attempted to combat the problem by means of various solutions.

290. The law provides for particular forms of insurance (Article 62, KVG) as a means of generally reducing costs and individually reducing premiums. Presently the insurer can offer three different models of insurance:

- Limited choice of the health care provider: Insured people can forfeit their right to choose their own health care provider (Article 62, paragraph 1, KVG in conjunction with Article 41, paragraph 4, KVG). They are then only allowed free choice of health care providers who their insurers select with respect to cost-efficient care. Furthermore, under this insurance model the standard services may not be limited under any circumstances, and in emergency medical cases another health care provider may be sought. More than 50% of adults have restricted their selections in this respect.

- Increased cost sharing: The insurer can offer insurance plans with selectable deductibles (Article 62, paragraph 2a, KVG). The maximum deductible for adults is presently CHF 2,500 (Article 93, paragraph 1, KVV). Insurance plans with selectable deductibles are widespread but far less popular than the plans with limited choice of health care providers.
- Bonus insurance plans: This designates an insurance plan in which the insurers reduce the premiums if the insured person has not made any claims on his insurance plan in the course of the previous year (Article 62, paragraph 2b, KVG). Conversely, if the insured person makes claims on his insurance, the premiums are raised. This form of insurance is not very widespread.

291. In order to reduce costs, there has been a move towards state demand planning in recent years, even among medical staff – albeit without any success. A so-called licensing moratorium (*Zulassungsstopp*) was put into effect in July 2002 in an attempt to prevent the feared sharp rise in the number of physicians after enactment of the FZA. An additional goal was to reduce costs. The relevant ordinance established a maximum number for every category of medical staff in each canton. This moratorium was originally intended to be in effect for three years, but has since been extended three times until the end of 2011. After removal of the moratorium the number of licenses given to physicians increased substantially in 2012. A modified form of licensing moratorium was reintroduced in July 2013 (Article 55a, KVG).

292. The KVG has other economic and quality controls (Articles 56 et seq., KVG). Among other things, the economic efficiency of the services performed is checked in order to prevent what is referred to as *Überarztung* ('over-doctoring') when someone is treated by a physician. *Überarztung* exists if the services provided are not limited to what is objectively necessary. An evaluation of the economic efficiency of the services is mostly undertaken by means of a comparison of average costs. Unnecessary medical services are ascertained when a considerable number of the doctor's bills sent to the health insurance are, on average, substantially higher than the bills of other physicians who are active in a similar region and who can demonstrate a similar patient base without there being anything in particular justifying the difference in cost. If unnecessary medical services are indeed ascertained, the insurer can refuse payment or demand reimbursement of past payments (Article 56, paragraph 2, KVG). It is even possible, as a last resort, to exclude the health care provider from invoicing services to the compulsory health insurance.

293. In parliament there are always various bills pending to revise health care insurance and to reduce costs. Reforms in the area of the financing of nursing and hospitals were enacted in 2012, together with reforms in the area of balancing risks. But a Federal Council proposal consisting of various 'measures for curbing costs' was rejected by a majority of parliament in 2010 – it included, for example, the introduction of a charge of CHF 30 per out-patient procedure and a commitment of two years instead of one with respect to increased deductibles. Furthermore, a reform which intended to introduce more managed care models into Swiss health insurance failed in the popular vote in June 2012.

Chapter 3. Conditions

294. Diverse prerequisites must be fulfilled for the health care provider to assume the costs of treatments or materials. These will be discussed below.

§1. Affiliation with a Health Insurer

295. Although health insurance is compulsory, individuals are not automatically insured by law; rather, they have an obligation to insure themselves – they must sign up with a health care insurer within three months of establishing their residency or within three months of the birth of a child (Article 3, paragraph 1, KVG). Persons with their residence in the EU/EFTA who are obliged to be insured in Switzerland (Article 1, paragraph 2e, KVG) have three months within which to fulfil this obligation. The insurance contract is governed by public law. The insured can freely choose an insurer and can change insurers at will (Articles 4 and 7, KVG).

296. The correlate to one's freedom in choosing an insurer is that with any voluntary change of insurer, the insured person must observe the regular or extraordinary (in the case of a new premium) cancellation period (Article 7, paragraphs 1 and 2, KVG).

297. Individuals who have accident insurance are not exempt from compulsory insurance as detailed in Article 3 of the KVG. So as to avoid a double burden from the fees paid for health and accident insurance, Article 8, paragraph 1, of the KVG provides for the possible suspension of the accident coverage within the health insurance for those insurees who are subject to social accident insurance. The premiums are lowered by 7% at most (*see* Article 91a, KVV). Any such suspension will only follow after application by the insured. No insurance gaps may result: as soon as the accident coverage ends within the framework of the accident insurance, the law decrees that the coverage be taken up by the compulsory health insurance (Article 8, paragraph 2, KVG).

298. Because health insurance is compulsory, no one may be denied coverage. Even people who fail to pay their contributions remain insured; however, they must expect sanctions, as detailed in Article 64a of the KVG (e.g., a deferment of services).

§2. Contribution Documents

299. Premiums must basically be paid by the insured, normally on a monthly basis and in advance (Article 90, KVV). If a person falls behind with payment, he is subject to the provisions in Article 64a of the KVG, which describe the legal consequences of not paying premiums (and thus sharing costs). Some of these are quite severe. If required, insurers may recover back premiums in a procedure designed to enforce their claims (Article 64a, paragraph 1, KVG). They may also delay covering the costs of services until the accrued debts are completely paid off (Article 64a, paragraph 2, KVG). Once the arrears are paid, the insurer must retroactively cover the costs of services provided during the time when premiums were not paid (Article 64, paragraph 3, KVG). The insured are not permitted to switch insurers as long as they are in arrears (Article 64a, paragraph 4, KVG; Article 105d, KVV), but they may also not be dropped by the insurer. The insured are still required to have health insurance coverage and pay premiums despite the fact that they must essentially pay for services themselves until they settle their accrued debts. The cantons' social assistance law and basic constitutional rights (Article 12, BV) apply.

300. The health insurers set insurance premiums, but these must be approved by the Swiss Federal Council (Article 61, paragraphs 1 and 5, KVG). Insurers essentially collect the same premium from all the insured (the so-called *Einheitsprämie*, or single premium; Article 61, paragraph 1, KVG). With just a few legal exceptions, insurers are not permitted to set premiums based on risk or income.

301. The law permits the following premium tiers:

- A tier based on the insured party's place of residence (Article 61, paragraph 2, KVG): the premiums may vary according to canton and region.
- A tier based on the insured party's age (Article 61, paragraph 3, KVG): premiums for persons up to the age of 18 (children) must necessarily be cheaper than those for older people (adults). In addition, insurers are permitted to reduce premiums for people up to the age of 25 (young adults). With the exception of these regulations, age may not play a role in determining premiums.
- A tier based on the selected insurance model: lower premiums may be granted for special forms of insurance pursuant to Article 62 of the KVG.
- A tier based on insurance coverage: premiums may be lower for insured parties without accident coverage (Article 8, paragraph 1, KVG; Article 91a, KVV).

302. For those insurees who have less financial wherewithal, the single premium can lead to an intolerable burden. Therefore, Article 65 of the KVG provides for state financial assistance in reducing premiums. Implementation of the reduction in premiums is left to the cantons, which establish binding standards in terms of income and assets. In 2017 some 37% of all Swiss households were supported by the state.

§3. Insured Risk

303. Social health insurance provides benefits in the event of illness, maternity and accidents unless such costs are borne by accident insurance (Article 1a, paragraph 2, KVG) or military insurance (cf. Article 3, paragraph 4, KVG; *see* Part VI). Birth defects are equated with illness (cf. Article 3, paragraph 2, ATSG; Article 27, KVG). Health insurance is therefore not limited to the social risk of illness. For people who do not have accident coverage, it is a comprehensive insurance programme that provides benefits whenever a person's health is impaired, regardless of whether the cause is accident or illness.

304. Maternity care is also a part of the health insurance programme since pregnancy causes a need for benefits similar to the need that arises when a person's health is impaired and he requires diagnosis and treatment (e.g., ultrasound examinations, hospital stays). However, in the case of maternity, any loss of income after delivery is covered by the maternity compensation provisions in the Law on Income Replacement (*Erwerbsersatzgesetz, EOG*; Articles 16b et seq.).[1]

305. Article 3, paragraph 1, of the ATSG defines illness as 'any impairment of physical or mental health that is not the result of an accident and requires a medical examination or treatment, or that results in the inability to work'. This legal definition contains an important medical component: the requirement that there be damage to a person's health and thus a physical or mental dysfunction. A restrictive proviso is the assumption that this dysfunction is not the result of an accident and leads to the need for an examination or treatment, or that it causes disability. These restrictions not only distinguish the concept of illness from that of accident under Article 4 of the ATSG but also add an objective, benefit-related component. The concept of illness is in line with the benefits offered by the social health insurance: defrayment of the costs for medical examinations and treatment as well as a daily allowance in the case of disability.

§4. Permissible Health Care Providers

306. Furthermore, health insurance only assumes the costs of those services provided by permitted parties or entities. Article 35, paragraph 2, of the KVG concludes with a list of permissible health care providers. The first group encompasses medical staff that practices an academic or non-academic medical profession. Pharmacists, physicians, dentists and chiropractors have an academic medical profession. Those practicing a non-academic medical profession include midwives and individuals who are active on orders of a doctor. If these medical workers fulfil the legal prerequisite – that is, if they have a Swiss diploma and accredited advanced training – then they are automatically permitted to bill their services to the health insurance.[2]

307. Hospitals, nursing homes and birth houses can be included in the second group of health care providers. A formal qualification procedure is provided for them, within whose framework the fulfilment of certain service and infrastructure prerequisites (adequate care by physicians, the necessary specialized staff, suitable medical establishments and pharmaceutical care) as well as the state's demand planning are examined (Article 39, KVG). The cantons are obliged to carry out their

1. *See* Part V, Ch. 4, § 1 II.
2. Presently the sole exception to this is in the sphere of the moratorium. *See* Part III, Ch. 2, § 4.

hospital planning so that they can reduce their excess capacity (cf. Articles 58a et seq., KVV). In so doing, they must coordinate their planning and formulate a nationwide plan – for example, in the area of highly specialized medicine (Article 39, paragraph 2 and 2*bis*, KVG). Should they fail to meet their obligations in this regard in a timely fashion, the responsibility for such devolves on the Federal Council. Such plans are necessary for nursing homes and birth houses in addition to hospitals.

308. Finally, insofar as they fulfil the necessary legal prerequisites, permissible health care providers also include laboratories; dispensary stations for the resources and materials used for examinations and treatment; health spas; and transport and rescue services. With the exception of health spas (Article 40, KVG; Articles 57 and 58 KVV), there is no formal qualification procedure.

§5. Service Catalogue and the 'List Principle'

309. Article 34, paragraph 1, of the KVG directs that, within the scope of compulsory health insurance, insurers are only permitted to cover the costs of legally defined services. The lists of services drawn up by legislators and regulators are seen as exhaustive and complete. As a consequence, insurers are not allowed to provide voluntary services but must adhere to the law and legal ordinances ('principle of legality'). Private insurance may be taken out to cover additional services.

310. The legislators did not content themselves with providing general criteria for services (Article 32, KVG) but went into greater detail, listing individual service categories and then the services themselves (Articles 25 et seq., KVG). These lists are considered exhaustive (Article 34, paragraph 1, KVG; 'list principle'). The costs of services that do not appear on the lists in Articles 25 et seq. of the KVG are not borne by the insurers. The legislators are not only authorized but required to further define these lists (Article 33, KVG).

311. Within the scope of Article 25, paragraph 2, of the KVG, the legislators have granted doctors and chiropractors a great deal of decision-making leeway. The services they provide under this Article are subject to a 'standard service assumption' (*Pflichtleistungsvermutung*; *see also* Ruling of the Federal Court (BGE) 129 V 167, 170 (2003)). This means that the law makes the refutable assumption that care providers apply treatment methods that are effective, appropriate and economical (Article 32, KVG). This assumption is not explicitly mentioned in the law. In Article 33, paragraph 1, of the KVG, regulators merely identify those medical and chiropractic services that are not covered by insurance or that are only covered under certain conditions. There is no genuine, exhaustive list of approved standard medical and chiropractic services ('positive list'). Rather, regulators only enumerate the medical and chiropractic services that do not fulfil the conditions of Article 32 of the KVG and are therefore not covered by health insurance or are covered only under certain conditions ('negative list' or 'exclusionary list').

312. This legal assumption plays no role in services that are not provided by doctors or chiropractors. Concerning these, regulators have both the authority and the duty to further define the lists of services described in Article 25, paragraph 2, of the KVG. They must also create exhaustive and complete lists of standard services (Article 33, paragraph 2, KVG). Health insurance only covers the costs of services appearing on these positive lists. The positive and negative lists touched upon in Article 33 of the KVG and Articles 33 et seq. of the KVV can be found in the KLV. Appendix 1 to this Ordinance contains the lists of medical services referred to in Article 33, paragraphs 1 to 3, of the KVG.

§6. Effective, Appropriate and Economical Services

313. Article 32 of the KVG contains a blanket clause defining the central requirements for services covered by the health insurance programme. It states that these services must be effective, appropriate and economical. If these conditions are not met, insurers are under no obligation to assume costs. Regulators only include those services on their list that fulfil these conditions. In concrete cases, care providers must always check whether the conditions are met. Article 32 of the KVG thus contains a universally valid regulation that must always be borne in mind, in both general evaluations by regulators and in assessments of concrete cases.

314. Medical services are considered effective if, from an objective standpoint, they are suitable for achieving the desired medical benefit – i.e., they have a diagnostic or therapeutic benefit, or support patient care. The central question is whether the aim of treatment (restoration or improvement of the patient's health) can be objectively achieved.

315. Appropriateness presupposes effectiveness and, as a criterion, is primarily intended to facilitate the selection of one of the available medical measures. The medical benefit of a measure is evaluated on the basis of its risks and by comparing this benefit to those of alternative measures. A measure is considered appropriate if, from an objective standpoint, it provides the best medical benefit – i.e., if it leads more quickly and effectively to success.

316. The notion of 'economical' presupposes effectiveness and appropriateness. If there are measures available with comparable medical benefits, the least expensive must be chosen. Objective criteria must be brought to bear in judgments of whether a measure is economical. Such judgments are also based on the assumption that one of several appropriate treatments will be markedly less expensive for the care provider.

§7. Fee Protection

317. The insured person has a right to have the health insurer assume all health care costs insofar as a permissible health care provider has performed legally defined standard services. Article 44, paragraph 1, of the KVG dictates that the health care providers adhere to the established fees and only enter claims for compensation that are in accord with these fees. These fees are legally binding regardless of whether health insurance assumes only a portion of the health care costs. If all the costs are assumed, the health care provider is fully remunerated according to the respective fee agreements. If the health insurance only assumes a portion of the costs, the health care provider can bill the insured for those costs that were not paid – but they must keep to the legally defined fees if they have performed standard services.

§8. Waiting Period

318. If a person signs up with an insurer in a timely fashion, insurance coverage extends back to the point when the requirement to take out insurance began (Article 5, paragraph 1, KVG). If a person delays in taking out insurance, insurance coverage begins at the point when he signs up (Article 5, paragraph 2, KVG). Moreover, in the case of inexcusable tardiness, the insuree must pay an extra amount over and above the premium (Article 5, paragraph 2, KVG and Article 8, KVV). Those who do not sign up with an insurer in a timely manner will be assigned to an insurer by the canton (Article 6, paragraph 2, KVG).

319. Apart from this rule and the already mentioned consequences of not paying the premiums (*see also* paragraphs 299 et seq.), compulsory health insurance has no waiting period. In contrast to supplementary insurance, insurance coverage cannot be deferred for certain health problems or for general reasons.

§9. Medical Prescription

320. If medical services are performed personally by the physician, they are recognized as standard services and the costs are assumed by the health insurance programme. Such services also include those performed by the practice's assistants as well as by medical employees who are not physicians themselves but are under the direct supervision of doctors who assume responsibility on the premises of the medical practice (delegated activity of the doctor). But there must be a basic legal or real subaltern relationship present.

321. By contrast, all diagnostic, therapeutic or nursing services that are not undertaken by a physician but by physiotherapists, ergotherapists, nursing personnel, logopedics or nutritionists must in principle be prescribed by a physician in order that these be regarded as standard services and that their costs be assumed by the health insurance programme. Accordingly, in this service sector, physicians play a key role in that: only they can order these diagnostic, therapeutic or nursing procedures if the costs for such are to be assumed by health insurance.

§10. Approval by a Medical Advisor

322. Health care providers are monitored in order to guarantee the lowest possible costs for high-quality health care providers. Since the insurers, as the entities paying the costs, have an interest in effective economic controls, it would be a mistake to assume that they are independent in this matter. It is for this reason that the legislators have created the office of the independent examining doctor as an independent authority for economic and quality controls.

323. Every medical insurer – in consultation with the cantonal doctor's society – must appoint an independent examining doctor (Article 57, KVG). Although the independent examining doctor is employed or commissioned by the insurer, he remains independent in his judgment and neither the insurer nor the health care provider may give him instructions. The main task of the independent examining doctor is to monitor the health care provider. He checks whether all the preconditions for payment have been met.

324. Apart from that, he also has an advisory capacity, for it is he who must give the go-ahead for certain services. His sphere of responsibilities is restricted to answering medical questions of a particular nature in order to convey the matters of fact of the case. A concrete task of the independent examining doctor consists – for example – in the sphere of physiotherapy: if physiotherapy after a treatment of thirty-six sessions is to be continued at the expense of the insurer, the independent examining doctor examines the proposal of the attending physician and determines whether, to what extent and for how long physiotherapy can be continued at the expense of the insurer until the next report (*see* Article 5, paragraph 4, KLV).

§11. Grounds for Exclusion

325. If an accident befalls the individual concerned and it is covered by accident insurance, his health insurance is not responsible for paying the health care services performed – the accident insurance bears the costs (cf. Article 1a, paragraph 2b, KVG). Health insurance only bears the costs associated with the medical treatments and benefits in kind if no other social insurance will assume them (Articles 64 and 65, ATSG). But in connection with benefits in kind, the health insurance has an obligation to make advance payment (Article 70, ATSG).

326. If a third party is liable for the event covered by the insured party's insurance, Article 72 of the ATSG states that, at the time of the event, the insurer takes over the claims of the insured person or his survivors up to the amount of the legal benefits. But the claims of the insuree are only transferred to the insurer insofar as the latter's payment exceeds the relevant damage together with the compensation owed by the third party for the same timeframe (Article 73, ATSG).

327. In principle, health insurance is not liable for services that are performed outside of Switzerland. Exceptions include emergencies, cases in which the relevant treatment is not offered in Switzerland, and pilot projects in which the costs for services performed abroad are assumed (Article 34, paragraph 2, KVG in conjunction with Articles 36 and 36a, KVV).

328. The obligation of every citizen to be insured is suspended if the person concerned is subject to the Military Insurance Law for more than sixty consecutive days (Article 3, paragraph 4, KVG). In such cases, any costs that arise are paid by the military insurance scheme.

329. Finally, the failure to pay one's health insurance premiums can lead to a suspension of benefits. If the insured person fails to pay his premiums and share of costs, he must be warned in writing and given a grace period of thirty days. Furthermore, he must be made aware of the consequences of delay in payment (Article 64a, paragraph 1, KVG). If he still fails to make the necessary payments and the insurer has instigated prosecution and has applied to continue proceedings, the insurer can postpone assuming the costs for any services performed until all outstanding debts are paid (Article 64a, paragraph 2, KVG; *see also* paragraph 299). If all these debts are paid by the insured person, however, the insurer is obliged to assume the costs for those services performed during the period of delay in payment (Article 64a, paragraph 3, KVG).

§12. Time Limit

330. Article 24, paragraph 1, of the ATSG dictates that a claim to outstanding benefits expires five years after the end of the month for which the benefits were owed. The expiration of the claim is suspended if the insured person registers to draw the benefit and does not then undermine the provision of the benefit by failing to cooperate (cf. Article 28, paragraph 1, ATSG).

331. The aforementioned regulation is tailored for periodical benefits. But since, within the framework of the health insurance programme, benefits are provided for certain services, the rule in Article 24, paragraph 1, of the ATSG is not really appropriate. Legal experts have proposed various possible solutions – for example, that the earliest possible point in time at which registration can be made to receive a benefit should be chosen as a criterion for determining the origin of a claim to the benefit. Another possibility is using the point in time when the claim to fees arose under a binding contract for treatment.

332. According to Article 25, paragraph 1, of the ATSG, wrongfully drawn benefits must be paid back. The claim to restitution lapses one year after the insurance provider has received knowledge of the wrongfully drawn benefit, or, at the latest, five years after provision of the individual benefit (Article 25, paragraph 2, ATSG).

Part IV. Family Allowances

Introduction

333. Since children are a financial burden and sometimes even increase the risk of poverty, the legislators have decided that the social insurance system should bear at least part of the additional family-related costs that constitute a social risk.

334. The federal government was given legislative powers in the area of family allowances in 1945. The FLG went into effect in 1953, but as the name suggests, it has only limited application. The aim of these family allowances was to ensure the maintenance of the country and to prevent migration into cities.

335. For years, family allowances for people outside agriculture were regulated only at the cantonal level, with every canton issuing its own set of regulations. It was not until 1 January 2009 that the Federal Law on Family Allowances (*Bundesgesetz über die Familienzulagen, FamZG*) went into effect, which is applicable to people outside agriculture. But this federal law provides only a general framework. It establishes the underlying principles of family allowances and stipulates, for example, that the assumption under this law is mandatory for certain groups of people. The cantons still have the power to define many aspects, such as the scope of benefits or the provision of family allowances for the self-employed persons. In addition, the cantons are responsible for organization, supervision and financing (*see* Articles 17 and 21, FamZG).

Chapter 1. Who Is Entitled to Family Allowances?

§1. Territorial Field of Application

336. Payment of family allowances is not dependent on whether the child for which a claim is asserted is a Swiss citizen or whether it is domiciled or being raised in Switzerland. The decisive factor is that the persons eligible to benefits meet one of the following conditions: they must be employees, self-employed or non-employed persons who are mandatorily insured in the AHV; they must work in Switzerland as agricultural workers, self-employed farmers, alpine herdsmen or professional fishermen; or they must be mandatorily insured in the AHV as non-employed persons.

§2. Personal Field of Application

337. According to the FLG and the Federal Law on Fishery (*Bundesgesetz über die Fischerei*), full- and part-time self-employed farmers, alpine herdsmen, professional fishermen and agricultural workers are insured (Articles 1a and 5, FLG; Article 14 of the Federal Law on Fishery).

338. The FamZG has a supplementary scope of application. This law covers employees outside agriculture, non-employed people and, since January 2013, also self-employed people (*see* Articles 13 and 19, FamZG).

Chapter 2. Eligible Children

§1. The Insured Person

I. Employees

339. The main group of people eligible for family allowances are employees. Nevertheless, most are not subject to the FamZG themselves, but are 'merely' the people who are eligible to receive the benefit. In most cases, it is their employer who is subject to the FamZG, provided they are required to pay contributions to the AHV by the AHVG.

340. It is a different matter if a person is in the employ of a company that is not required to pay contributions to the AHV. In this case, the employee himself is subject to the FamZG (*see* Article 11, paragraph 1, FamZG).

341. Everyone who is subject to the FamZG is required to join a Family Compensation Agency (*Familienausgleichskasse*) in that canton, whose Family Compensation Regulation (*Familienzulagenordnung*) he is subjected to (Article 12, paragraph 1, FamZG). The FamZG specifies which cantonal family allowance regulation applies to an employer or employee (Article 12, paragraphs 2 and 3, FamZG).

342. With regard to employees, an important requirement for receipt of a family allowance is that they be mandatorily insured in the AHV (cf. Article 13, FamZG). Furthermore, AHV contributions must be paid on an income amounting to at least CHF 7,050 per year or at least CHF 586 per month (as of 2018; *see* Article 13, paragraph 3, FamZG in conjunction with Article 34, paragraph 5, AHVG). The legislators made a conscious decision to pay the full benefit even if employees have very small incomes or a slight workload.

343. If an employee works for different employers, his earnings are added together in order to determine whether the minimum income level has been reached. People who do not earn the minimum annual income level are not eligible for a family allowance, but in this case the cantons have the power to provide an allowance under the same conditions that are applicable to non-employed people.

344. Eligibility for a family allowance is accessory to an entitlement to a salary; eligibility only exists if there is an entitlement to a salary. If a position is filled in the middle of a month, the family allowance is paid in proportion to the number of days during which the salary is earned. This means that in Switzerland eligibility for the allowance is not tied to the child, but – with the exception of non-employed persons – to the employment status of the parents or the person raising the child. However, if a person is prevented from working through no fault of his own or if an employed person dies, family allowances continue to be paid during the current month and the three following months. They are also paid during maternity leave (*see* Article 10 of the Ordinance on Family Allowances (*Familienzulagenverordnung, FamZV*)).

II. Self-Employed People

345. Until the end of 2012 family allowances were not provided at the national level for self-employed people outside agriculture. In some cases, family allowances were paid to self-employed people at the cantonal level. Thirteen out of twenty-six cantons had family allowance regulations that included provisions for the self-employed. However, there were notable differences between the regulations.

346. In 2010, Parliament passed a bill extending eligibility to the self-employed outside agriculture (in force since January 2013). The political goal of the extension was to grant an allowance to every child, independent from the insurance status of its parents.

III. In Agriculture

347. Agricultural workers are one of the groups of recipients named in the FLG. The term 'agricultural worker' refers to people who are employed for pay by an agricultural enterprise and who mainly carry out agricultural tasks (Article 1a, paragraphs 1 and 4, FLG in conjunction with Article 1 of the Ordinance on Family Allowances in Agriculture (*Verordnung über die Familienzulagen in der Landwirtschaft, FLV*)).

348. Under the FLG, family allowances are also granted to self-employed farmers, regardless of whether they work full- or part-time (*see* Article 5, paragraph 1, FLG). They are deemed to work full-time if their agricultural activities provide the primary economic foundation for their existence.

349. Finally, the FLG includes two other groups of recipients: first, self-employed alpine herdsmen, which refers to people who tend livestock in an alpine meadow on a self-employed basis for at least two months a year without interruption (Article 5, FLG in conjunction with Article 3, paragraph 4, FLV); and second, full-time professional fishermen, regardless of whether they are self-employed or in the employment of others (Article 14 of the Federal Law on Fishery).

350. In order to be eligible for family allowances, agricultural workers must earn a specific minimum income. As of 2018, this minimum income is CHF 7,050 per year (*see* Article 4, sentence 2, FLG in conjunction with Article 34, paragraph 5, AHVG). An additional requirement not found in the FamZG is that wages must conform to the usual local rates paid to agricultural workers (Article 4a, FLG). Finally, as in the FamZG, allowances are always paid in full (Article 4, sentence 1, FLG). If an agricultural labourer works by the day, the eligibility for an allowance is also calculated by the day (cf. Article 2, FLV).

IV. Non-employed People

351. Certain groups of non-employed persons are also eligible for family allowances within the scope of the FamZG. These groups include people who are mandatorily insured in the AHV and are registered there as non-employed (Article 19, paragraph 1, FamZG).

352. Non-employed people are primarily defined as those who are not engaged in a gainful activity (cf. Article 16, FamZV). Evaluations are more difficult in the case of people who, for example, do seasonal work or work on a part-time basis. In such cases, a comparison is made between the contributions paid to the AHV on the basis of the gainful activity and those paid on the basis of the person's non-employed status.

353. Employees who earn less than CHF 7,050 per year (as of 2018) are not awarded family allowances on the basis of their employee status. Although the FamZG (still) lacks explicit regulations addressing this group of people, they should in fact be categorized as non-employed and granted the right to family allowances. It is inexplicable why this group is denied benefits while people who earn nothing at all or more than CHF 7,050 receive allowances.

354. Under certain circumstances, employees with small income who are not employed on a permanent or full-time basis are regarded as non-employed. This occurs when the employee in question is categorized as non-employed on the basis of a comparative calculation.

355. Non-employed people are only subject to the contribution regulations of the AHV after completion of their 20th year since they are only required to pay contributions from that point on (Article 3, paragraph 1, AHVG). Given the history of the law and the purpose of family allowances – and contrary to the wording of the law – it is to endorse that non-employed parents under the age of 20 are also eligible for family allowances.

356. Moreover, eligibility extends to social assistance recipients.

357. Non-employed spouses have no claim to allowances if their employed spouse pays a certain level of contributions to the AHV. In this case, the AHV contributions of the non-employed spouses are regarded as paid and the spouses are not registered as 'non-employed' by the AHV (cf. Article 16, letter c, FamZV in conjunction with Article 3, paragraph 3, AHVG). Nor do people who receive retirement benefits from the AHV after reaching the usual retirement age have any claim to family allowances (cf. Article 16, letter a, FamZV). The reason is that if these people are no longer gainfully employed, they are no longer required to pay contributions to the AHV.

358. Finally, in the case of non-employed people, eligibility for family allowances is linked to two additional requirements. First, their taxable income may not amount to more than CHF 42,300 (as of 2018; *see* Article 19, paragraph 2, FamZG in conjunction with Article 34, paragraphs 3 and 5, AHVG). This requirement is meant to ensure that the people who receive family allowances are actually in need of support. Second, non-employed people are not permitted to receive supplementary benefits in addition to benefits from the AHV or the IV (*see also* part 10).

359. The FamZG is a federal law that is merely meant to provide general guidelines, and the cantons have the power to frame more generous regulations with respect to the eligibility of non-employed persons (Article 18, FamZV). They can, for example, raise the income limit or pay allowances in addition to supplementary benefits. Nevertheless, the cantons are not permitted to impose stricter conditions on recipients.

V. Coordination

360. A fundamental principle is that the same type of allowance can only be paid once for each child. In other words, the same type of benefit cannot be accumulated.

361. The FamZG does not contain regulations addressing people who are eligible for several allowances. This situation can exist, for example, if a parent has two jobs, each in a different canton. But in such cases solutions can be derived from the *Kaskadenordnung* ('cascade system') that is legally defined in the FamZG. The *Kaskadenordnung* is applicable to situations in which several people are entitled to allowances for the same child (Article 7, FamZG). If the same person is eligible for a family allowance under the FamZG and the FLG, the claim from the FamZG takes precedence over that from the FLG (cf. Article 2a, FLG).

362. If several people have a claim to allowances for the same child, the FamZG rules that the person who is employed has primary eligibility (Article 7, paragraph 1a, FamZG). The problematic aspect of this solution is that this person can become unexpectedly ineligible due to the loss of his job, illness or an accident. The next in line is the person who has parental authority over the child (Article 7, paragraph 1b, FamZG) – in other words, the person who is responsible for and takes care of the child, whether on the basis of legal regulations, a court ruling or a contract. If the question of entitlement still cannot be resolved, the person eligible for the allowance is deemed to be that person with whom the child primarily lives (Article 7, paragraph 1c, FamZG). The fourth level of claims regulation states that the allowance is paid to the person to which the family allowance regulations in the child's canton of residence are applicable (Article 7, paragraph 1d, FamZG). This level is mainly of relevance in cases where both parents are employed, have joint custody of the child, and live together with the child in one canton, but where one parent is employed in another canton. After all, for cases in which both parents are employed in the same canton, have joint custody and live together with their child, the right to receive the allowance is granted to the person who has the higher income subject to AHV contributions (Article 7, paragraph 1e, FamZG).

363. The FLG cites the above-mentioned regulations of the FamZG in cases where different claims by several people must be coordinated (Article 9, paragraph 2b, FLG).

364. Since the cantons may introduce allowances that differ from the minimum amounts, the person with primary eligibility under the legal *Kaskadenordnung* may receive a smaller family allowance than a person with secondary eligibility. In such situations the law stipulates that the person with secondary eligibility (and only this person, not other eligible persons lower in the hierarchy) is granted the right to a differential payment (cf. Article 7, paragraph 2, FamZG). In order to determine whether a right to a differential payment exists, it must first be examined whether several people are eligible for family allowances. If this is affirmed, the people with primary and secondary eligibility must be defined. It must be noted that the right to a differential payment is ruled out if the person with secondary eligibility is non-employed.

365. Concerning relations between Switzerland and the EU/EFTA states, Article 76 of Regulation 1408/71 (concerning EFTA) and Article 68 of Regulation 883/2004 stipulate that, in principle, the child's country of residence is liable for payment. This means that the right to benefits is suspended in the country of employment if the child is also eligible for family allowances in his country of residence in accordance with the legal system there.

§2. The Child

366. Article 4 of the FamZG describes which children generally establish eligibility for family allowances. Concerning such children, the FLG cites Article 4 of the FamZG. The child's nationality plays no role in establishing eligibility for family allowances.

I. Biological and Adopted Children

367. It is usually a biological child that entitles a person to family allowances. 'Biological' refers to a relationship that emerges between the mother and child at birth under civil law. The child's relationship with the father is based on the father's marriage to the mother, his recognition of the child as his own or on a ruling on fatherhood.

368. The child can also enter into a relationship with the mother and father through adoption. In regard to the law, biological and adopted children are equal.

II. Stepchildren

369. Stepchildren are the spouse's children who were born out of wedlock, were adopted, or who originate from an earlier marriage. The child of the registered partner as defined in the Partnership Law (*Partnerschaftsgesetz*) is also considered a stepchild. In this case, the conditions applicable to the payment of allowances are the same as those applicable to the stepchild of a spouse. By contrast, the child of a domestic partner is not considered a stepchild.

370. One additional requirement must be fulfilled for a person to be eligible for family allowances for a stepchild: the child in question must mainly live in the stepparent's household or at least have lived with this parent until maturity (Article 4, paragraph 1, FamZV). The background to this rule is the assumption by the legislators that the stepparent makes a contribution to supporting the child in a joint household or that he made this contribution until the child reached maturity. It is irrelevant whether a third party pays benefits such as alimony.

III. Foster Children

371. A child is considered to be fostered by a couple if he has been taken into the foster parents' home for permanent care and upbringing and not for work or occupational training. In this sense, the child has the status of a biological child. He entitles the foster parents to receive family allowances if the fostering relationship is permanent and not based on remuneration (Article 5, FamZV). It is irrelevant whether the foster child is under age or related to the foster parents. It must be noted that the domestic partner's child is never considered a foster child in the sense of the FamZG.

372. If, from the outset, the foster child's stay is limited to less than one year, the criterion of permanence is essentially not fulfilled. But even if it is uncertain whether the child will really remain with his foster parents until he begins working life, the foster parents' intention to keep the foster child with them permanently is generally sufficient to meet this requirement.

373. The condition that payment may not form the basis of the relationship between the foster parents and the child is considered to be met if any contributions by third parties to the foster parents (support payments, advance child support payments, social insurance benefits) amount to less than one-quarter of the actual costs of supporting the child.

IV. Siblings and Grandchildren

374. Finally, people can be entitled to family allowances because of siblings or grandchildren, but only on the condition that they are primarily responsible for supporting their sibling or grandchild. This is considered to be the case if the child lives in the household of the recipient and all financial contributions by third parties to the support of the child do not exceed the amount of a maximum full orphan's pension from the AHV. Even if the child does not live in the household, though, the recipient can still assert a claim to family allowances if he makes a contribution to the child's support that equals or exceeds the maximum full orphan's pension from the AHV (Article 6, FamZV).

V. Children Residing Abroad

375. According to the regulations of the FamZG, children who reside abroad may also establish eligibility for family allowances. The determination of whether a child resides abroad is based on the Federal Law on International Private Law (*Bundesgesetz über das internationale Privatrecht, IPR, SR 291*).

376. The Swiss Federal Council has the power to define the conditions under which the children in question establish eligibility for family allowances (Article 4, paragraph 3, FamZG). An important point is that under the regulations of the FamZG and the FamZV, the nationality of the children and the person eligible for the benefit is irrelevant. Likewise, the provisions can also be applied to Swiss children and Swiss nationals who reside in Switzerland. The only condition stipulated by the FamZG is that the amount of the allowance must be based on the purchasing power in the country of residence. This applies not only to the minimum amount specified by federal law but also to possible higher amounts in the cantons.

377. The Swiss Federal Council has created regulations pertaining to claims to allowances for children residing abroad. It has selected a very restrictive solution, decreeing that family allowances can only be paid to children residing abroad if this is prescribed by international agreements (Article 7, FamZV). As a result, Switzerland only 'exports' family allowances if it is required to do so by agreements with other states.

378. The restriction that family allowances be adapted to the purchasing power in the country of residence and the further requirements detailed by the Swiss Federal Council are not applicable in the field of application of international agreements because other possible conditions arise from the treaties in these areas.

379. Important treaties in this regard are the FZA, as well as the EFTA-Agreement. The principle of the country of employment is generally applicable within the scope of these agreements, which means that employed people are in principle subject to the legal system of the country where they work. Switzerland has also signed agreements with different states outside the EU/EFTA. A part of these agreements covers only family allowances in the agricultural sector.

380. In special cases, family allowances can be paid to children domiciled abroad even if Switzerland is not obliged to do so under agreements with other states (Article 7, paragraph 2, FamZV). But this exception only applies to special groups of employees, such as Swiss citizens who work abroad in the service of either the Swiss Confederation, an international organization, or a relief organization, and who are mandatorily insured in the AHV during this period (Article 1a, paragraph 1c, AHVG). This rule also applies to Swiss or foreign nationals who have been sent abroad on a temporary basis by an employer based in Switzerland and who remain insured in the AHV (Article 1a, paragraph 3, AHVG). But in these cases the eligibility for family allowances is subsidiary to other possible claims to allowances in the country of residence. In addition, there must be a relationship between the child and the employee in the sense of the ZGB, which is why, for example, stepchildren, foster children, siblings and grandchildren are excluded.

381. As concerns the payment of child and education allowances for the children of agricultural employees who reside abroad, the FLG cites the germane regulations in the FamZG (Article 1a, paragraph 3, sentence 2, FLG).

382. According to the FLG, household allowances are paid regardless of where the child resides. Nevertheless, the agricultural employee must live in Switzerland with his family (Article 1a, paragraph 3, sentence 1, FLG) and meet one of the following three conditions: He must live in a shared household with his spouse and/or children; live in a household community (*Hausgemeinschaft*) with his employer while his spouse and/or children run a household, whose costs he covers; or live in a household community with his employer together with his spouse and/or children (Article 3, paragraph 1, FLG). If the family members are EU or EFTA citizens, entitlement to a household allowance also exists if the spouse and the children live in an EU or EFTA state.

§3. The Person Receiving the Benefit

383. Depending on who has primary eligibility, the right to receive family allowance is granted to either of the parents of the child who entitles them to child allowance. In principle, the family allowance is thus paid to the insured person.

384. However, under certain conditions, payment can also be made to third parties. This can occur, for example, when the paid family allowances are not used to meet the needs of the person for whom they are intended, in violation of their purpose (Article 9, paragraph 1, FamZG).

385. In order to clarify whether a payment to a third party is possible, an attempt must be made to determine who there is the decisive person. This can be the child or another person such as a parent who takes care of the child. Then, the most important needs must be defined. Since family allowances are meant to cover additional family-related expenses, in most cases the needs consist of paying for at least part of the child's support. If the paid family allowances are not used for the needs of the central person, it is possible to pay the allowance to a third party. But the third party in question must file a request for payment.

386. Another case of a 'third-party payment' exists when education allowances are paid directly to the adult child (Article 9, paragraph 2, FamZG). The requirement for this payment is a well-founded request, though it must be noted that the law does not define what exactly this means. According to the Federal Council, a third-party payment should be possible, for example, if the parent and child have a troubled relationship or if the people required to provide support do not perform their duty. The possibility of a third-party payment exists only for education allowances, not for child allowances, and is only possible for adult children.

Chapter 3. The Amount of the Benefit

387. Both the FamZG and the FLG include provisions on child and education allowances (Articles 3 and 5, FamZG; Articles 2, 7 and 9, FLG). The age limits specified in these laws are compulsory for the cantons, which have regulatory freedom only when it comes to setting the amount of the benefits (Article 3, paragraph 2, FamZG; Article 24, FLG). Furthermore, the FLG provides for a household allowance (Articles 2 and 3, FLG). Under the FamZG, the cantons are free to provide birth and adoption allowances in addition to child and education allowances.

388. Within the scope of the FLG, family allowances are funded through different sources. On the one hand, employers pay contributions; on the other, the federation and the cantons provide subsidies (Articles 18 et seq., FLG).

389. By contrast, under the FamZG, the method of funding the allowance is not regulated at a federal level, but left to the cantons (Article 16, paragraph 1, FamZG). In practice this means that the family allowances for employees are financed by employers and by the self-employed persons. There is only one canton in which employees participate in financing. The contributions are set as a percentage of the salary upon which employees pay AHV contributions (Article 16, paragraph 2, FamZG). The levels differ significantly per canton, ranging from 0.5% to 3.1% (as of 2015).

390. Family allowances for non-employed people must be funded by the cantons (Article 20, FamZG). It can be inferred indirectly from the FamZG that the federal government cannot be called upon to provide financing. At the same time, FamZG stipulates that, under certain circumstances, the cantons are free to require non-employed people to pay a contribution. Furthermore, the cantons can also call on the municipalities to share in financing.

§1. Basic Amounts

I. Child Allowances

391. Child allowances are paid beginning in the month in which the child is born (Article 3, paragraph 1a, FamZG). The condition for the start of payment is that the child is recorded as a live birth in the civil registry. If the child is stillborn, no right exists to a child allowance for the month of birth. In other cases, the right to receive payments exists up to the month in which the child completes his 16th year or up to the end of the month in which the child dies.

392. If the child is unable to earn a living, the child allowance is paid until completion of his 20th year. A child is considered unable to earn a living if, after treatment and integration efforts, he must contend with a partial or complete loss of his ability to earn a living in a well-balanced labour market due to an impairment of his physical, mental or emotional health (Article 7, ATSG). This benefit is designed to provide economic support for families with a disabled child.

393. Under the FLG, the child allowance amounts to at least CHF 200 per month. In mountainous regions it is topped off by a monthly amount of CHF 20 (Article 2, paragraph 3, and Article 7, FLG in conjunction with Article 5, paragraph 1, FamZG).

394. Under the FamZG, the specific amount of the monthly child allowance can differ depending on the canton. It is irrelevant whether the beneficiary is an employed, a self-employed or a non-employed person. The FamZG stipulates that the child benefit must amount to at least CHF 200 per month (Article 5, paragraph 1, FamZG). The majority of cantons pay only this minimum amount, but a few cantons pay higher benefits, with the amounts ranging from CHF 210 to CHF 400 (as of 2018). Some of the cantons pay less for children under the age of 12 than for older children. Other cantons pay more for the third and subsequent child than for the first two children.

II. Education Allowances

395. In order to receive education allowances, a young person must be older than 16 and enrolled in a school or occupational training programme (Article 3, paragraph 1b, FamZG; Article 1, FamZV in conjunction with Article 25, paragraph 5, AHVG and Article 49*bis* AHVV; Article 2, paragraph 1, and Article 7, FLG). This programme must last at least one month and the young person must intend to complete a fixed programme of study. If he is gainfully employed and only attends courses or school on the side, he is not deemed to be in an educational programme and is therefore ineligible for education allowances. Nor is he eligible for the benefit if he is enrolled in an occupational training programme but earns more than CHF 28,200 per year (as of 2018). The right to an education allowance expires upon the death of the child, upon completion of the educational programme, or, if the programme is only completed after his 25th birthday, at the end of the month in which the child ends his 25th year.

396. Under the FLG, the people eligible for the education allowance receive an amount of at least CHF 250 per month. In mountainous regions this amount is topped off by a monthly amount of CHF 20 per month (Article 2, paragraph 3, and Article 7, FLG in conjunction with Article 5, paragraph 2, FamZG).

397. The FamZG provides for a minimum education allowance of CHF 250 per month (Article 5, paragraph 2, FamZG). Once again, the majority of the cantons do not exceed this minimum amount. In the cantons that do, the monthly payments range from CHF 270 to CHF 525 (as of 2018). A number of cantons pay different education benefits based on the age of the child (younger/older than 18) or the number of benefits per family (higher benefits for the third and subsequent child).

III. Household Allowances

398. Under certain circumstances, agricultural employees who are subject to the FLG are eligible for a household allowance. To qualify, they must meet one of three conditions: they must run a joint household in Switzerland with their spouse and/or children; live in a household community (*Hausgemeinschaft*) with their employer while their spouse and/or children run a household, whose costs they cover; or live in a household community with their employer together with their spouse and/or children (Article 3, FLG). The household allowance, which amounts to CHF 100 per month (Article 2, paragraph 2, FLG), is meant to make it easier for people to establish and cover the costs of a household – and thus prevent rural depopulation.

§2. Birth Allowance

399. Birth allowances are not provided at the national level. It is left to the individual cantons to make such grants available (Article 3, paragraph 2, FamZG; Article 2 FamZV). Ten cantons currently pay a birth allowance (2018).

400. The purpose of the birth allowance is to offset at least part of the special costs associated with giving birth to a child. In contrast to the child and education allowances, it is a one-time benefit. The general rule is that one grant is paid per child, and it is left to the cantons to decide whether they wish to pay a grant for all the children from a multiple birth.

401. However, the FamZG requires that various conditions be met for the payment of a birth allowance (Article 3, paragraph 2, FamZG; Article 2, FamZV):

- First, a right to the grant must exist under the applicable cantonal regulations governing family allowances.
- Second, the right to child allowances must exist under the FamZG.
- Third, during the nine months directly preceding the birth, the mother must have been domiciled or had her habitual residence in Switzerland. This requirement is meant to prevent abuse and is applicable even if the father or a third party asserts a claim to the birth allowance in the place of the mother. In the case of premature births, the mother must be domiciled or have had her habitual abode in Switzerland for a shorter time.
- Fourth, the child must be born alive or after a pregnancy of at least twenty-three weeks. This means that the right to a birth allowance exists after a pregnancy lasting twenty-three weeks, regardless of whether the baby is a live birth or stillborn.

402. The amount of the birth allowance varies widely – from CHF 850 to CHF 3,000 (as of 2018) – in the cantons that provide such a benefit. Some cantons have different rules for multiple births or for the first, second and third child. The amount of the birth allowance can vary accordingly.

403. Like birth allowances, adoption allowances are not prescribed at the national level. Here, too, it is left to the cantons to determine whether they want to provide such allowances. However, under the FamZG, an adoption allowance can be granted only if, at a minimum, the five following conditions are met (Article 3, paragraphs 2 and 3, FamZG; Article 3, FamZV):

- First, the applicable cantonal regulations governing family allowances must include such a benefit. At the moment, eight cantons have applicable regulations (as of 2018).
- Second, a claim to a child allowance must exist under the FamZG.
- Third, the child that is to be adopted must be a minor, meaning the child may not be 18 when it is considered for subsequent adoption.
- Fourth, adoption allowances are granted only if the adopted child is not a stepchild.
- Fifth, the final approval for taking in the child must be granted and the underage child must in fact have been taken on in Switzerland. It is not necessary for the adoption to have taken place. It is sufficient that the parents had permission to take in the child for the subsequent adoption and that child was actually taken in.

404. Depending on the canton, the amount of the allowance ranges from CHF 850 to CHF 3,000 (as of 2018) – whereas higher benefits are paid for the third and subsequent adopted child or in the case of multiple adoptions, as compared to the adoption of just one or two children.

405. If, for whatever reason, the adoption is not finalized, the adoption allowance must not be paid back. It must be emphasized that the adoption of a stepchild does not establish eligibility for an adoption allowance.

§3. Socio-Pedagogical Allowance

406. As already mentioned, only the child and education allowances are stipulated at the national level. The cantons are free to provide additional benefits. These benefits can include, for example, advance child support payments, benefits for single parents, scholarships and housing allowances. Most cantons offer a variety of such benefits.

407. Finally, it is possible for individual employers – on the basis of collective or individual employment agreements – to provide additional benefits for the support of families. But in contrast to the family allowances regulated in the FLG and FamZG, this support is subject to private and not public law.

Chapter 4. Collective Services

408. There continues to be a lack of childcare slots to assist families. As a result, not all mothers – or fathers – who would like to work are able to do so, as they are unable to enrol their children in childcare. Recognizing this need, the federation passed the Federal Law on Financial Assistance for Childcare outside the Family (*Bundesgesetz über Finanzhilfen für familienergänzende Kinderbetreuung, SR 861*) in 2002. On the basis of this law, the federation provides financial assistance in the form of approved loans to create childcare slots. The goal is to help reconcile family and working life.

409. Financial assistance is paid to childcare centres, facilities that care for children after the lessons until the end of the mandatory school days, structures that coordinate care in day care families, and natural persons, cantons, municipalities and further legal persons for projects with innovation character in the field of preschool age childcare (Article 2, paragraph 1). Funding goes to new institutions or to existing ones that plan to significantly expand their offerings (Article 2, paragraph 2).

410. Financial assistance is permitted to make up a maximum of one-third of capital and operating expenses and may not exceed CHF 5,000 per slot per year. Furthermore, assistance is granted for a maximum of three years (Article 5, paragraph 4). This impetus programme was initially limited to eight years. It would have expired at the end of 2011, but the legislators extended the programme by an additional four years, followed by another four (until 31 January 2019; Article 10), since the results of the first few years had been very positive.

Chapter 5. Guaranteed Family Allowances

411. Mothers or fathers may experience hardship as the result of their child's birth and may be forced by economic circumstances to engage in a gainful activity, although they would prefer to attend to their child's care and upbringing personally. Such financial bottlenecks cannot be adequately compensated for by the family allowances, which are not based on need and do not take the beneficiary's specific circumstances into account.

412. In order to support parents who are experiencing difficult economic circumstances, half of the cantons currently provide special benefits in addition to family allowances.

413. These are needs-based benefits that take different forms in the various cantons. In general, they are hybrid forms that combine social insurance benefits and social assistance benefits. Some are paid only to mothers, others also to fathers. In principle, the question of whether a person is eligible for these types of need-based benefits depends on that person's income and assets. The specific level of support is determined on the basis of the identified need. Nevertheless, some cantons have also specified maximum monthly amounts. In many cases, certain waiting periods must also be observed, meaning that the mother or father must be a resident of the canton or municipality for a defined period of time. In addition, in some cases specified workloads may not be exceeded, so as to ensure that the mother or father can really attend to the child's care and upbringing personally. The duration of the benefits differs depending on the canton. In some cantons, benefits are paid for a maximum of six months after the child's birth. In others, benefits are paid for two, three or even six years after birth.

414. Ticino stands out among these cantons. On the one hand, it offers benefits for young children in order to help families cover their special needs. This benefit is paid for three years after the child's birth. On the other hand, supplementary benefits can also be paid that are explicitly designed to cover the child's needs. If required, these benefits can continue until the age of 15. In most cases, the need-based benefits paid at the cantonal level are financed by the beneficiaries' cantons or municipalities.

415. Different political efforts at the national level to provide families in economically difficult circumstances with need-based benefits in addition to a family allowance have not been successful until now.

Chapter 6. Provisional Payment

416. If it is not clear at the beginning of the year whether an employee will earn the minimum income for the entire year, the family allowance is initially disbursed to him for those months in which his income exceeds CHF 588 (i.e., one-twelfth of 7,050; all figures as of 2018). At the end of the year, an additional payment can be made for the remaining months if he has earned the minimum income of CHF 7,050 per year.

417. If it is not clear whether the person with primary eligibility will reach the necessary minimum income level for the entire year, the responsible Compensation Offices must reach agreement on paying the family allowance to the person whose income clearly exceeds the minimum income. The purpose of this regulation is to ensure that the recipient of the family allowance does not constantly change.

Part V. Incapacity to Work

Introduction

418. In the Swiss social insurance system there is no insurance which solely and conclusively covers the risk of an incapacity to work. Rather, there are several types of insurance, namely, health insurance, accident insurance, military insurance, disability insurance, compensation for lost income, and the occupational pension system (occupational pension funds), which are responsible for covering risks, depending on the cause of the incapacity to work.

419. A person's incapacity to work can be the consequence of unemployment, sickness, accident, maternity or the performance of a service (e.g., military service).

420. The benefits that the Swiss social insurance system provides to cover these risks can be subdivided into cash benefits and in-kind benefits. The following chapter focuses on cash benefits.

421. The statutory in-kind benefits provided in the event of an incapacity to work or earn a living are also covered in Part III, 'Health Care', Part VI, 'Industrial Accidents and Occupational Diseases', as well as Part IX, 'The Handicapped Persons'. The risk of unemployment will not be dealt with in this chapter (*see* Part VII).

Chapter 1. Field of Application

§1. Territorial Field of Application

422. The cash and in-kind benefits for people who cannot work do not necessarily depend on whether their place of residence is in Switzerland; these people may receive benefits if they are covered by the responsible social insurance scheme.

423. The place of residence, however, does play a role in the disability and health insurance schemes. In principle, the entire resident population of Switzerland has a right to statutory benefits. Additionally, people who do not have their principal residence in Switzerland but work in the country may join the disability and health insurance schemes.

424. In the accident insurance scheme and the occupational pension system, coverage is linked to dependent employment, not the place of residence. Both the compensation scheme for lost income and the military insurance scheme also insure persons independent of their place of residence if – generally speaking – they perform military service or serve in the civil defence.

425. According to the EOG, maternity benefits can be granted to women who are insured by the old-age and survivors' or IV. The place of residence therefore only has a certain importance for disability and health insurance.

426. Since one's place of residence is often irrelevant to the provision of benefits, these benefits can be provided outside Switzerland if the insured person does not have his residence in Switzerland. But there are certain exceptions to this rule. For example, in the IV, pension benefits for degrees of disability under 50% are paid only to those insured people who have their domicile and habitual residence in Switzerland (Article 29, paragraph 4, IVG).

427. These explanations of the territorial field of application apply only to relations with third countries. Switzerland's relations with EU and EFTA Member States are subject to the coordinating body of European social law, in which applicability is essentially based on the place of work and not on residence. If a person is employed in several states, the applicable law is that of the state in which the person in question lives. As far as benefit law goes, the application of European coordinating rules means that cash benefits can generally be provided abroad. Under the rulings of the Federal Supreme Court, this also holds for benefits for disability levels under 50%. However, with respect to in-kind benefits, so-called *Sachleistungsaushilfe* comes into play; that is to say, those persons who live in a state other than the one in which they are insured are granted in-kind benefits at the expense of the relevant insurance in the state where they live.

§2. Personal Field of Application

428. People who are unable to work qualify for benefits if they are insured by one of the insurance schemes responsible for benefits and fulfil the legal prerequisites.

429. People are insured if they have their place of residence in Switzerland, earn their living there or are in the Swiss military or other service. As concerns the insurance coverage and the related obligation to pay premiums on the part of employed people, it makes no difference whether they are employees or civil servants.

430. With respect to self-employed people, it must be noted that they are not always compulsorily insured in all branches which are relevant for the incapacity to work. They are compulsorily insured under old-age and survivors' insurance, disability insurance and the compensation scheme for lost income, but not under accident insurance or the occupational pension system. If they wish, they can voluntarily insure themselves in both these programmes.

431. In the individual insurance schemes, the groups subject to contributions are not necessarily the same as the groups that are eligible for benefits. In the case of disability insurance, the occupational pension system and the compensation scheme for lost income, the employer and employee each pay half of what is owed for the employee. The (voluntary) insurance for a daily sick-pay allowance is generally co-financed by the employer and the employee, but only the employee may claim benefits.

432. In the case of accident insurance, the employer assumes the premiums for industrial accidents and the employee for non-industrial accidents, but in both cases the benefits go to the employee.

Chapter 2. Specific Risks

433. Depending on the reason why a person cannot work or the length of the limitation, different risks are in play:

– Short-term incapacity to work due to sickness or accident.
– Military service, service in the civil defence, etc.
– Maternity.
– Long-term incapacity to work or earn a living (disability).
– Death.

434. In Switzerland various insurance programmes offer protection against these risks. Coordination of the individual branches of insurance is therefore of utmost importance.

§1. Funeral Benefit

435. In Swiss social insurance law there is no special life insurance. Rather, if an insured person dies, various social insurance schemes provide for partial or entire payment of the costs of transporting the corpse, of the funeral or of supporting the survivors by means of survivors' benefits.

436. Whether or not a certain insurance programme is obliged to pay benefits depends on the cause of the insured person's death. A more detailed discussion can be found elsewhere regarding the survivors' benefits provided by old-age and survivors' insurance, the occupational pension system, accident insurance and military insurance. The following focuses solely on the costs reimbursed by the accident insurance and military insurance schemes for the transport of the corpse and the funeral of one of their insured. Relatives of the insured do not profit from these benefits in the event of their own death.

I. Transport of the Corpse

437. If the insured person dies as the result of an industrial accident, a non-industrial accident or an occupational disease, the accident insurance scheme assumes the necessary costs of transporting the corpse to the place of burial (Article 14, paragraph 1, UVG). Within Switzerland itself there is no limit on the costs that are assumed. If the costs are incurred abroad, these are reimbursed up to a maximum of one-fifth of the maximum insured annual income, which is presently set at CHF 29,640 (as of 2018). An individual is eligible for reimbursement of the costs incurred in transporting a corpse if he can prove that he himself has assumed the costs (Articles 21 and 22, UVV).

438. If the insured person has died as the result of an insured health impairment, the military insurance scheme also reimburses the costs of transporting the corpse from the place of death to the place where the corpse is laid out or buried. There is no provision limiting the costs.

II. Burial Costs

439. Along with the costs of transporting the corpse, accident insurance also assumes the burial costs of insured people upon advent of the insured risk. Compensation is set on the basis of the costs that have been effectively incurred. But the law provides for an upper limit to this compensation, namely, sevenfold the maximum insured daily earnings (Article 14, paragraph 2, UVG). The maximum insured earnings are CHF 406 per day (as of 2018; Article 22, paragraph 1, UVV). In other words, a maximum of CHF 2,842 can be paid for a burial.

440. If the insured person dies as the result of an insured injury, not only the accident insurance but also the military insurance scheme provides compensation for burial costs (Article 60, MVG). As is the case with accident insurance, the compensation provided by military insurance has an absolute limit, which is presently set at CHF 15,228 (as of 2018). This equates to one-tenth of the maximum annual earnings insured by military insurance (*see* Article 15, paragraph 1, of the Ordinance on the Military Insurance (*Verordnung über die Militärversicherung, MVV*)). However, in contrast to accident insurance, compensation is not based on the actual costs. Rather, a lump sum is paid. Compensation is paid to the person who has assumed the burial costs – this need not be a relative or friend of the deceased, but can also be a third party. Nevertheless, a legal entity such as a municipality is ineligible for compensation.

§2. Incapacity to Work

I. Incapacity to Work (*Arbeitsunfähigkeit*)

441. Article 6 of the ATSG describes the incapacity to work as an impairment of one's physical, mental or psychological health that results in the partial or complete inability to perform reasonable work in one's previous occupation or area of responsibility. This is the basic definition for evaluating employed, self-employed, and non-employed individuals.

442. The capacity to work allows a person to perform reasonable work in their previous occupation or area of responsibility. If physical, mental or psychological impairments to a person's health restrict his capacity to work, there can be certain repercussions under social insurance law.

443. The decision as to whether an individual is possibly incapable of working is not based on a theoretical medical evaluation but rather on the particular case at hand and whether and to what degree the impairment of the individual's health will affect his concrete activities. The health impairment must have been caused by sickness or accident and must, moreover, be the reason for the person's full or partial incapacity to perform reasonable work in his previous occupation or area of responsibility.

444. In accord with Article 6 of the ATSG, in the health insurance, disability insurance and accident insurance schemes, the incapacity to work is viewed as the loss of capacity to perform functionally. A comparison of income or function with regard to the concrete activity last performed is undertaken in order to assess the degree of a person's incapacity to work. This has the result that the degree of the disability does not always coincide with the theoretical medical restriction. In the case of non-employed people, the degree of disability is judged on the basis of how restricted the individual might be in their area of responsibility (keeping a household, raising children, etc.). The decisive factor is the degree to which the person concerned is restricted in the performance of housekeeping duties or child-rearing or in pursuing their education and training.

445. In terms of measuring the degree of an individual's incapacity to work, military insurance provides an exception to Article 6 of the ATSG (Article 28, paragraph 3, MVG). It undertakes a comparison between the income that the insured is presumably still capable of earning and the income that he would have earned in his previous occupation or field of activity without any impairment of his health. Consequently, it is based on the degree to which the person is economically disadvantaged in his previous occupation. A loss of earnings is thus (for working people) the prerequisite for any payment of daily allowances.

II. Incapacity to Earn a Living (*Erwerbsunfähigkeit*)

446. The incapacity to earn a living is defined in Article 7 of the ATSG as the loss of employability in a balanced labour market that results from the impairment of a person's physical, mental or psychological health and that remains in effect after reasonable efforts at treatment and integration. It is only the effects of the damage to a person's health that may be considered in judging whether an incapacity to earn a living exists. Moreover, this incapacity exists only if it cannot be overcome based on an objective judgment. Article 7 of the ATSG does not address non-employed individuals.

447. In Article 7 of the ATSG, the concept of an incapacity to earn a living is applied only to self-employed and employed people. First, there must be an impairment of the individual's health. This includes physical, mental and psychological impairments. It is important to note that the health impairment is judged on the basis of the 'reasonableness' criterion. A check is made as to whether the insured person, acting in good faith, can adequately perform work. Furthermore, the incapacity to earn a living is only evaluated if appropriate treatment and integration efforts have already taken place.

448. Under Article 7 of the ATSG, the 'opportunities to earn a living' are defined as the subjective opportunities that an individual has to pursue gainful employment. These depend on the person's age, education, experience and certain health factors. Under Article 7 of the ATSG, only health impairments may be considered when judging the incapacity to earn a living; so-called non-disability factors may not be considered.

449. There must be a natural and adequate causal connection between the damage to a person's health and the loss of the opportunity to earn a living. Judgment is based on the segment of the labour market 'under consideration', which is determined with a view to the insured individual and the concrete situation. Moreover, this judgment must proceed from the assumption of a balanced labour market; that is to say, from a balance between supply and demand. In this way a distinction is drawn between the risk of an inability to earn a living and that of unemployment.

450. When it comes to answering the question of whether an inability to earn a living can be overcome, an objective judgment must be made that has nothing to do with the subjective feelings of the person concerned.

III. Disability

451. 'Disability' is described in Article 8 of the ATSG, though it must be noted that it is a performance-related concept. Article 8, paragraph 1, of the ATSG applies it to working people and states that a disability exists if a person is entirely or partially incapable of earning a living for the foreseeable future or over a longer period of time. In such a case no distinction is made between the employees or self-employed people.

452. Article 8, paragraph 3, of the ATSG addresses non-employed people, who are seen as having a disability if they are entirely or partially unable to perform the duties in their previous area of responsibility. Once again, only the consequences of a health impairment may be considered, and the impossibility of performing one's duties must be objectively insurmountable.

453. The definition of disability, when applied to working and non-employed people, consists of various elements. On the one hand, a medical element must be present, namely, a health impairment. On the other hand, there needs to be an economic element, which is reflected in the effects on a person's ability to engage in gainful work or his field of responsibility. Furthermore, there must be a connection between both of these elements. Finally, a temporal element plays a role, namely, the duration of the impairment.

454. In other words, in contrast to an incapacity to work, there is a temporal criterion for the concept of disability. A permanent incapacity to earning a living presupposes that the individual's health be stable. This cannot be the case as long as the ailment is still being treated. The ATSG does not define what is meant by 'a longer-term incapacity to earn a living'. In order to understand the precise meaning of this term, it is therefore necessary to give due regard to the applicable individual laws. One only has the right to a pension in the IV after the period of one year (Article 28, paragraph 1, IVG), whereas in the accident insurance scheme, the decisive factor is the point in time at which the continuation of medical treatment is not expected to bring about any substantial improvement in the patient's condition (Article 19, paragraph 1, UVG).

455. In various branches of social insurance, a disability often only becomes relevant under benefits law if the loss of the functional ability to perform tasks in one's previous occupation or area of responsibility has reached a certain percentage rate. There can be considerable variations in the level of this percentage rate among the various insurance programmes (e.g., 10% in accident insurance, 40% in disability insurance).

456. With respect to cash benefits, the Swiss social insurance system makes a clear distinction between an incapacity to work and a disability. Whereas a claim to a daily allowance may exist in the event of an incapacity to work, the payment of a pension must be reviewed in the case of a disability.

IV. Maternity

457. Under Article 5 of the ATSG, the risks associated with maternity encompass pregnancy, the delivery of a child and the mother's subsequent convalescence. What is important here is that a woman who does not work because she has just had a child is not incapable of working in the sense of Article 6 of the ATSG. In other words, maternity is not characterized as an illness.

458. Article 5 of the ATSG does not specify how long the mother's convalescence lasts. This is left to the individual laws that provide for maternity benefits.

459. Under Swiss labour law, mothers are prohibited from working during the first eight weeks after giving birth to their child. According to labour law regulations, it is only with their consent that they may be employed within the eight weeks following these first eight weeks after delivery. The various social insurance programmes have given only limited consideration to these timeframes when structuring their benefits. For instance, the daily allowance for mothers can be dispensed for a maximum of fourteen weeks.

V. Military Service, Civil Defence and Similar Forms of Service

460. People may serve (or be required to serve) in the Swiss Army, civil defence or Red Cross, or they may do alternative service, take part in specialized training for 'Youth + Sport' at the federal or cantonal level, or attend a course for trainers of young marksmen.

461. During this period the person concerned may not be able to work in their occupation or area of responsibility. This type of incapacity to work is also covered by social insurance benefits (*see* Article 1a, EOG). They are available to employed, self-employed and non-employed individuals.

Chapter 3. Certification of the Incapacity to Work

§1. Primary Incapacity to Work

I. Incapacity to Work (or Inability to Earn a Living) as the Result of Sickness or Accident

462. Should an employee become sick or have an accident, it is his responsibility to demonstrate the existence of conditions requiring the employer to continue payment of his salary. The law itself does not dictate just how the employee is to prove an incapacity to work. As a rule, the employee must show that he is incapable of work due to sickness or accident by presenting a medical certificate.

463. The employment contract often contains an agreement requiring the employee to present a medical certificate if he is absent from work for more than two or three days. But even without such a clause in the contract, the employer can demand a medical certificate. If he has doubts as to the veracity of this certificate, he can then demand that the employee undergo examination by a medical examiner. The employer can refuse to continue paying the employee's salary as long as the employee is unable to show that he is incapable of work. In principle this also holds for public employees. The concrete requirements are specified in the law applicable to personnel.

464. But it is often not the employer, but an insurance provider, who is obliged to continue paying an employee's salary. In other words, the insurance provider reimburses the employer for the cost of continued payment of the salary. This can be the health insurance provider (in the case of someone voluntarily entering into a contract for a daily sick-pay allowance) or providers of accident, military or disability insurance.

465. Many employers take out an insurance policy for a daily sick-pay allowance for their employees. After a predefined period, these policies release them from their obligation to continue paying their employees' salaries in case of sickness. If an employee is sick for a certain number of days and the waiting period expires, it is up to the employer to inform the insurer that the employee is sick. In most cases there are forms for reporting this circumstance that can be downloaded directly from the Internet. In each case, an employee's incapacity to work must be documented by a physician who is authorized by the insurer. The insurers often have special forms for sick reports that are to be filled out by the insured people and their attending physician.

466. The UVG holds that the insured employee must immediately inform his employer or insurer of any accident that has made medical treatment necessary or that results in an incapacity to work (Article 45, paragraph 1, UVG). The employer, for his part, is likewise obligated to inform the insurer upon learning that an employee has had an accident and requires medical treatment or is incapable of work (Article 45, paragraph 2, UVG). Self-employed insured people who are voluntarily insured in the accident insurance scheme must report any accident directly to the insurer (Article 45, paragraph 3, UVG). Should there not be any legitimate excuse for the insured person's failure to report the accident, benefits can be reduced or even denied entirely (Article 46, UVG). In reporting the accident, the employer and the attending physician must fill in the relevant forms, which provide information that serves to clarify the sequence of events leading to the accident as well as the medical consequences of the accident (Article 53, paragraph 3, UVV). The insured person has an obligation to cooperate with the insurer. He must provide the insurer with all the necessary information and all those documents that might assist in clarifying the facts and consequences of the accident and in determining the insurance benefits. He must also authorize all those persons and offices that are able to provide relevant information for clarifying benefits to provide such information. Additionally, he must submit to those measures dictated by the insurer so as to clarify the case (*see* Article 55, UVV).

467. Insofar as claims can be made for potential benefits from the military insurance scheme in the event of sickness or accident, the insured person has the obligation, during his service, to report all known health impairments to the army doctor or the doctor responsible for his course, or, after his service, to a doctor, dentist or chiropractor (Article 83, paragraphs 1 and 2, MVG). If the reporting obligation is wilfully ignored and results in increased costs to the military insurance scheme, the benefits can be reduced accordingly (Article 83, paragraph 3, MVG). If there appears to be a connection between any reported impairments of the individual's health and his service, the physician, dentist or chiropractor who has been consulted is required to immediately report the case to the military insurance scheme (Article 84, MVG). Special forms are available for such cases. If the doctor neglects to do this, he is then responsible for any possible consequences. The insured person must then provide all necessary information for clarifying the claim and determining the benefits. Moreover, he must authorize all persons and offices to provide all the information that is necessary to clarify his eligibility for benefits (Article 28, ATSG).

468. Anyone who wishes to receive benefits from the IV must register with the disability insurance offices using an official form (Article 65, paragraph 1, IVV). The IV then undertakes to clarify the particular circumstances of the case, for which it can demand reports and other information, obtain expert evaluations, carry out investigations in situ, and summon the insured person to a meeting (*see* Article 69, IVV). Additionally, regional medical services have been set up to assist the disability insurance offices in judging whether the medical requirements for benefit claims are in evidence (*see* Article 59, IVG). It is their task to determine the relevant functional capacity of the insured person. In order to prevent the wrongful receipt of benefits, the IV may also bring in specialists – that is, private detectives for observing the insured – when doubts as to the true state of the insured person's health cannot be eliminated in any other way. The insured person, for his part, is not only required to furnish all information demanded of him to clarify the claim and determine any possible benefits, but also to authorize all relevant persons and offices to provide information considered necessary for determining eligibility for benefits (*see* Article 6a, IVG). The decision regarding the awarding of benefits is made by an interdisciplinary team. In the case of integration or occupational measures, the individual's personal and occupational situation is evaluated together with his capabilities. An expert evaluation may also be carried out. The IV must reach a decision within twelve months after the filing of claims as to whether integration measures should be undertaken or whether the person concerned is eligible for a pension. If the IV decides to award integration measures, it reviews eligibility for daily allowances of its own motion. The insured person is not obliged to undertake any action on his own.

469. Self-employed individuals do not have an employer who can pay their salaries for a certain period of time in the event of sickness or accident. No third party takes out an insurance policy for a daily sick-pay allowance for them; nor are they compulsorily insured by the accident insurance scheme. But they can take out a sick-pay policy themselves and voluntarily insure themselves in the accident insurance scheme (*see* Article 4, paragraph 1, UVG). If this is the case, the above explanations of procedures in the health, accident, military and IVs also apply to them.

470. Any claims to social insurance benefits – that is, from accident, military, disability and health insurance (if it is about insurance policies for daily sick-pay allowances based on the KVG) – expire after the end of five years starting from the end of the month for which the benefits are owed (Article 24, paragraph 1, ATSG). If the insurance policy for a daily sick-pay allowance is based on private law, the claim expires two years after occurrence of the circumstances that led to a duty to provide benefits.

II. Military Service, Civil Defence, Etc.

471. The person performing service receives an application from the compensation scheme for lost income for the days in service or the days of his course, regardless of whether he is self-employed, non-employed or employed by others (*see* Article 15, EOV).

472. The pay clerk is responsible for handing out this registration form. He notes on the form the number of service or course days for which the person is eligible for compensation (*see* Article 16, EOV). If the period of service lasts fewer than thirty days, the form must be given to the person just before he is released from service. If service lasts longer, the form is handed out at the end of the first ten days and then at the end of each calendar month (Article 15, paragraph 3, EOV). The person performing service must complete some of the information on the form and then forward the registration either to his employer or the responsible compensation agency of the AHV (regardless of whether he is self-employed, non-employed or employed by others). If necessary, the employer completes the registration form and then submits it to the compensation agency (*see* Article 19, EOV).

473. Compensation is paid only if the registration form has been submitted. If the registration form gets lost or its submission is delayed, the person performing service must bear the consequences. The claim for compensation expires five years after the end of the period of service (Article 20, paragraph 1, EOG). Compensation benefits are generally paid directly to the eligible person, but payment can be directed to the employer if the person performing service receives salary payments from him during his period of service (*see* Article 19, EOG).

§2. Maternity

474. During pregnancy, a woman may decide not to work at any time without getting a note from her doctor, but her employer is only required to continue paying her salary if she is absent from work due to health reasons. This is why a note from the doctor is required in such cases.

475. Since 1 July 2005, women have been entitled to maternity benefits based on the norms of the EOG. Before this law was passed, mothers continued to receive payment of their salaries from their employers under the provisions of private labour law, but these sometimes clashed with the duration of the ban on work in federal labour law (Articles 35 et seq., ArG). This problem has now been (partially) resolved by the regulations on maternity benefits.

476. To receive maternity benefits, the woman in question must file a claim at the compensation agency of the AHV. If she is employed, she must do so through her employer, completing the registration form together with her employer, who then submits it to the compensation agency. Self-employed or unemployed women, as well as women who are unable to work, must report directly to the compensation agency. If the woman in question neglects to take the necessary steps to register, her employer may register her on her behalf, provided he pays her a salary for the duration of her claim to maternity benefits. If a mother does not fulfil her duty to support her child, members of her family may also file the claim with the compensation agency of the AHV (*see* Article 17, EOG).

477. In the case of women who are employed, unemployed or unable to work, the current or previous employer must provide information on the duration of the employer-employee relationship and the salary relevant to determining the benefit (Article 34, paragraphs 1 and 2, EOV). The employer must also indicate whether he will pay the woman a salary for the period during which she receives the daily allowance. The registration must include a variety of documents: a copy of the woman's ID, a copy of the child's birth certificate, a medical certificate indicating the duration of the pregnancy (for cases where the baby was still born or born prematurely), and pay cards. A claim for maternity benefits may be asserted up to five years after the end of the fourteen-week maternity leave (Article 20, paragraph 1, in conjunction with Article 16d, EOG).

§3. Disability

478. If an insured person, due to a disability, lodges a claim with the accident, military or IVs, he must follow a prescribed procedure and provide certain supporting documents. The reader is referred to the above discussion concerning the verification of an incapacity to work or earn a living in the accident, military and IVs.

479. In the event of a disability, the occupational pension system may also provide benefits. The social insurance rules applicable to the occupational pension system do not make clear when and how an employee must register with the occupational pension system if he is unable to earn a living. This registration procedure is left up to the individual pension funds. Often these funds have special forms that must be completed by both the employer and the employee. In most cases, various documents must also be submitted, including confirmation of registration with the IV, daily allowance statements and medical certificates. The pension funds are also permitted to obtain reports from an independent medical examiner. If an insured person refuses to cooperate, the pension funds may, under certain circumstances, base their decision solely on the documents available to them.

480. If an insured person's health changes in such a way that it is relevant to benefits, he must report the changes to the insurance provider or the responsible implementation body. With respect to long-term benefits, it is possible in such cases to modify the original decision that served as the basis for awarding benefits.

481. The insured person's claims against the responsible social insurance scheme expire five years after the end of the month for which the benefit was owed (Article 41, paragraph 2, BVG).

Chapter 4. Benefits

§1. Wage-Earners

482. The following applies in general to both employees and civil servants. As far as the duties of the employer are concerned some special rules of the federal, cantonal or communal legislation on civil servants apply.

I. Primary Incapacity

A. *Benefits from the Employer*

483. If an employee is unable to work, he has a right to receive continued payment of his salary from his employer, provided he is prevented from working through no fault of his own and the employer-employee relationship has lasted more than three months or was entered into for longer than three months. This claim is based on the rules on individual employment contracts in the OR – that is, on private law (Article 324a and 324b, OR). Continued payment of a salary is guaranteed for a limited time, depending on the length of the employer-employee relationship. If there is an obligation to continue making salary payments, it takes effect on the first day of work. There is no waiting period.

484. The claim for continued payment of a salary arises anew each year of employment. In the case of a longer incapacity to work, the employee may reach the time limitations imposed on continued payment of his salary in the old year and no longer receive his salary. But after the start of the new year of employment, he has a new balance in his account.

485. In practice, employers often take out a daily allowance policy with an insurance provider to cover the risk of employees becoming unable to work due to illness. If the employer is subject to a collective agreement, there may even be circumstances under which he is obliged to take out a daily allowance policy. In many cases employees contribute to the payment of premiums themselves. However, under the law, employers are not allowed to shift their payment obligation entirely to their employees. Rather, under any insurance model, employees may not be worse off than with the continued payment.

486. There are also situations in which employees are compulsorily insured under statutory regulations against the risk of incapacity to work. This applies if they have had an accident, are pregnant or are performing military or a similar form of service. In such cases, different branches of social insurance – i.e., accident insurance, military insurance and the compensation scheme for lost income – may provide compensation. The employer is required to continue paying the person's salary only during the waiting period or in cases where the insurance benefits cover less than four-fifths of the insured person's lost earnings.

487. In principle, the above explanations also apply to public employees. The personnel law applicable to the specific case determines when, how long and on what scale continued salary payments are guaranteed when an employee is unable to work. But standards are often based on the corresponding regulations in private law.

B. Benefits from an Insurance Contract for a Daily Sick-Pay Allowance

488. If an insurance policy exists for a daily sick-pay allowance based on Articles 67 et seq. of the KVG, the insured person is eligible for a daily allowance only if he is 50% unable to work. Moreover, if not subject to any other agreement, the claim arises on the third day after the illness. During the waiting period, the employer is required to continue paying the person's salary. If the insurance benefits begin later, the premiums are cheaper (*see* Article 72, paragraph 2, KVG). The daily allowance, whose contractually stipulated amount is often not very high, is paid for a minimum of 720 days within a 900-day time frame (Article 72, paragraph 3, KVG).

489. If the daily allowance policy is based on the VVG, the parties have greater freedoms in structuring it. The daily allowance usually amounts to at least 80% of the lost salary, but it can be increased to 100%. The parties to the contract can agree that a daily allowance is also paid if the person concerned is less than 50% disabled. Furthermore, in contrast to the provisions of the KVG, the waiting period need not amount to three days, but can be flexibly defined, depending on the insurer.

C. Benefits from the Accident Insurance Scheme

490. The daily allowances from the accident insurance scheme amount to 80% of the insured salary (Article 17, paragraph 1, UVG). The maximum insured salary is currently set at CHF 148,200 per year, or CHF 406 per day (as of 2018; *see* Article 22, paragraph 1, UVV). Any earnings above this amount are not replaced by the daily allowance payments from the accident insurance scheme. In such situations, the employer is required to pay the difference between the daily allowance and four-fifths of the person's salary (Article 324b, paragraph 2, OR). If a person is only partially unable to work, the daily allowance is reduced accordingly. The daily allowance is paid for all days, even for Sundays and holidays (Article 25, paragraph 1, UVV).

491. Unlike the daily sick-pay allowances, there is no maximum number of daily allowances paid by the accident insurance scheme. The claim to a daily allowance expires as soon as the person is fully able to work, dies or begins receiving a pension from the accident insurance scheme (Article 16, paragraph 2, UVG).

D. Benefits from the Military Insurance Scheme

492. If the insured person is unable to work due to a health problem that is insured under the MVG, he is eligible for a daily allowance from the military insurance scheme (Article 28, paragraph 1, MVG). If he is entirely unable to work, the daily allowance amounts to 80% of his insured salary. For a partial incapacity to work, the daily allowance is reduced accordingly (Article 28, paragraph 2, MVG). At the moment, the maximum insured salary per year is CHF 152,276 (Article 15, paragraph 1, MVV). In this scheme, too, the employer is required to make up the difference between the daily allowance and four-fifths of the salary if the daily allowance amounts to less than 80% of the actual salary due to the cap on insured annual earnings. There is no waiting period for the start of the claim in the military insurance scheme.

493. The daily allowance is paid for every day, even for Sundays and holidays (Article 18, MVV). In contrast to the daily sick-pay allowance or the daily allowance from the accident insurance scheme, this military insurance benefit is subject to contributions to old-age and survivors' insurance, disability insurance, the compensation scheme for lost income and unemployment insurance (Article 29, paragraph 3, MVG).

494. The claim for a daily allowance expires if the person is able to work again, if there are no longer any lost earnings, or the daily allowance is replaced by a disability pension or lump-sum settlement.

E. Benefits from the IV

495. In the event of an incapacity to work or earn a living, the IV offers two categories of benefits: integration measures and daily allowances.

496. The possible integration measures include:

- Medical measures, whose purpose is to protect a person against major impairments of his health or to permanently and substantially improve his employability or capacity to engage in his field of responsibility. Such measures are meant to eliminate or correct persistent or at least relatively persistent defective states. In terms of type and scope, the medical measures are similar to those offered by the health and accident insurance schemes (*see also* Part III and Part VI). One difference is that disability insurance provides the measures only until the insured person completes his 20th year (*see* Article 12, IVG).
- Furthermore, measures are provided to prepare for integration into working life (Article 14a, IVG). Insured people who have been 50% disabled for at least six months are eligible for such integration measures if they enable the person concerned to take part in occupational measures. Integration measures are defined as those measures designed to familiarize a person with the work process, enhance job motivation, stabilize the person's personality, improve basic social skills or

provide work to bridge time (Article 4*quinquies*, IVV). Integration measures may not last more than one year, or 230 integration measure days (i.e., work days).

- Integration measures may also include occupational measures, such as career counselling, reimbursement of any substantial additional costs connected to a person's first occupational training programme, retraining, job placement, job orientation subsidies and capital assistance for disabled people who aim to become self-employed (Articles 15 et seq., IVG).
- An additional integration measure is the provision of any technical aids that the insured person requires to pursue gainful employment or engage in his area of responsibility; or that he requires to maintain or improve employability or pursue schooling, training or advanced training (Article 21, IVG). Possible technical aids are described in an exhaustive list compiled by the Swiss EDI (*see* Article 14, IVV).

497. Most of these integration measures are also accessible to people who are receiving a disability pension (Article 8a, IVG). The legislators strengthened the idea of reintegration into labour market with the 6*th* revision of the IVG which entered into force 2012.

498. The daily allowances from the IV are accessory to integration measures. In other words, they are basically only paid if integration measures are in fact carried out. The daily allowances are intended to help the beneficiary cover expenses during this period. Daily allowances are provided if the insured person is prevented from working on at least three consecutive days because of the integration measure, or if he is at least 50% disabled in his usual activity (Article 22, paragraph 1, IVG). Insured people who are enrolled in their first occupational training programme and underage insured people who have not yet begun working receive a daily allowance if a disability-related loss of employment exists (Article 22, paragraph 1*bis*, IVG). Non-employed people may at most claim compensation for the cost of care (Article 11a, IVG).

499. The daily allowance is made up of two parts: basic compensation to which all employed insured people are entitled, and a child benefit for those insured people with children (Article 22, paragraph 2, IVG). Basic compensation generally replaces 80% of the income the insured person last earned from employment without an impairment of his health, but no more than 80% of the maximum insured daily earnings under the UVG (Article 23, paragraph 1, IVG in conjunction with Article 22, paragraph 1, UVV).

500. For insured people in their first occupational training programme and for those who have not completed their 20th year and are as yet unemployed, it amounts to 30% of the maximum daily allowance (the so-called small daily allowance; Article 23, paragraph 2*bis*, IVG).

501. The maximum daily allowance is equal to the maximum insured daily earnings under the UVG – currently fixed at CHF 406 per day (as of 2018; Article 24, paragraph 1, IVG in conjunction with Article 22, paragraph 1, UVV). If the insured person received a daily allowance from the accident insurance scheme until disability insurance integration measures began, the principle of protecting acquired rights applies: the daily allowance from the IV must at least match the previously drawn daily allowance from the accident insurance scheme (Article 24, paragraph 4, IVG). The daily allowance can be reduced if it exceeds the relevant earned income, including the statutory child and education benefits (Article 24, paragraph 2, IVG). It may also be reduced if the insured person pursues a gainful activity during integration measures and his earnings, together with the daily allowance, exceed the relevant employment earnings (Article 24, paragraph 5, IVG in conjunction with Article 21*septies*, IVV).

502. The child benefit paid for the insured person's children amounts at most to 2% of the maximum daily allowance (Article 23*bis*, IVG). However, the benefit is not paid if statutory child or education benefits are already provided for the child (*see* Article 22, paragraph 3, IVG and Article 22*quinquies*, IVV).

503. As in the military insurance scheme, contributions to old-age and survivors' insurance, disability insurance, unemployment insurance and the compensation scheme for lost income must be paid on the daily allowances from the IV (Article 25, IVG). The insured person and the IV each pay half of these contributions.

504. Non-employed people who take part in integration measures do not qualify for daily allowances. However, during the measures, they may incur additional costs for the care of children younger than 16 or for family members with whom they live in a shared household. In such cases, the costs of care are reimbursed – i.e., the costs of meals, travel, accommodation, crèches, wages for family and household helpers, as well as travel by third parties (Article 11a, IVG and Article 22*quater*, IVV). Generally the actual incurred costs are reimbursed, subject to a limit of 20% of the maximum daily allowance per effective integration day.

F. Benefits Provided by the Compensation Scheme for Lost Income to People Performing Service

505. The following describes the compensation provided for people performing service. The maternity benefit that is also provided by the compensation scheme for lost income is treated in the next section.

506. The benefit for people performing service is made up of different components. To begin with, all individuals performing service are eligible for basic compensation, regardless of whether they interrupt gainful work to perform service (Article 4, EOG). The amount of compensation varies.

507. If the insured person is enrolled in a military training school or another basic training programme, he receives basic daily compensation amounting to 25% of maximum overall compensation, which is currently set at CHF 61 per day (as of

2018; Articles 9 and 16a, EOG). During other periods of service, the basic daily compensation paid to working people essentially amounts to 80% of the average pre-service employment earnings, though it must be noted that minimum and maximum amounts apply (Article 10, paragraph 1, EOG). In addition, minimum amounts apply to people who were not engaged in gainful work before performing service (Article 10, paragraph 2, EOG).

508. In addition to basic compensation, people performing service are eligible for a child benefit for each of their children that are not yet 18 or are still in an education or training programme and have not completed his/her 25th year (Article 6, EOG). This also applies to foster children who have been taken in for permanent care and upbringing without remuneration. Compensation amounts to CHF 20 per day (as of 2018; *see* Articles 13 and 16a, EOG).

509. In addition to child benefits, benefits are paid for the cost of care if the person performing service lives in a shared household with one or several children younger than 16 and demonstrates that additional costs have been incurred for the care of his children (Article 7, EOG). Furthermore, the person must serve for at least two consecutive days. The costs of care include the cost of meals provided to children outside the home, the travel and accommodation costs of the children or the third parties who look after the children, the wages of family or household helpers, as well as the costs of day care centres, etc. (*see* Article 12, EOV). In general, the actual incurred costs are reimbursed, thought it must be noted that maximum and minimum amounts apply. In other words, at most, 27% of the maximum total daily compensation is reimbursed, or CHF 66 per day (as of 2018). Expenses under CHF 20 are not reimbursed (Article 13, EOV).

II. Maternity Benefit

510. The compensation scheme for lost income has provided a federally regulated maternity benefit since 1 July 2005.

511. Beginning on the day of delivery, women are eligible for a maternity benefit provided their child is born alive or their pregnancy lasted at least twenty-three weeks (Article 16c, paragraph 1, EOG in conjunction with Article 23, EOV). If the child stays for a longer period in the hospital, the mother can apply to defer payment of the benefit until the child comes home (Article 16c, paragraph 2, EOG).

512. The claim exists for a maximum of ninety-eight days (Article 16d, EOG). It ends prematurely if the mother dies or returns to her job before this period is over – regardless of how many hours she works.

513. The maternity benefit is provided in the form of a daily allowance and is paid for every weekday (Article 16e, paragraph 1, EOG). The daily allowance basically amounts to 80% of the person's average earnings from employment, but the maximum amount paid per day is CHF 196 (as of 2018; Article 16e, paragraph 2, and 16f, EOG).

514. These benefits are subject to contributions to old-age and survivors' insurance, disability insurance, the compensation scheme for lost income and, if applicable, unemployment insurance (Article 19a, EOG).

515. The EOG explicitly allows the cantons to provide more generous maternity or adoption benefits, pay these benefits for a longer period of time, and collect special contributions to finance them (Article 16h, EOG). But such supplementary rules are not very widespread.

III. Disability

A. Benefits from the IV

516. Pensions from the IV are graduated according to the degree of disability. If a person is assessed as being at least 40% disabled, he receives a quarter pension; from 50%, a half pension; from 60%, a three-quarter pension; and from 70%, a full pension (Article 28, paragraph 2, IVG).

517. The amount of the disability insurance pension is equal to that of the old-age pensions in the AHV (Article 37, paragraph 1, IVG). This means that a full regular pension amounts to at least CHF 1,175 and at most CHF 2,350 per month (as of 2018; Article 34, paragraphs 3 and 5, AHVG). A quarter pension is equal to one-fourth of the corresponding full regular pension.

518. If both spouses receive a pension, their pensions, taken together, are capped at 150% of the maximum amount, i.e., CHF 3,525 a month (Article 37, paragraph 1*bis*, IVG in conjunction with Article 35, paragraph 1, AHVG). The individual pensions are reduced accordingly.

519. A special rule applies to young insured people who become disabled before turning 25 if they can demonstrate payment of contributions for the required period: their disability pension amounts to at least 133.3% of the minimum applicable full pensions (Article 37, paragraph 2, IVG). The extraordinary pension generally corresponds to the minimum applicable regular full pension. As a rule, pensions are adapted to salary and price developments every two years.

520. The IV also provides disabled insured people with children's pensions in addition to disability pensions. The children's pensions amount to 40% of the corresponding disability pension (Article 38, paragraph 1, sentence 1, IVG). But under certain circumstances a children's pension can be reduced – namely, when together with the eligible parent's disability pension it exceeds 90% of the average annual income underlying the pension (Article 38*bis*, IVG). If both parents are eligible for a children's pension, the two children's pensions are reduced if the sum of both exceeds 60% of the maximum disability pension (Article 38, paragraph 1, sentence 2, IVG).

521. If an eligible person is able to earn income once again or increase existing income, the pension is modified – but only if earnings increase by more than CHF 1,500 per year. In addition, only two-thirds of the amount exceeding CHF 1,500 is taken into account when the pension is reviewed (Article 31, IVG).

B. Benefits from the Occupational Pension System

522. The occupational pension system also provides insured people with benefits in the event of disability. These benefits consist of disability and children's pensions (Articles 23 et seq., BVG). As set forth in Article 24, paragraph 1, of the BVG, the disability pensions are divided into full, three-quarter, half and one-quarter pensions according to the degree of disability – as in the IV. The individual pension funds are free to apply a more precisely graduated scale in their regulations as long as the minimal statutory benefits are guaranteed.

523. In order to determine the amount of the pension, the disabled person is attributed, in addition to acquired credits, the fictive credits that he would have received by the regular retirement age (*see* Article 24, paragraph 3, BVG).

524. The conversion rate used to compute the disability pension is the same as the rate used to compute old-age pensions (Article 24, paragraph 2, BVG). In other words, the accumulated capital – or, in the case of disability, the fictively attributed capital – is converted to an annual pension using a 6.8% conversion rate (Article 14, paragraph 2, BVG).

525. Precise information on the amount of pensions can only be provided in individual cases since the amounts depend on a variety factors: not only on the degree of disability, but also on the insured salary, the available retirement assets, the future retirement credits, the conversation rate and the insured person's age. The law dictates that the disability pension must be periodically adapted to price developments (Article 36, BVG).

526. In addition, it must be noted that the majority of insured people enjoy better insurance coverage than what is provided by the minimum specifications in the BVG. In other words, the statutory minimum benefits are calculated on the basis of the applicable regulations of the occupational pension fund, not on the basis of the statutory regulations.

527. The children's pensions are calculated according to the same rules used in the disability pension scheme (Article 25, BVG).

C. Accident Insurance Benefits

528. If the insured person is 100% disabled, his disability pension amounts to 80% of his insured salary – though it is important to note that the maximum insured salary is currently set at CHF 148,200 (as of 2018; Article 22, paragraph 1, UVV). If a partial disability exists, the pension is reduced accordingly (Article 20, paragraph 1, UVG).

529. If a disability prevents a person from beginning an occupational training programme that he can prove was planned and that would have suited his abilities, or if it keeps him from concluding a programme that has already been started, the statutory regulations stipulate that the degree of disability is determined on the basis of the income that the person could earn in his profession without his disability (Article 28, paragraph 1, UVV).

530. The disability pensions can be structured in a variety of ways. If the insured person's degree of disability cannot be assessed with sufficient certainty and occupational integration measures are provided only later by the IV, the accident insurance scheme provides a transitional or interim pension after medical treatment has been completed (Article 30, UVV). Eligibility expires when the insured person receives a daily allowance from the IV, this scheme decides against occupational integration, or the final pension is set.

531. The final pension can be structured as a permanent or a temporary pension. Under the law, the pension must be adjusted for inflation (Article 34, UVG).

532. If the insured person is also eligible for a pension from the disability or AHV, the accident insurance scheme pays a complementary pension (Article 20, paragraph 2, UVG). In this case, the disability pension from the accident insurance scheme is equal to the difference between 90% of the insured salary and the pension from the disability or AHV (including children's pensions). However, it may not exceed the amount provided for a full or partial disability.

533. As a special option, the accident insurance scheme may provide a settlement instead of a disability pension (Article 23, UVG). This is possible if based on the type of accident and the accident victim's behaviour, it can be concluded that one-time compensation will enable the victim to work again. The maximum settlement is equal to triple the amount of the insured annual salary. In practice, though, settlements are hardly ever granted.

D. Benefits from the Military Insurance Scheme

534. Military insurance provides various benefits for people who are unable to earn a living due to a disability. On the one hand, these include integration benefits, such as the assumption of the cost of treatment and the provision of technical aids

(Articles 16 et seq., MVG). On the other hand, they encompass specific occupational integration measures, including career counselling, reimbursement of the additional costs of the first occupational training programme, as well as the assumption of the cost of retraining measures (Articles 33 et seq., MVG). Furthermore, military insurance also helps cover the cost of work clothes and personal tools that arise in connection with the start of gainful employment (Article 39, paragraph 1, MVG). If the insured person must move as a result of a disability-related change of jobs, military insurance pays the transportation costs (Article 39, paragraph 2, MVG). Finally, the insured person is eligible for reimbursement of the disability-related additional costs of commuting or practicing his profession (Article 39, paragraph 3, MVG).

535. One special type of benefit is the follow-up support measures (*Nachfürsorgemassnahmen*). Follow-up support consists of additional cash benefits that are provided if the insured person is unable to work through no fault of his own after occupational integration measures have been successfully carried out (Article 34, paragraph 2, MVG). These benefits are similar to unemployment insurance benefits. As is only proper, the benefits that the insured person receives from the ALV are taken into account when follow-up support is awarded. The amount of the follow-up support is limited to the amount of the daily allowance for half a year.

536. Furthermore, the military insurance scheme pays disability pensions. In the case of full disability, the annual disability pension from this scheme amounts to 80% of the insured annual salary (Article 40, paragraph 2, MVG). In the case of a partial disability, the pension is reduced accordingly. However, in contrast to the IV and the occupational pension system, military insurance has no graduated pension scale. Moreover, unlike accident insurance, it is required to provide compensation for degrees of disability less than 10%. The maximum insured annual salary is currently set at CHF 152,276 (as of 2018; Article 15, paragraph 1, MVV). The salary that the insured person would presumably have earned for the duration of his disability if he had not had the insured health problem is used as the basis for determining the insured annual income (Article 40, paragraph 3, MVG).

537. The pension can be paid for an indefinite or definite period of time (Article 41, paragraph 1, MVG). A disability pension is paid for a definite period of time if the scope of the disability cannot be assessed due to an unstable health condition or because employment conditions cannot be predicted reliably for the future (Article 23, paragraph 1, MVV). Such temporary pensions are generally awarded for one to two years. Moreover, a pension is not awarded for an indefinite period of time if the insured person starts to draw the pension after achieving the retirement age in the AHV (Article 23, paragraph 2, MVV).

538. The pensions paid for an indefinite period of time are adjusted to the nominal wage index (for people younger than the regular retirement age and for spouses and orphans) or to the national index of consumer prices (Article 43, MVG). This adjustment is made by increasing or reducing the annual salary underlying the pension and is performed at the same time as adjustments to pensions in the old-age and survivors' and IVs.

539. If an insured person becomes disabled and, just before the start of his pension, earned less than a fully able member of his profession, he is subject to a special provision in the MVG: in such cases, the law provides the option of calculating the pension starting in the period in which the insured person, without damage to his health, would presumably have earned as much as a fully able member of his profession and to use these higher earnings as a basis for calculations (Article 41, paragraph 2, MVG). Otherwise the assumed annual earnings that have been lost – once they are fixed – apply for the entire duration of the pension, subject to adjustments for wage and price developments. New hypotheses about earnings can only be considered within the scope of a revision of the pension if there is a high probability of their correctness (Article 41, paragraph 4, MVG).

540. If the recipient of a disability pension reaches the retirement age applicable in the AHV, the disability pension awarded for an indefinite time is now paid as an old-age pension whose purpose is to compensate for disability-related losses of income. Half the annual earnings underlying the disability pension are used as a basis for setting this pension (Article 47, paragraph 1, MVG). The result is a de facto halving of the pension claim. This rule is meant to prevent excessive compensation from being paid to insured people who also receive an old-age pension from the AHV and possibly from the occupational pension system as well.

§2. Self-Employed Workers

I. Primary Incapacity

A. No Benefits from an Employer

541. If, through no fault of their own, self-employed people are prevented from working, they have no employer who is obliged to continue paying their salary.

B. Benefits from an Insurance Policy for a Daily Sick-Pay Allowance

542. There is no compulsory insurance scheme that pays a daily sick-pay allowance to self-employed people, but they may insure themselves on a voluntary basis. This is advisable, since, as mentioned, they have no employer to fall back on to continue paying their salary at least temporarily in the event of illness.

543. On the one hand, self-employed people may take out an insurance policy for a daily sick-pay allowance based on Articles 67 et seq. of the KVG. In such cases, they are eligible for a daily allowance if they are at least 50% unable to work. Due to the three-day waiting period, daily allowances are paid only from the third day after the onset of the illness. The amount of the benefit can be set in the contract, and the allowances are then paid for at least 720 out of 900 days.

544. On the other hand – and this occurs more frequently in practice – self-employed people may take out a private policy for a daily sick-pay allowance based on the VVG. No general information can be provided here on the amount of these daily allowances, since they depend on the individual terms of the contract.

545. Since this latter insurance contract is governed by private law, the statutory social insurance regulations do not apply. As a result, the parties have a degree of freedom when setting the terms of the contract and are not bound to the provisions of social insurance law. This also means that self-employed people have no right to be insured by a private insurance company. In addition, private insurance companies are free to introduce restrictions for existing health risks.

C. Benefits from the Accident Insurance Scheme

546. Self-employed people are not compulsorily insured in the Swiss accident insurance scheme. If due to their work or place of residence they are insured by the compulsory health insurance programme, this programme covers all the costs of treatment in the event of an accident (cf. Article 1a, paragraph 2, KVG).

547. However, under the UVG, self-employed people may insure themselves voluntarily with an insurer against the risk of accidents (Article 4, paragraph 1, UVG). In such cases, the voluntarily insured people are eligible for a daily allowance under the same conditions as those applicable to employees.

548. Cash benefits are based on the insured salary, which is set when the contract is concluded and can be adjusted at beginning of every calendar year.

D. Benefits from the Military Insurance Scheme

549. If self-employed people have a health impairment that is covered by military insurance, they, too, are eligible for a daily allowance from the military insurance scheme amounting to 80% of their insured salary. The term 'insured salary' is defined in the MVV (Article 16). The daily allowance is paid for every day of the disability (not just working days) and is subject to contributions to old-age and survivors' insurance, disability insurance, and the compensation scheme for lost income. The claim to a daily allowance arises on the day on which all eligibility requirements are met. There is no waiting period under military insurance.

550. If a self-employed person receives a daily allowance from the military insurance scheme, there are circumstances under which he may also be eligible for additional compensation. This is the case if he incurs additional losses during his incapacity to work due to fixed operating costs and the structure of his company –

losses that are unavoidable despite careful management (Article 32, paragraph 1, MVG). If neither the daily allowance nor this compensation is sufficient to keep the company running, the military insurance scheme may grant further compensation, provided the insured person has taken all reasonable measures to remedy the situation and can be expected to run the company again on his own in due time (Article 32, paragraph 2, MVG). These benefits cover the specific risks faced by the self-employed. The amount of compensation is based on the concrete facts of the case. Combined, they may not exceed twice the amount of the maximum applicable annual salary, currently set at CHF 304,552 (as of 2018; Article 32, paragraph 3, MVG).

E. Benefits from the IV

551. In contrast to military insurance, the IV does not provide any special benefits for self-employed people. The reader is therefore referred to the description above of the benefits provided to employees under the IV.[3]

F. Benefits from the Compensation Scheme for Lost Income

552. Both employees and self-employed people are eligible for benefits from the compensation scheme for lost income. The reader is referred to the descriptions of related employee benefits.[4]

553. In addition, people performing service who earn most of their income from self-employment are eligible for company grants (Article 8, EOG). To qualify, they must be the owners, leasees or beneficiaries of a company; partners in a collective; partners with unlimited liability in a limited partnership; or partners in a group with a commercial purpose that is not a legal entity. Furthermore, they must actively take part in managing operations. This grant amounts to 27% of maximum overall compensation, or CHF 66 per day (as of 2018; Articles 15 and 16a, paragraph 1, EOG).

II. Maternity Benefit

554. As regards maternity benefits, self-employed mothers are treated in the same way as employed mothers. The reader is therefore referred to the explanations above.[5]

3. Part V, Ch. 4, § 1, I E.
4. Part V, Ch. 4, § 1, I F.
5. Part V, Ch., § 1, II.

III. Disability

A. *Benefits from the IV*

555. If a self-employed person becomes disabled, he must meet the same eligibility criteria as an insured employee if he wishes to receive a pension from the IV. There is no difference in the benefits provided for both groups. The reader is therefore referred to the explanations above.[6]

B. *Benefits from the Occupational Pension System*

556. Although self-employed people are not compulsorily insured in the occupational pension system, they may voluntarily join an occupational pension fund and insure themselves in this manner against the risk of disability.

557. The minimum statutory benefits for employees do not apply to voluntarily insured self-employed people. As a result, the amount of the possible disability and children's pensions is based solely on the regulations of the individual pension fund. For this reason it is impossible to provide precise information in this treatment on the scope of possible benefits.

C. *Benefits from the Accident Insurance Scheme*

558. As mentioned above, self-employed people are not compulsorily insured in the accident insurance scheme. However, under the UVG, they may voluntarily take out accident coverage with an insurance provider. In the case of disability, they are eligible for the same benefits as compulsorily insured employees.[7]

D. *Benefits from the Military Insurance Scheme*

559. The military insurance scheme provides an additional integration measure for self-employed people besides integration measures, follow-up support, career counselling and retraining. It consists of capital assistance to begin or expand a self-employed activity or to finance disability-related modifications within a company (Article 38, MVG). A key requirement is that the capital assistance must be necessary due to the damage to a person's health. It can be flexibly structured as an interest-free, interest-bearing or non-repayable loan. Furthermore, instead of cash benefits, the scheme can provide equipment or guarantees. The form of the assistance is left to the military insurance scheme.

6. Part V, Ch. 4, § 1, III A.
7. Part V, Ch. 4, § 1, III C.

560. Self-employed people are also eligible for a disability pension if no improvement can be expected from continued medical treatment and, after integration measures, the health problem that arose during service or was reported or discovered elsewhere causes what is likely to be a permanent or long-term impairment of their ability to work.

E. Benefits from an Occupational Disability Insurance Policy

561. Self-employed and permanently employed people are free to take out an occupational disability insurance policy. This is a form of private, not social, insurance. This type of insurance policy is especially advisable for self-employed individuals who are not voluntarily insured in the occupational pension system or the accident insurance scheme.

562. The framing of the specific insurance contract lies in the private autonomy of the contracting parties. Generally this type of contract contains the agreement that, at the onset of a disability, the insurer will provide the insured person with a pension to replace lost income.

Chapter 5. Conditions

563. One requirement that applies to all insurance schemes is that a person who aims to claim an insurance benefit must register with the responsible social insurance scheme in the proper manner (Article 29, ATSG). To this end, the responsible programmes provide forms free of charge.

§1. In the IV

564. As mentioned on several occasions, the IV is intended for all members of society. This means that everyone who resides or works in Switzerland is insured. In terms of coverage and eligibility for benefits, it makes no difference whether the person in question is employed or self-employed.

565. But in addition to being insured in the scheme, the person in question must fulfil other conditions depending on the benefit.

I. Integration Measures

566. People who are disabled or directly threatened by a disability are eligible for integration measures (Article 8, IVG). Such measures must be necessary and suitable for restoring, maintaining or improving their capacity to work or to engage in their field of responsibility. The various measures are subject to additional special conditions (e.g., in order to qualify for career counselling, a person must have a disability that limits his choice of professions or prevents him from practicing his previous profession; *see* Article 15, IVG).

567. Integration measures are generally only granted in Switzerland, but in special cases they can also be approved for abroad (e.g., the measure only takes place outside Switzerland; *see* Article 9, paragraph 1, IVG and Article 23*bis*, IVV). A claim for occupational integration measures arises when the person validly registers with the IV (Article 10, paragraph 1, IVG). In the case of the other integration measures, the insured person is eligible if such measures can be regarded as appropriate given his age and health (Article 10, paragraph 2, IVG). The claim for integration measures expires when the person receives an old-age pension from the AHV or is no longer covered by disability insurance (*see* Article 10, paragraph 3, IVG).

II. Daily Allowance

568. Daily allowances are paid while a person takes part in integration measures (*see* Article 22, paragraph 1, IVG). They are meant to replace the earnings lost during these measures and to cover living expenses. In addition, the insured person must be at least 50% unable to work in his usual activity or unable to work for three consecutive days due to the integration measure. Even if the three days are not consecutive, a daily allowance is still paid, provided the person is unable to work for the entire day because of the measure (*see* Article 17*bis*, IVV). The insured person is also eligible for a daily allowance if he is required to undergo an examination ordered by the disability insurance office and this examination lasts at least two consecutive days (Article 17, IVV).

569. Eligibility for a daily allowance begins on the first day of the month following completion of the insured person's 18th year. It expires if one of the eligibility requirements is no longer met, or, at the latest, when the insured person receives an old-age pension (Article 22, paragraph 4, IVG).

570. If the person in question is taking part in his first occupational training programme, he is paid a 'small daily allowance', provided he is fully or partially unable to earn a living. The same applies to people who have not completed their 20th year and have not yet begun to work (Article 22, paragraph 1*bis*, IVG).

571. Non-employed people are not paid a daily allowance, but they may request reimbursement of the costs of care if they can prove that, due to their participation in an integration measure, they have incurred additional costs for the care of children (including foster children) younger than 16 or of family members with whom they live in a shared household (Article 11a, IVG). A further requirement is that the integration measures must last at least two consecutive days.

III. Child Benefit

572. An insured person is eligible for a child benefit if he has a child of his own who is younger than 18. If the child is in enrolled in a training or educational programme, the claim for a child benefit is good until the end of the programme but no longer than completion of the child's 25th year. The same applies to foster children who are taken in for permanent care without remuneration (Article 22, paragraph 3, IVG).

573. However, it must be noted that the claim to a child benefit from the IV expires if the child simultaneously receives legally stipulated child or education benefit.

IV. Disability Pension

574. A person is eligible for a disability pension if reasonable integration measures do not enable him to restore, maintain or improve his ability to work or engage in his field of responsibility. This also applies to people who are on average at least 40% unable to work for a period of one year (without any significant interruption) and have at least a 40% disability after the end of this year (Article 28, paragraph 1, IVG).

575. In the case of working people, the degree of disability is determined by the income comparison as defined in Article 16 of the ATSG (Article 28a, paragraph 1, IVG). The income that the person would theoretically be able to earn in a reasonable job in a balanced labour market after onset of the disability, subsequent medical treatment and all integration measures, is compared with the income that he would be able to earn without the disability.

576. For non-employed people, the degree of disability is based on the extent to which they are they unable to engage in their field of responsibility (Article 28a, paragraph 2, IVG). A so-called activity comparison is performed in order to determine the degree of disability for such people.

577. If a person works only part-time, his degree of disability is determined using a mixed method (Article 28a, paragraph 3, IVG). Roughly speaking, the income comparison is used for the area of work and the activity comparison for the area of responsibility. The degrees of disability in both areas are added together on a pro rata basis.

578. Under the law, a pension claim arises six months after the claim is registered but no earlier than the month following the completion of the person's 18th year (Article 29, paragraph 1, IVG).

579. The principle of 'integration before pension' continues to apply in the IV, which means that a claim for a disability pension is subsidiary to the claim for integration measures. As long as the insured person claims a daily allowance, he is ineligible for a disability pension (Article 29, paragraph 2, IVG).

580. The disability pension is paid starting in the month in which the pension claim arises (Article 29, paragraph 3, IVG). If the beneficiary dies or becomes eligible for an old-age pension from the AHV, his claim to a disability pension expires (Article 30, IVG).

581. Pensions are paid for disability ratings under 50% only if the insured person has his domicile and habitual residence in Switzerland (Article 29, paragraph 4, IVG). An exception to this rule applies to relations with members states of the EU and the EFTA. The Federal Supreme Court has ruled that quarter pensions must be paid in these states due to the obligations assumed by Switzerland under the FZA.

582. People who have paid contributions for at least three years before the onset of a disability receive a regular pension (Article 36, paragraph 1, IVG). All others receive an extraordinary pension (Articles 39 et seq., IVG).

V. Children's Pensions

583. If an insured person is eligible for a disability pension from the IV, he may, under certain circumstances, also receive a children's pension. This is the case if he has a child who would be able to claim an orphan's pension from the AHV in the event of his death – that is, if the child is younger than 18 or not yet 25 and still enrolled in an training or educational programme (Article 35, paragraph 1, IVG in conjunction with Article 25, AHVG). The same applies to foster children who have been taken in for permanent care without remuneration (*see* Article 49, AHVV; cf. also Article 35, paragraph 3, IVG).

§2. In the Occupational Pension System

I. Disability Pension

584. Employees who have completed their seventeenth year and earn more than CHF 21,150 per year (as of 2018) are compulsorily insured in the occupational pension system (Article 2, paragraph 1, BVG). Employees who do not meet these conditions and self-employed people may voluntarily join the occupational pension system (Article 4, paragraph 1, BVG).

585. The BVG uses the provisions of the IVG in order to determine who is eligible for disability benefits in the occupational pension system. This means that disability benefits are granted to people who are at least 40% disabled as defined by the IV and who were insured in the occupational pension system at the onset of the work impairment that led to them being classified as disabled (Article 23, letter a, BVG). There are special rules for people with birth defects or for people who were disabled as minors (Article 23, letters b and c, BVG).

586. A further requirement is that a close factual and temporal connection must cumulatively exist between the incapacity to work that began while the person had insurance coverage and the disability that establishes eligibility for a pension.

587. The pension claim expires when the beneficiary dies or is no longer disabled (Article 26, paragraph 3, BVG). However, in contrast to the IV, the disability pension from the occupational pension system does not end when the insured person reaches retirement age. In other words, unless stipulated by regulations, the disability pension from the occupational pension system is not replaced by an old-age pension from occupational pension system.

II. Children's Pension

588. Furthermore, an insured person is eligible for a children's pension if he draws a disability pension and has a child who is not yet 18 or who has not completed his 25th year and is still in a training or educational programme (Article 25, BVG).

§3. In the Accident Insurance Scheme

589. For a person to claim accident insurance benefits, he must of course be insured in the scheme. This is the case if he is an employee in Switzerland (Article 1a, paragraph 1, UVG). If he works more than eight hours a week for his employer, he is insured against industrial and non-industrial accidents in the accident insurance scheme (Articles 7 and 8, UVG; Articles 13 and 14, UVV). If he works for an employer for fewer than eight hours a week, he is only insured against industrial accidents and not against non-industrial accidents. Self-employed people may insure themselves voluntarily, provided they reside in Switzerland (Article 4, paragraph 1, UVG).

I. Daily Allowance

590. An insured person is eligible for a daily allowance from the accident insurance scheme if he is partly or fully unable to work due to an accident (Article 16, paragraph 1, UVG). There must be a causal connection between the accident and the disability. If such an accident-related disability exists, the employee is eligible for a daily allowance starting on the third day after the accident occurred (Article 16, paragraph 2, sentence 1, UVG). It must be noted, though, that the claim exists only if the employee is more than 25% unable to work (Article 25, paragraph 3, UVV). During the waiting period, the employer must continue to pay 80% of the employee's salary (Article 324b, paragraph 3, OR). The claim expires as soon as the insured person regains his full capacity to work, receives a pension, or dies (Article 16, paragraph 2, sentence 2, UVG).

II. Disability Pension

591. To qualify for a disability pension from the accident insurance scheme, the insured person must be disabled due to an accident. In contrast to the IV and the occupational pension system, a disability of at least 10% suffices (Article 18, paragraph 1, UVG). The person becomes eligible once continued medical treatment can no longer be expected to bring a substantial improvement to his health and all possible integration measures from the IV have been completed (Article 19, paragraph 1, UVG).

592. The claim for medical treatment and a daily allowance normally expires once the pension is paid. However, there are special cases where benefits for care may be provided and costs may be reimbursed after the pension is set – e.g., if the insured person has an occupational illness; if he has a relapse of a condition related to the accident or suffers from its long-term consequences and his capacity to work can be substantially improved by medical measures; or if medical treatment guards against major impairments of his health (Article 21, UVG).

593. The pension claim expires if a full settlement is paid, the pension is bought out, or the insured person dies (Article 19, paragraph 2, UVG). As in the occupational pension system, the disability pension from the accident insurance scheme is not converted into an old-age pension when the insured person reaches retirement age.

§4. In the Military Insurance Scheme

594. Anyone performing service as defined by the law (Article 1a, MVG) is insured in the military insurance scheme for the period of service. An insured person who becomes disabled or unable to work due to an insured health problem is eligible for military insurance benefits.

I. Daily Allowance

595. To qualify, an insured person must have a disability that was caused by an insured health problem (Article 28, paragraph 1, MVG). One special feature of the MVG is that the degree of the inability to work is determined by comparing the salary that the insured person is still able to earn performing reasonable work with the salary that he would have been able to earn in his previous profession or area of responsibility without the health impairment (Article 28, paragraph 3, sentence 1, MVG). In addition to the actual inability to work, the person must also suffer a loss of earnings in order to be eligible for a daily allowance. By contrast, in other branches of insurance, the degree of the inability to work is not determined by economic loss, but by the actual restrictions in the person's previous activity (Article 6, paragraph 1, ATSG).

596. In the case of people who mainly work in the household or raise children, the degree of disability is based on the extent to which they are unable to perform this work (Article 28, paragraph 3, sentence 2, MVG).

II. Integration Measures

597. To qualify for integration benefits, a person must be disabled or directly threatened by a disability (Article 33, paragraph 1, MVG). In addition, these benefits must be necessary and suitable for preserving or improving social integration or the person's residual capacity to work. Finally, in principle, such measures are conducted only in Switzerland. As in the IV, the principle of 'integration before pension' applies. If an insured person refuses to take part in integration measures or fails to make a reasonable commitment, the benefits may be reduced or revoked after the person is warned in writing and granted to consider his situation (Article 21, paragraph 4, ATSG; *see also* Article 66, MVG).

598. Since the military insurance scheme offers integration measures that are similar to those of disability insurance, it is permitted to consult the disability insurance offices and the medical and occupational observation centres (*Abklärungsstellen*) when undertaking to clarify a person's capacity for integration and organizing and coordinating occupational integration measures (Article 22, MVV).

599. In order to qualify for career counselling, the insured person must be limited by the disability in his choice of professions or prevented from pursuing his previous profession (Article 35, MVG). Military insurance covers any additional disability-related costs of the first vocational training programme if the programme suits the person's abilities and there are reasonable prospects for the commercial utilization of his work afterward (Article 36, MVG). Eligibility for retraining measures also depends on whether the disability has made them necessary and whether it is likely that the measures will preserve or considerably improve the person's ability to work (Article 37, MVG). For the person to be eligible for retraining, case law requires that the feared permanent loss of earnings caused by the disability amount to at least 20% of previous earnings. Finally, if the insured person intends to claim capital assistance within the scope of the integration measures, a number of conditions must be met: he must be suited for self-employment in terms of his expertise and character; the proper economic conditions must exist for him to earn a living on a permanent basis; and adequate funding must be guaranteed (Article 38, MVG).

III. Disability Pensions

600. A disability pension is paid if continued medical treatment can no longer be expected to bring a significant improvement to the insured person's health and, after reasonable integration efforts, the damage to his health results in what is likely to be a permanent or long-term impairment of his capacity to work (Article 40, paragraph 1, MVG). Eligibility for a disability pension is based solely on health restrictions. Factors unrelated to the disability such as a weak labour market are not taken into account.

601. If medical treatment is resumed for certain reasons and results in a worsening of a person's incapacity to work, the pension may be increased for the duration of medical treatment or a daily allowance may be paid in its place (Article 42, MVG).

602. Finally, a buyout of the pension is possible at any time for the actual cash value of the pension if the degree of disability does not amount to more than 10% (Article 46, paragraph 1, MVG). If the degree of disability is more than 10%, the insured person must file an application for a full or partial buyout (Article 46, paragraph 2, MVG). The application may be approved if the buyout seems appropriate taking a medical evaluation and the insured person's personal, economic and social situation into account. This may be the case, for example, if the bought-out pension is used to purchase an owner-occupied home. The buyout may be turned if it is foreseeable that the degree of disability will decrease or disappear altogether in the near future. If a pension is bought out and the insured person's degree of disability then increases substantially, the person may request payment of an additional pension (Article 46, paragraph 3, MVG). The buyout takes the form of a capital payment.

§5. Under an Insurance Contract for a Daily Sick-Pay Allowance

603. As mentioned above, employers have the option of taking out a policy for a daily sick-pay allowance and thereby transferring the risk of continued salary payments to an insurance provider. This solution is generally also advantageous to employees since in most cases the insurance benefits are more favourable than the statutory obligations of the employer. Self-employed people are also free to insure themselves against the risk of an incapacity to work by purchasing a policy for a daily sick-pay allowance. The contract can be based on the KVG or the VVG. If the policy is based on the VVG, there is more leeway in the way it is structured than if it is based on the KVG. In case of illness, a daily allowance must be paid for every calendar day and not, for example, only for working days.

604. Daily allowance benefits are only paid by the health insurance provider if the corresponding contract exists. The specific requirements that must be met for an insured person to receive the daily sick-pay allowance are spelled out in the terms of the contract.

§6. In the Compensation Scheme for Lost Income

I. Compensation for Lost Income

605. Any person claiming compensation for lost income from this scheme must perform one of the forms of service listed in Article 1a of the EOG or be enrolled in a special training course. As far as basic compensation goes, it is immaterial whether the eligible person works or not.

606. By contrast, child benefits are only provided to people performing service who have their own children or have taken in foster children for permanent care and upbringing without remuneration – provided the children are not yet 18 or are still in a training or educational programme and not yet 25 (Article 6, EOG).

607. To claim benefits for care, the person in question must prove that he has incurred additional costs for care due to service, which must last at least two consecutive days. Furthermore, he must live with his children in a shared household and the children cannot be older than 16 (Article 7, EOG).

II. Maternity Benefit

608. According to Article 16b of the EOG, employed and self-employed women are generally eligible for a maternity benefit. The woman in question must have been compulsorily insured as defined in the AHVG for the nine months prior to delivery and must have worked for at least five months during this same period. In addition, at the time of birth, the woman must meet the following conditions concerning employment status: she must be an employee as defined in Article 10 of the ATSG; self-employed as defined in Article 12 of the ATSG; or work in her husband's company for monetary compensation. In the event of a premature birth, the nine-month insurance period may be shortened accordingly.

609. Within the scope of the FZA and the revised EFTA-Agreement, the periods in which the eligible mother is compulsorily insured in another state are taken into account when determining the minimum insurance and employment periods.

610. Unemployed women are eligible for a daily allowance if, up to the birth of their child, they have drawn a daily allowance from the ALV or, on the day of birth, they fulfil the contribution period requirements for receiving a daily allowance. Under certain circumstances, mothers who are unable to work are also eligible for a daily allowance – namely, if, until the birth of their child, they have received compensation for lost income due to illness or accident from a social or private insurance provider or have drawn a daily allowance from the IV (Article 16b, paragraph 3, EOG in conjunction with Articles 29 and 30, EOV).

Chapter 6. Accumulation Rules

§1. General Remarks

611. The ATSG contains a number of intersystem coordination rules. To the extent that these rules are declared applicable by the individual laws, they are used to coordinate the benefits of the different social insurance programmes.

612. Article 64 of the ATSG addresses the coordination of medical treatment. Treatment is provided exclusively by a single branch of social insurance, in the following order: military insurance, accident insurance, disability insurance and, finally, health insurance. The liable social insurer must assume benefits completely, even if the health impairment is only partially attributable to an event it covers.

613. Article 65 of the ATSG stipulates that other in-kind benefits, particularly integration measures, are assumed first by military insurance or accident insurance, then by disability insurance or old-age and survivors' insurance, and lastly by health insurance.

614. Daily allowances may be granted together with the pensions of other social insurance schemes, provided that they do not result in excessive compensation (Article 68, ATSG).

615. Under Article 66, paragraph 1, of the ATSG, the pensions and settlements provided by the various social insurance programmes may be awarded cumulatively, as long as no excessive compensation results. The payment of pensions is governed by the regulations in the respective laws and is undertaken in the following order: old-age and survivors' insurance or disability insurance; military insurance or accident insurance; occupational pension system.

616. The coordination rule of Article 66, ATSG, is of major importance for the whole system of coordination between the different schemes which grant disability pensions. In a 'normal' case of an accident, three schemes are involved: the IV, the accident insurance scheme and the occupational insurance scheme. Therefore the accident insurance scheme normally does not pay 'normal' pensions but complementary pensions in addition to the pension of the IV. These complementary pensions amount to 90% of the insured income (Article 20, paragraph 2, UVG). For the rest – or if there is no accident insurance in a special case – the occupational pension scheme pays a pension which amounts in maximum to 90% of the lost income (Article 24, Ordinance on the Occupational Old-Age, Survivors' and Disability Provision (*Verordnung über die berufliche Alters-, Hinterlassenen- und Invalidenvorsorge, BVV 2*)). As a result, the insured person receives pensions from up to three different insurers.

617. There is no coordination rule in the ATSG pertaining to the daily allowances from the various social insurance programmes. Their coordination must be based on the rules of the individual laws, to the extent that such rules exist. A discussion of the different regulations of the individual laws would go beyond the scope of this treatment, yet one basic principle applies: daily allowances are generally not combinable. As a result, the individual laws define which insurance scheme is solely responsible for providing daily allowances.

§2. In the IV

618. As long as an insured person has a claim for a daily allowance from the IV, no claim arises for a pension from the same scheme (Article 29, paragraph 2, IVG). If the insured person has a claim for both a daily allowance and a pension from the IV, the amounts of both benefits are compared, and if the daily allowance (including the child benefit) is less than the previously drawn pension, the pension continues to be paid (Article 20*ter*, IVV).

619. In most cases, a disabled person who participates in integration measures is eligible for a daily allowance under the IVG. But if he is already receiving a pension from the IV, this pension continues to be paid during the integration measures instead of the daily allowance.

620. If, due to accident, illness or maternity, the insured person is forced to interrupt the integration measure, he continues to receive the daily allowance from the IV provided he has no claim to a daily allowance from another compulsory social insurance programme or to a daily allowance from a voluntary insurance policy that pays at least the same amount as provided by disability insurance (Article 20*quater*, paragraph 1, IVV). A maximum of thirty daily allowances are paid for each case of illness, but no more than sixty daily allowances per year. The same applies to accidents or maternity (Article 20*quater*, paragraph 2, IVV). However, after delivery, the mother is eligible for an additional fifty-six daily allowances and the one-year restriction does not apply (Article 20*quater*, paragraph 3, IVV). If it becomes evident that the integration measures will not be continued, the claim for daily allowances is no longer valid (Article 20*quater*, paragraph 4, IVV).

621. If an insured person is eligible for compensation from the compensation scheme for lost income or a daily allowance from the unemployment or military insurance schemes, his claim to a daily allowance from the IV is no longer valid (Article 44, IVG in conjunction with Article 18, paragraph 4, and 39*bis*, IVV; Article 16g EOG).

622. The opposite applies if daily allowance benefits from the accident and IVs converge. In such cases the IV has the primary responsibility for providing the benefit (*see* Article 16, paragraph 3, UVG). If the insured person received a daily allowance from the accident insurance scheme prior to integration measures by the IV, the principle of protecting acquired rights applies. In this case the daily allowance from the IV must at least match the previously received daily allowance from the accident insurance scheme (Article 24, paragraph 4, UVG).

623. For the coordination rules for disability pensions the reader is referred to paragraphs 611 et seq.

§3. In the Occupational Pension System

624. In its regulations an occupational pension fund may offer the option of a pension deferral for the period in which a disabled person receives a daily allowance from the health insurance or accident insurance schemes. But this is permissible only if the daily allowance replaces at least 80% of the lost earnings and the employer has co-financed at least half of the insurance for a daily allowance (Article 26, BVV 2).

625. For the coordination rules for disability pensions the reader is referred to paragraphs 611 et seq.

§4. In the Accident Insurance Scheme

626. If an employee has an accident and is prevented from working through no fault of his own, the employer is required to continue paying his salary, as discussed above. But when, on the third day after the accident, the accident insurance scheme begins paying the employee a daily allowance, the employer is released from his duty to continue making salary payments, provided the daily allowance covers at least four-fifths of the lost earnings (*see* Article 324b, OR).

627. The UVG stipulates that the daily allowance from the accident insurance scheme is not paid if the insured person is simultaneously eligible for a daily allowance from the IV or for maternity benefits under the EOG (Article 16, paragraph 3, UVG).

628. By contrast, a daily allowance from the accident insurance scheme can be combined with a pension from the IV – unless this results in excessive compensation being paid by the accident insurer.

629. For the coordination rules for disability pensions the reader is referred to paragraphs 611 et seq.

§5. In the Military Insurance Scheme

630. If an employee falls ill or has an accident during work hours and is therefore prevented from working through no fault of his own, his employer is basically required to continue paying his salary. But if the military insurance scheme provides daily allowance benefits in such situations, the employer is released from his duty to make salary payments, provided the military insurance benefits cover four-fifths of the lost earnings (*see* Article 324b, OR).

631. If an insured person has a claim to pay or compensation from the compensation scheme for lost income, any simultaneous claim to a daily allowance from the military insurance scheme is deferred (Article 9, paragraph 3, MVG in conjunction with Article 10, paragraph 4, MVV).

632. If a person is eligible for a disability pension, this pension takes the place of the daily allowances paid up to then (cf. Article 40, paragraph 1, MVG).

633. Even if an insured person draws a disability pension, it does not mean that medical treatment can no longer be provided. Rather, medical treatment can be ordered if it is medically indicated or if it can be expected to bring about a substantial improvement to the insured person's capacity to work (Article 16, paragraph 4, MVG). The resumption of medical treatment may lead to an additional incapacitation, which is why, for the duration of treatment, the pension is increased or a daily allowance is paid in its place (Article 42, MVG). Generally speaking, the military insurance scheme pays a daily allowance in addition to the ongoing disability pension.

634. For the coordination rules for disability pensions the reader is referred to paragraphs 611 et seq.

§6. Under an Insurance Contract for a Daily Sick-Pay Allowance

635. Under Article 324a of the OR, the employer is obliged to pay his employee's salary if due to illness the employee is prevented from performing his job through no fault of his own. By taking out insurance for a daily sick-pay allowance, the employer can shift this risk to an insurance provider. The employer is then released from his duty to make continued salary payments, provided the insurance benefits are at least equal to the continued pay.

636. The following principle is anchored in the KVG: if, at the occurrence of the insured event, health insurance benefits converge with the same type of benefits from the accident, military or AHVs, or with those of the compensation scheme for lost income, the benefits from these other social insurance programmes are provided first. This means that the daily allowance from the health insurance programme is paid only if the insured person does not receive a daily allowance from any other social insurance programme (Article 78, KVG; Article 110, KVV).

§7. In the Compensation Scheme for Lost Income

637. If an employee is prevented from performing his job through no fault of his own because he must fulfil a public duty (service), the employer must generally meet his obligation to continue paying his salary. The same applies to cases of maternity. But if the employee receives compensation from the compensation scheme for lost income, the employer is released from this obligation, provided the insurance benefits cover at least four-fifths of the relevant salary (*see* Article 324b, OR).

I. Compensation for People Performing Service

638. In the case of working people, overall compensation, which consists of basic compensation and child benefits, may not exceed CHF 245 per day (Article 16a, paragraph 1, EOG). In the case of non-employed people, it may generally not exceed CHF 123 a day (*see* Article 10, paragraph 2, and 16, EOG). Company grants and benefits for care are paid in addition to overall compensation and are not reduced (Article 16, paragraph 6, EOG).

639. In the case of employees, overall compensation is reduced if it exceeds the person's average earnings before he performed service (Article 16, paragraph 5, EOG). If the person received a daily allowance from the disability or accident insurance schemes before recruitment, overall compensation must at least match the amount of the previous daily allowance (Article 9, MVV).

II. Maternity Benefit

640. Article 16g of the EOG states that the receipt of maternity benefits rules out the receipt of compensation from the compensation scheme for lost income or a daily allowance from the disability, accident or military insurance schemes. The daily allowances are therefore subsidiary to maternity benefits.

641. If, until the claim arises for a maternity benefit, a woman was eligible for a daily allowance from the IV, from a (voluntary) insurance policy for a daily sick-pay allowance based on the KVG, or from the accident or military insurance schemes, the amount of the maternity benefit must at least match the amount of the previously drawn daily allowance.

Part VI. Industrial Accidents and Occupational Diseases

Introduction

642. In the Swiss social insurance system, industrial accidents and occupational diseases are generally covered by the statutory accident insurance scheme.

643. A special feature of the Swiss system – one that can only be explained historically – is that non-industrial accidents are also covered by statutory accident insurance if the worker is insured under the scheme and works at least eight hours a week with the same employer. If the accident victim is not insured against accidents, the statutory health insurance programme pays for medical treatment. It must be noted, though, that health insurance does not provide cash benefits (daily allowances, pensions, etc.).

644. In some cases, military insurance, not accident insurance, may be responsible, but only if the non-industrial accident occurred in conjunction with military service or with an activity covered by military insurance.

645. Accident insurance is one of the oldest branches of social insurance in Switzerland. The first accident insurance law – the KUVG) – was enacted in 1911. Seventy years later, in 1981, legislators passed the Federal Accident Insurance Law (*Bundesgesetz über die Unfallversicherung, UVG*), which went into effect on 1 January 1984 and is still in force today.

646. The oldest form of social insurance in Switzerland is military insurance. The first Federal Military Insurance Law (*Bundesgesetz über die Militärversicherung, MVG*) went into effect on 1 January 1902 and has been completely revised several times since.

§1. Field of Application

I. Territorial Field of Application

647. Accident insurance is subject to the principle of territoriality. Within the scope of the programme, benefits are essentially provided only if the accident has occurred in Switzerland.

648. But there are a number of exceptions to this rule – for example, when Swiss law is applicable, even though the accident occurred abroad. This can be the case if a Swiss employer sends an employee abroad for a limited time (Article 2, paragraph 1, UVG). An additional exception concerns situations in which foreign law is applicable, even though the accident occurred in Switzerland. This is the case if a foreign employer sends a foreign employee to Switzerland for a limited time (Article 2, paragraph 2, UVG).

649. Furthermore, between Switzerland and EU/EFTA states European coordination law in the area of social security is applicable. This body of law contains special norms regarding the territorial field of application for certain constellations (*see*, e.g., Articles 11 et seq. and Articles 36 et seq., Regulation 883/2004).

650. Military insurance is not subject to the principle of territoriality. The MVG's territorial field of application is partially determined by the personal and material scope of the law. This is the case, for example, when the law extends insurance coverage to activities that at least partially take place abroad.

II. Personal Field of Application

A. *Compulsory Insurance*

651. As regards accident insurance, a distinction is made between compulsory and voluntary insurance.

652. All employees in Switzerland are compulsorily insured in the accident insurance scheme (Article 1a, paragraph 1, UVG). Employees are defined as people who are gainfully employed as defined in the *AHVG*; Article 1 of the Accident Insurance Ordinance (*Verordnung über die Unfallversicherung, UVV*). This means that in most cases the employer and employee have entered into an employment contract or an employee-employer relationship exists under public law.

653. As regards the applicability of the UVG, it is irrelevant whether the employee works on a full or part-basis, though this criterion plays a role in defining the specific scope of insurance coverage.

654. Nevertheless, there are a number of exceptions to the rule of compulsory employee insurance, and the Swiss Federal Council is responsible for defining them

(Article 1a, paragraph 2, UVG). For example, co-working family members who do not receive cash wages or do not pay contributions to the AHV are not compulsorily insured (Article 2, paragraph 1a, UVV).

655. Housewives, full-time students, pensioners and children are not covered under the accident insurance scheme.

656. Finally, the scope of accident insurance must be distinguished from that of military insurance. During the time in which a person is insured by military insurance, accident insurance coverage is suspended (Article 3, paragraph 4, UVG). The MVG's personal scope of application is defined, not by a blanket clause but by an exhaustive list of categories for insured people (*see* Article 1a, MVG). One can roughly distinguish between people who are insured on a temporary or a permanent basis. A person is considered permanently insured if his insured status results from his being assigned to a certain category of people. A person is considered only temporarily insured by military insurance if the MVG links insurance coverage to certain activities or circumstances. Concerning this second group, it is important to note the differences to the scope of accident insurance. If a person from this second group has a non-industrial accident, in most cases the accident insurance scheme is responsible for providing benefits. But if the damage to a person's health crops up during military service and is reported by the person or discovered in some other way, military insurance is responsible (Article 5, paragraph 2, MVG). The same applies if the damage to a person's health is discovered only after military service, but there is a preponderance of evidence suggesting it was caused or aggravated during military service; or if the person suffers from the long-term consequences or a relapse of the insured damage to his health (Article 6, MVG). Finally, military insurance is also liable for a previous impairment of a person's health discovered during the medical examination for military service – provided that the insured person is accepted into the military despite this previous condition and it worsens (Article 7, MVG).

B. Voluntary Insurance

657. Voluntary accident insurance coverage is available to self-employed people who reside in Switzerland and to their co-working family members who are not subject to compulsory insurance (Article 4, paragraph 1, UVG). But the residence restriction cannot be applied to people who are self-employed in Switzerland but reside in an EU state. Explicitly excluded from voluntary insurance coverage are non-employed 'employers' who hire only household servants (Article 4, paragraph 2, UVG).

658. Voluntary coverage is also possible under the military insurance scheme, but it is available only to people insured by military insurance due to their profession and after they retire (Article 2, paragraph 2, UVG). This voluntary insurance replaces statutory health insurance for the insured people. However, within the scope of voluntary insurance coverage, the MVG's list of benefits is restricted to medical treatment, dental treatment, the reimbursement of travel and rescue costs, home care benefits, cures, attendance allowances and technical aids. Insured people have no claim to daily allowances or disability pensions.

C. Scope of Insurance Coverage

659. In the event of an industrial accident or occupational illness, benefits are provided to all people covered by the accident insurance scheme provided that all the other eligibility criteria for the individual benefits are met.

660. By contrast, benefits for non-industrial accidents are restricted to the group of insurees who work for more than eight hours a week for an employer (*see* Article 8, paragraph 2, UVG and Article 13, UVV). Part-time employees who do not fulfil this criterion are not covered for non-industrial accidents under the accident insurance scheme. They must cover this risk through health insurance. This is why it is impossible in their case to suspend accident coverage in the health insurance programme.

661. According to the MVG, military insurance is liable for all physical, mental and psychological damage to a person's health and for the immediate economic results, regardless of whether the damage is caused by illness or an accident (Article 4, paragraph 1, MVG).

§2. THE CONCEPT OF 'INDUSTRIAL ACCIDENT'

I. The Accident

662. The following definition of 'accident' is applicable in the accident and military insurance schemes, but it is not as important in military insurance, which covers damage to a person's health regardless of whether it is caused by illness or an accident.

663. By contrast, both the definition of 'accident' and the resulting distinction between 'accident' and 'illness' play an important role in the accident insurance scheme. If a person's health has been damaged by an accident, the accident insurance scheme provides in-kind and cash benefits. But if an illness has caused the health problem, the health insurance programme is responsible. Since the benefits offered by the accident insurance scheme are much more comprehensive than those provided by health insurance – and since, furthermore, there is no cost sharing in the accident insurance scheme – the question of whether an accident or illness has damaged an insured person's health has far-reaching consequences. It is therefore not surprising that a great deal of effort has gone into distinguishing accidents from illnesses in legal practice.

664. For decades, the Swiss Federal Supreme Court has used the same formula to define an accident. In 2003 this definition was even taken up in Article 4 of the ATSG: 'An accident is the sudden, unintentional and damaging effect of an unusual external factor on the human body, resulting in an impairment of the person's physical, mental or psychological health or leading to death.' This definition contains five elements that must all be present for an accident to exist. The following section discusses each element individually.

A. *Damaging Effect*

665. For an accident to exist, a person's health must be damaged. This damage can be of a physical, mental or psychological nature. Although the legal definition of an accident only addresses the accident's effects on the body, intense effects on the mind can also damage a person's health (e.g., shock).

666. However, a person is eligible for insurance benefits only if the damage to his health makes medical treatment necessary or leads to an incapacity to work or earn a living or death.

667. If a person's teeth are damaged in an accident, the accident insurance scheme is liable for benefits – in contrast to the health insurance programme (*see* Article 10, paragraph 1a, UVG).

668. If the accident has a damaging effect on an object that replaces a part of the body or a bodily function (e.g., leg prostheses), the insured person also has a claim for compensation (Article 12, UVG).

B. *Unintentional Damage*

669. An additional requirement for benefits is the unintentional nature of the damage to the person's health. If the insured person harms himself deliberately, an accident is ruled out. However, 'intention' presupposes that the person is mentally competent.

670. In connection with suicides, in particular, an attempt must be made to assess mental competence. In case of doubt, due to the human drive to live, it is commonly assumed that there was no suicide. If it is clear that the person committed suicide, the general presumption applies that a person acts mentally competent (Article 16, ZGB). In these cases it must be proved that the person was not mentally competent when he committed suicide.

C. External Factor

671. An external factor such as a blow or a fall must have an effect on the body. In many cases this requirement does not pose a major problem, but there are situations in which the existence of an external factor cannot be so readily assumed. It is certainly legitimate, for example to question whether infections, stings or bites are external factors.

672. Case law has determined, for example, that clearly defined skin injuries resulting from the sting of a bee, wasp, hornet or tick constitute external factors.

673. Furthermore, regarding sports accidents, in legal practice the concept of damage through movement of the person's own body has developed. But this bodily movement is regarded as an external factor only if it occurs 'contrary to plan', such as when a football player misses the ball and tears a muscle.

D. Unusual Factor

674. A criterion for 'unusualness' is that the factor goes beyond what is considered commonplace or usual in a certain area of life. It should be noted, however, that the factor must be unusual in itself, not in its effect on the body. If foot blisters, for example, are caused by a hike that has proceeded as planned, they are not recognized as an unusual factor.

675. The following example can be cited by way of illustration: In connection with the intake of food, 'unusualness' exists if the damage to a person's teeth was caused by an object that is not usually found in the food, such as a bone fragment in a sausage. But if a person must expect to find the object in the food, such as a bit of nut shell in nut bread, the question of unusualness is negated.

E. Suddenness

676. The unusual external factor must suddenly affect the human body. This element of the definition is crucial to distinguishing an accident from an illness that may have been caused by an external factor but generally progresses slowly.

677. The sudden effect can last for a few moments, a few minutes, or even a few hours. What is crucial is that it is a one-time temporary effect. The effect itself must be sudden, not, for example, the damage or pain it causes. In the case of Lyme disease caused by a tick bite, for example, the criterion of suddenness is recognized as existing since the bite and the penetration of the infectious agents into the body are seen as a unit, even if the infection manifests itself only a few days later.

F. Accident-Like Injuries

678. Accident-like injuries are certain kinds of injuries that either occur after accidents or are sustained without there being an accident in a legal sense since there is insufficient evidence of an unusual external factor. Such injuries fall within the boundary between accident insurance and health insurance.

679. Article 6, paragraph 2, of the UVG defines which accident-like injuries are covered by accident insurance. These injuries are treated as accidents even without there being an unusual external effect – provided that the remaining conditions for an accident are met and the damage to the person's health cannot be clearly attributed to degeneration or illness. The listed injuries include broken bones, dislocated joints, ruptures of the meniscus, torn and pulled muscles, torn tendons, ligament lesions and eardrum injuries.

680. An example of an accident-like injury is a skier who tears his Achilles tendon while skiing down a slope, without experiencing anything unusual such as a hard blow.

II. Link to the Contract of Employment

681. For individual employees, coverage begins the day they start work or on the first day they are entitled to payment. At any rate, coverage begins when the employee sets out for work (Article 3, paragraph 1, UVG).

682. Industrial accidents are defined as all those accidents that an insured person sustains while performing tasks on his employer's orders or in his employer's interests. They include accidents that an insured person has during breaks from work and before and after work while he is on the company's premises (and authorized to be there) or in a danger zone linked to his occupational activity (Article 7, paragraph 1, UVG). Industrial accidents also include accidents that an insured person has between the time he leaves and returns from a business trip or while he is on a company excursion that is organized or financed by his employer (*see* Article 12, UVV).

683. Non-industrial accidents are defined as all other accidents besides industrial accidents (Article 8, paragraph 1, UVG). In contrast to most other accident insurance systems, the Swiss system does not attach any great importance to the distinction between industrial accidents and non-industrial accidents since most insured people are covered for non-industrial accidents in the accident insurance scheme and receive the same benefits.

684. Insurance coverage ends the thirtieth day following the day on which the claim for at least half the person's salary expires (Article 3, paragraph 2, UVG). But the insured person may extend coverage for non-industrial accidents by 180 days (Article 3, paragraph 3, UVG).

III. Accidents on the Way to Work

685. Contrary to a widespread belief, accidents that occur on the way to work are generally not regarded as industrial accidents. In the Swiss system – in which a person who is insured against accidents is also compulsorily insured against non-industrial accidents – they are considered non-industrial accidents.

686. One exception pertains to insured part-time employees who do not work for their employer for a minimum of eight hours per week. In this case – as an extension of accident insurance coverage – accidents on the way to work are also regarded as industrial accidents (Article 7, paragraph 2, UVG in conjunction with Article 13, UVV).

687. The distinction between industrial and non-industrial accidents is important for various aspects of accident insurance. For example, it plays a role in prevention, the setting of premiums and the denial or reduction of benefits in the event of extreme dangers or risks. Benefits can only be reduced or denied in the case of non-industrial accidents (*see* Articles 39, 88 and 92, paragraph 6, UVG).

§3. The Concept of 'Occupational Disease'

688. In addition to accidents, the accident insurance scheme is also responsible for diseases that are closely linked to employment. Such 'occupational diseases' are illnesses that have been caused solely or primarily by harmful substances on the job or by certain tasks carried out at work (Article 9, paragraph 1, UVG).

689. The Swiss Federal Council is responsible for clarifying what is meant by occupational disease, harmful substance and work. Appendix 1 of the UVV contains a list of harmful substances and occupational diseases. The various illnesses on this list must be partially caused by specific types of work to be recognized as occupational diseases. Since a qualified causal connection must exist (either primarily or solely) between the illness and the harmful substances or specific work, a probability of more than 50% is required.

690. Since this list is naturally incomplete, the UVG contains a blanket clause to supplement the listed items. Under this clause, additional illnesses may also be regarded as occupational diseases if it can be proven that they have been mainly or exclusively caused by occupational activities (Article 9, paragraph 2, UVG). Here even stricter requirements are imposed on the causal connection: 'mainly' is taken to mean that the occupational activity contributed 75% to the cause of the occupational disease.

691. If an insured person, in his spare time, uses any of the damaging substances listed in appendix 1 of the UVV and subsequently falls ill, his illness is not considered an occupational disease and is not covered by insurance.

§4. Medical Care

I. Under Accident Insurance

692. If an accident occurs, the accident victim has a right to appropriate treatment of his injuries (Article 10, UVG). This treatment includes:

- Out-patient treatment by a doctor or dentist, by a medical assistant acting on the doctor's or dentist's orders, and by a chiropractor.
- Medication and analyses prescribed by a doctor or dentist.
- Treatment, accommodation and meals in the general ward of a hospital.
- Follow-up and spa treatment ordered by a doctor.
- Any resources or objects beneficial for treatment.

693. The insured person may freely choose his doctor, dentist, chiropractor, pharmacist and hospital, but with respect to hospitals, he is entitled only to treatment, accommodation and meals in the general ward (Article 10, paragraph 2, UVG in conjunction with Article 15, UVV). If treatment is provided abroad, the maximum amount paid is equal to double the costs that would have been incurred in Switzerland (Article 10, paragraph 3, UVG in conjunction with Article 17, UVV).

694. In addition, the insured person has a right to any technical aids that compensate for the physical damage to his health or the loss of bodily functions (Article 11, UVG). Under the UVG, the Swiss Federal Council is permitted to draw up a list of permissible aids. To be approved, an aid must be simple and appropriate. The list includes, for example, hand and arm prostheses, leg equipment, surgical corsets, insoles, ear reconstruction, magnifying glasses, walkers, etc.

695. If the doctor prescribes home care for the insured person, the accident insurance scheme assumes the cost of a licensed care provider (Article 10, paragraph 3, UVG in conjunction with Article 18, UVV).

696. The insured person is reimbursed for all necessary travel, transport and rescue costs (Article 13, UVG). Additional travel expenses and transportation may also be assumed if family circumstances justify the coverage of costs. Expenses incurred abroad are assumed up to CHF 29,640 (as of 2018; *see* Article 20 in conjunction with Article 22, UVV).

II. Under Military Insurance

697. If, due to an accident, the military insurance scheme is responsible for providing benefits, the insured person has a claim to appropriate and economical treatment provided this treatment is suitable for improving his condition or his capacity to earn a living or for protecting him against further impairments of his health

(Article 16, paragraph 1, MVG). The exact scope of treatment is not exhaustively defined by law, but at a minimum it must match the benefits provided under the UVG.

698. Under the military insurance scheme, the insured person can freely choose his doctor, dentist, chiropractor, pharmacist and hospital, though in the case of in-patient care he is eligible only for treatment, accommodation and food in the general ward of a hospital (Article 17, MVG).

699. Military insurance assumes the necessary costs of travel and transport as well as search and rescue operations. In exceptional cases, it contributes to the costs of visits by close family members (Article 19, MVG). Grants may also be paid to the insured person for additional costs incurred in connection with home care or spa treatments (Article 20, MVG).

700. Finally, the insured person is entitled to technical aids, provided that they improve his health, enable him to practice a profession or promote his education, training, mobility or contact with the environment (Article 21, MVG).

§5. Incapacity to Work

I. Temporary Full Incapacity

A. *Under Accident Insurance*

701. If an insured person is fully or partially unable to work because of an accident, he is eligible for a daily allowance from the accident insurance scheme (Article 16, paragraph 1, UVG). His claim arises the third day after the accident has occurred and ends once he has regained his full capacity to work, receives a pension or dies (Article 16, paragraph 2, UVG).

702. Beginning on the day of the accident, an employee has a claim against his employer for continued payment of 80% of his salary provided the employer-employee relationship has existed for more than three months or was entered into more than three months earlier (*see* Article 324a and 324b of the OR). The daily allowance from the accident insurance scheme is paid as long as is necessary – a maximum number of days are not stipulated.

703. If the insured person is fully unable to work, the daily allowance amounts to 80% of his insured salary (Article 17, paragraph 1, UVG). The basis for calculating the allowance is his last salary (Article 15, paragraph 2, UVG). However, there is a cap on insured earnings, currently set at CHF 406 per day (as of 2018). If in specific cases the salary exceeds this amount, the daily allowance from the accident insurance scheme will no longer cover 80% of the salary and the employer is required to pay the difference between the daily allowance and 80% of the employee's salary (Article 324b, paragraph 2, OR).

704. There are special rules for determining the applicable salary for people who, due to military service, receive only a reduced salary or no salary at all or whose salary is subject to wide fluctuations (Article 23, UVV). These rules also apply to trainees, interns and people who work at occupational integration centres for the disabled.

705. At the onset of incapacitation, it is not uncommon for the insured person to be treated in hospital. Under certain circumstances, a deduction can be made from the daily allowance in order to pay for the hospital costs (Article 27, UVV).

B. Under Military Insurance

706. If the insured person is unable to work due to damage to his health, the military insurance scheme provides a daily allowance (Article 28, paragraph 1, MVG). In contrast to the accident insurance scheme, the claim for benefits arises on the first day the person is unable to work and suffers a loss of earnings (Article 9, paragraph 1, MVG). It ends when the relevant conditions (incapacity to work, lost earnings) no longer exist or the insured person dies (cf. Article 18, MVV).

707. The degree of incapacitation is determined by comparing the income the insured person can reasonably be expected to earn with the income he earned without damage to his health in his previous occupation or field of responsibility (Article 28, paragraph 3, MVG). If his incapacity to work continues for a longer time and he cannot reasonably be assumed to use what is left of his capacity to work, other areas of activity must be considered in the evaluation (*see* Article 6, ATSG). If the insured person is fully unable to work, the daily allowance amounts to 80% of his insured earnings (Article 28, paragraph 2, MVG) – as in the accident insurance scheme. The insured earnings are determined by examining the income that the person would have earned for the duration of incapacitation without the insured injury (Article 28, paragraph 4, MVG). At the moment, the maximum insured salary is CHF 152,276 per year (as of 2018), which means that a maximum of CHF 334 (80% of the maximal daily insured earning of CHF 417) is paid per day. Special rules apply to unemployed people and participants in training or advanced training programmes (Article 28, paragraphs 6 and 7, MVG).

708. If the insured person receives the daily allowance while in the hospital and the military insurance scheme covers the costs of accommodation and meals, it may make a deduction from the daily allowance after factoring in the insured person's family expenses (Article 31, MVG).

709. If damage to an insured person's health results in his being delayed by at least six months in beginning occupational training, the military insurance scheme pays compensation for the delayed start of working life once the person is able to take part in training again (Article 30, MVG).

710. The military insurance scheme provides special assistance for self-employed people if they must pay fixed operating costs and thus incur additional damages while they are incapacitated due to the structure of their businesses (Article 32, paragraph 1, MVG). If the business's survival is at risk – despite the daily allowance and special assistance – the military insurance scheme can pay additional compensation (Article 32, paragraph 2, MVG).

II. Temporary Partial Incapacity

A. *Under Accident Insurance*

711. In the case of a partial incapacity to work, the daily allowance is reduced accordingly (Article 17, paragraph 1, sentence 2, UVG). Under Article 25, paragraph 3, of the UVV, the full benefit is provided to people who are at least 50% unable to work, a half benefit to people who are between 25% and 50% unable to work, and no daily allowance to people who are less than 25% unable to work.

712. The attending physician determines the extent of the employee's incapacity to work.

713. Accident insurance does not offer any special occupational integration measures. If a person is at least partially able to work, the scheme supports integration by means of treatment, technical aids and a daily allowance. Furthermore, the insured person is eligible for support from the IV for occupational integration (cf. Article 19, UVG in conjunction with Articles 15 et seq., IVG).

B. *Under Military Insurance*

714. Even if the insured person is only partially unable to work, he is nonetheless eligible for a daily allowance. But in comparison to the daily allowance for a full incapacity to work, in this case it is paid according to the determined degree of incapacitation (Article 28, paragraph 2, sentence 2, MVG).

715. In addition to daily allowances, people covered by military insurance have a right to integration measures if such measures are necessary and suitable for maintaining or improving their social integration or remaining capacity to earn a living. This means that the insured person must either be disabled or threatened by a disability (Article 33, paragraph 1, MVG). The law provides for various integration measures, including (Articles 34 et seq., MVG):

- Follow-up support (cash benefits in addition to a daily allowance or pension if the insured person is unable to work through no fault of his own).
- Career counselling.
- Reimbursement of any significant additional costs of occupational training.
- Retraining.

- Capital assistance to begin or expand a self-employed activity or to finance changes in the business required by a person's disability.
- Reimbursement of the costs of work clothes and personal tools; a move due to a change of jobs made necessary by the disability; and the additional disability-related costs of commuting or practicing a profession.

III. Permanent Incapacity

716. If the insured person's full or partial incapacity to earn a living is likely to remain permanent or exist for a long time, he is considered disabled as defined in Article 8 of the ATSG. In other words, a permanent incapacity to earn a living leads to the categorization of 'disabled'.

717. The degree of disability is determined by comparing the income the insured person would have been able to earn without his disability and the income he is able to earn after the onset of the disability and after medical treatment and all possible integration measures (Article 16, ATSG).[8]

A. Under Accident Insurance

718. In some cases, an insured person may remain permanently unable to earn a living due to an accident. If he is at least 10% disabled, he is eligible for a disability pension from the accident insurance scheme (Article 18, paragraph 1, UVG). A claim arises if continued medical treatment cannot be expected to improve his health in any substantial way and he has completed all possible integration measures provided by the IV (Article 19, paragraph 1, UVG).

719. If an insured person is 100% disabled, he receives a disability pension equal to 80% of his insured salary (Article 20, paragraph 1, UVG). The cap on the insured salary is currently set at CHF 148,200 (as of 2018; *see* Article 22, paragraph 1, UVV). In the case of a partial disability, the pension is reduced accordingly.

720. If the disabled person also draws a pension from the disability insurance or AHVs, the disability pension of the accident insurance scheme is structured as a complementary pension (Article 20, paragraph 2, UVG). This means that it covers the difference between 90% of insured earnings and the pension from disability insurance or old-age and survivors' insurance. However, the maximum amount provided is equal to that specified for a full or partial disability.

721. A lump-sum settlement can be paid instead of a pension (Article 23, UVG). This option is chosen when it can be inferred from the insured person's behaviour that the one-time payment will result in his regaining his capacity to earn a living.

---

8. For more detailed explanations, please *see* part V, Ch. 2, § 2 III.

The maximum settlement paid is equal to triple his insured annual earnings. In practice, though, this model is hardly ever used.

722. In addition to a claim for a disability pension,[9] the insured person continues to be eligible for medical treatment if:

- he has an occupational disease (Article 21, paragraph 1a, UVG);
- he has a relapse of his condition or suffers its long-term consequences and his capacity to earn a living can be improved by such treatment or this treatment can prevent major impairments of his health (Article 21, paragraph 1b, UVG);
- ongoing treatment or care is necessary to maintain his capacity to work (Article 21, paragraph 1c, UVG);
- if preventative medical measures can substantially improve the person's health or protect against major impairments (Article 21, paragraph 1d, UVG).

B. Under Military Insurance

723. The military insurance scheme also pays a disability pension to insured people if continued medical treatment cannot be expected to improve their health in any substantial way and the damage to their health results in a disability as defined in Article 8 of the ATSG (Article 40, paragraph 1, MVG). Military insurance does not specify any minimal degree of disability for the insured person to be eligible for a disability pension.

724. In the case of full disability, the disability pension covers 80% of the insured annual salary (the cap on the insured salary is currently (2018) set at CHF 152,276; *see* Article 40, paragraph 2, MVG and Article 15, paragraph 1, MVV). In the case of a partial disability, the pension is reduced accordingly. The pensions are set for a definite or indefinite period (Article 41, paragraph 1, MVG). The military insurance scheme contains a special rule for disabled insured people who have reached the retirement age in the AHV (Article 23, paragraph 2, MVV). At this time, a disability pension awarded for an indefinite period is converted into an old-age pension, which is computed on the basis of half the annual salary underlying the pension (Article 47, paragraph 1, MVG).

725. If medical treatment is provided and results in an additional incapacity to work, the pension is increased for the duration of this additional incapacity to work or a daily allowance is paid (Article 42, MVG).

726. Finally, a buyout of the pension is possible if the person is not more than 10% disabled (Article 46, paragraph 1, MVG). A buyout is also possible in other cases but requires an application from the insured person, a medical evaluation and

9. For further discussion of the disability pension from the accident insurance scheme, please *see* Part V, Ch. 4, § 1, III. C.

the existence of personal, economic and social conditions that demonstrate the appropriateness of the buyout (Article 46, paragraph 2, MVG).[10]

§6. Death

I. Transport of the Corpse and Funeral Expenses

A. *Under Accident Insurance*

727. If an insured person dies as the result of an industrial accident, a non-industrial accident or an occupational disease, the accident insurance scheme assumes the costs of transporting the corpse to the place of burial (Article 14, paragraph 1, UVG). There is no limit on the costs reimbursed for transporting the corpse within Switzerland. If costs are incurred abroad, these are capped at one-fifth of the maximum insured annual earnings, or CHF 29,640 (as of 2018; *see* Article 14, paragraph 1, sentence 2, UVG in conjunction with Article 21, UVV). The person who demonstrates that he has paid the costs of funeral transports abroad is the one who is eligible for reimbursement.

728. If the insured person dies, the accident insurance scheme assumes his funeral costs in addition to the costs of transporting the corpse (Article 14, paragraph 2, UVG). This benefit is paid on the basis of the costs that are actually incurred, subject to a legally defined maximum amount. This maximum amount is equal to seven times the maximum daily allowance insured under the accident insurance scheme. Currently (2018), the maximum insured income is CHF 406 per day. This means that a maximum of CHF 2,842 is paid for the funeral.

B. *Under Military Insurance*

729. If the insured person dies as a result of an insured injury, the military insurance scheme also reimburses the costs of transporting the corpse from the place of death to the place of burial. There is no cap on the reimbursement amount.

730. Like accident insurance, military insurance also provides a funeral benefit if the insured person dies as the result of an insured injury (Article 60, MVG). As in the accident insurance scheme, this benefit is subject to a maximum amount and is currently capped at CHF 15,228 (2018), or one-tenth the maximum annual salary insured under the military insurance scheme. However, in contrast to the accident insurance scheme, the actual incurred costs are not used as a basis for reimbursement. Rather, a lump-sum benefit is provided. The person who has paid the funeral

10. Additional explanations of the disability pension paid by the military insurance scheme can be found in Part V, Ch. 4, § 1, III D.

expenses receives the benefit; he does not necessarily have to be a relative or friend but may be a third party. Nevertheless, legal entities such as a local community are ineligible for reimbursement.

II. Survivors' Pension

A. *Under Accident Insurance*

731. If an insured person dies as a result of an accident, the accident insurance scheme provides a pension for the surviving spouse and children (Article 28, UVG).

732. But the pension is not automatically awarded to the surviving spouse. The law requires certain conditions to be met for a claim to arise (Article 29, paragraph 3, UVG). For example, at the time of the insured person's death, the surviving spouse must:

- have children who are eligible for a pension or live in a shared household with other children who are eligible for a pension due to the spouse's death;
- be at least two-thirds disabled or become two-thirds disabled within two years after the spouse's death.

733. In addition, the widow (though not the widower) is eligible for a pension if, when her spouse dies, she has children who are no longer eligible for a pension or she has completed her 45th year. If she does not meet these eligibility criteria, she is awarded a one-time lump settlement. The amount of this settlement depends on the length of the marriage (Article 32, UVG).

734. The law stipulates that the divorced spouse is treated the same way as the widow or widower if the accident victim was required to pay support for him or her (Article 29, paragraph 4, UVG).

735. The pension for widows and widowers amounts to 40% of the insured salary (Article 31, paragraph 1, UVG). The survivors' pension for divorced surviving spouses is lower and amounts to 20% of the insured earnings (Article 31, paragraph 2, UVG). But the maximum paid is the amount of alimony.

736. Like the disability pensions for accident victims, the survivors' pensions represent complementary pensions if the survivors continue to be eligible for pensions from the old-age and survivors' insurance or the IVs (Article 31, paragraph 4, UVG). If this is the case, they are equal to the difference between the pension from these schemes and 90% of the insured earnings. However, a maximum of 40% of the insured salary is paid.

737. If several survivors' pensions are paid, they are not, when taken together, permitted to amount to more than 70% of the insured salary (Article 31, paragraph 1, UVG).

738. The claim to a survivors' pension arises either in the month after the insured person dies or at that point in time when the surviving spouse becomes two-thirds disabled (Article 29, paragraph 6, UVG). The right to a pension expires with the death of the eligible person, the buyout of the pension, or the remarriage of the surviving spouse. But the claim arises again if this new marriage ends in divorce after less than ten years or is declared to be invalid (Article 33, UVG).

739. The deceased person's children are eligible for an orphan's pension if they are not yet 18 or in an education or training programme and younger than 25 (Article 30, UVG). The claim to such a pension ends when the age limits are reached, the training programme is completed, the orphan dies, or the pension is bought out. These conditions also apply to foster children who have been taken in for permanent care and upbringing without remuneration (Article 40, UVV).

740. The half-orphan's pension amounts to 15% of the insured earnings, the full orphan's pension to 25% of insured earnings (Article 31, paragraph 1, UVG).

B. Under Military Insurance

741. Under the military insurance scheme, there are certain circumstances in which spouses and children are eligible for survivors' benefits. The same applies to the parents of the deceased person (Article 51, paragraph 1, MVG) – a feature that distinguishes military insurance from accident insurance.

742. The widow or widower is automatically eligible for a survivors' pension if the insured person's death resulted from an insured injury (Article 52, paragraph 1, MVG). If he or she remarries, the pension claim is suspended for the duration of the new marriage (Article 52, paragraph 2, MVG). The pension amounts to 40% of the deceased person's insured annual earnings and is generally paid for life, barring the spouse's remarriage (Article 52, paragraphs 1 and 3, MVG). A divorced spouse may also be entitled to a survivor's pension, provided the deceased person was required to pay alimony at the time of his death (Article 52, paragraph 4, MVG). In this case, the pension amounts to the alimony owed, but may not exceed 20% of the deceased person's insured annual earnings. In addition, the pension is paid only as long as there would have been an obligation to pay alimony.

743. The deceased person's children, stepchildren and foster children are entitled either to a half-orphan's pension equal to 15% of his insured annual earnings or to a full orphan's pension equal to 25% of these earnings (Article 53, MVG). This claim is good until they complete their 18th year or, if they are in an education or training programme, until they complete their 25th year. If the orphan is at least 50% disabled, the pension is paid until the disability falls below the 50% level but it is not paid after completion of his 25th year.

744. If the deceased person received a disability pension for a period of five years and his death was not the result of an insured injury, the military insurance scheme may still pay survivors' benefits to the spouse and children if they are ineligible for additional pension benefits or these benefits are insufficient due to the deceased person's disability (Article 54, MVG). But the maximum amount of these pensions equals half the regular rates.

745. Finally, it is only the military insurance scheme that pays survivors' pensions to the parents of the deceased (Article 55, MVG). However, it provides such benefits only if the deceased had no spouses or children who are eligible for pensions and the parents require financial support – i.e., their income is below the poverty level. The maximum pension for the father and mother is 20% of the deceased person's insured annual earnings.

746. If several people are eligible for survivors' pensions from the military insurance scheme, the pensions are reduced equally if, when added together, they exceed the deceased person's insured annual earnings (Article 56, paragraph 1, MVG).

§7. Prevention of Occupational Disease and Industrial Accidents

I. Under Accident Insurance

747. Accident insurance law contains extensive regulations on the prevention of industrial accidents and occupational diseases. These regulations apply to all companies that employ workers in Switzerland (Article 81, paragraph 1, UVG). The UVG requires employers to take all measures that experience has shown to be necessary for the prevention of industrial accidents and occupational diseases; that can be employed given the current state of technology; and that are suited to existing conditions (Article 82, paragraph 1, UVG).

748. At the same time, employees are required to support the employer in implementing these measures (*see* Article 82, paragraphs 2 and 3, UVG). They must, for example, use personal protective equipment, operate safety systems properly and not modify or remove such systems without the employer's permission.

749. The regulations issued by the Swiss Federal Council include precisely defined rules on technical, medical and other measures designed to prevent industrial accidents and occupational diseases in companies (*see* Article 83, UVG in conjunction with the Ordinance on the prevention of accidents and occupational diseases (*Verordnung über die Unfallverhütung, VUV*)).

750. In addition, the UVG requires the Swiss Accident Insurance Fund (*Schweizerische Unfallversicherungsanstalt, Suva*) and other insurers to operate a joint institution that contributes to preventing non-industrial accidents through education and general safety measures (Article 88, paragraph 1, UVG).

751. In order to finance the prevention work, additional premiums may be charged for both industrial and non-industrial accident insurance (Articles 87 and 88, paragraphs 2 and 3, UVG). These premiums go to preventing industrial and non-industrial accidents and occupational diseases.

II. Under Military Insurance

752. Under the law, the military insurance scheme has been assigned a general prevention mandate, which it fulfils by promoting and supporting measures to prevent damage to human health (Article 62, MVG). The military insurance scheme works together with the responsible bodies in this field, particularly those in the army and the civil defence. It can also make a contribution to financing measures designed to prevent damage to human health.

753. Moreover, for the purpose of targeted prevention, medical examinations can be undertaken at the expense of the military insurance scheme if the enlistee's health justifies the attempt to clarify his fitness for service in this manner before recruitment (Article 63, paragraph 1, MVG). If preventive medical measures are ordered in this context, they can also be billed to the military insurance scheme to the extent that they serve to prevent specific damage to human health (Article 63, paragraph 3, MVG).

§8. Supplementary Benefits

754. The accident and military insurance schemes provide other benefits besides those described above. They are listed briefly in the following.

I. Under Accident Insurance

755. In addition to the above-mentioned benefits, accident insurance offers:

- Compensation for damage to integrity (Articles 24 and 25, UVG): This benefit is awarded if the insured person, as the result of an accident, suffers substantial permanent damage to his physical, mental or psychological integrity. Compensation consists of a one-time payment that is capped at CHF 148,200 (for the most severe injuries; as of 2018). Percentages of this amount are paid on a graduated scale based on the severity of the injury. For example, an insured person who has lost a hand in an accident is eligible for 40% of the maximum compensation, or CHF 59,280. Compensation for damage to integrity is paid in parallel with other benefits (daily allowances, disability pensions) and, to a certain extent, is a form of fixed-rate compensation.
- Attendance allowances (Articles 26 and 27, UVG): Such allowances go to people who, due to a health impairment, permanently depend on the help of third parties for everyday tasks or personal supervision.

- Cost-of-living bonus (Article 34, UVG): Pension recipients are granted bonuses as part of their pensions in order to offset inflation.
- Compensation for damage to property (Article 12, UVG): If an accident results in damage to objects that replace a part of the body or a bodily function, the insured person has a right to compensation for this damage. However, in the case of eyeglasses, hearing aids and dentures, they are only eligible for compensation if they have sustained an injury that requires treatment. This latter restriction protects against insurance fraud.

II. Under Military Insurance

756. Military Insurance offers the following additional benefits:

- Compensation for damage to integrity (Articles 48 et seq., MVG): If the insured person suffers substantial permanent damage to his physical, mental or psychological integrity, he is eligible for a pension for damage to integrity (i.e., benefits are not restricted to one-time compensation as in the accident insurance scheme).
- Compensation for damage to property (Article 57, MVG): Military insurance covers damage to clothes, eyeglasses, watches, prostheses and other objects that are usually worn or carried on the body and are closely and directly linked to the sustained injury.
- Settlement (Article 58, MVG): In exceptional cases, a settlement can be paid to cover the insured event.
- Compensation (Article 59, MVG): Under special circumstances, military insurance may award a severely injured person or, in exceptional cases, his closest family members an appropriate sum as compensation. In the case of death, the family members are eligible. But damages may not be awarded in combination with a pension for damage to integrity.
- Compensation for the cost of occupational training (Article 61, MVG): If the insured person's parents or spouse have incurred substantial costs for his occupational training and he dies before or within three years after completing the training programme, the military insurance scheme can grant the parents or spouse an appropriate contribution to these costs.

§9. No-Fault Insurance

I. Under Accident Insurance

757. It is essentially immaterial whether an employee or employer is to blame for an accident or illness. The accident insurance scheme provides benefits in both cases. However, there are a number of exceptions to this rule:

- If the insured person has deliberately caused damage to his health or brought about his own death, he has no claim for insurance benefits, except for funeral expenses. In this case no 'accident' exists in the legal sense (Article 37, paragraph 1, UVG).
- In the event of an industrial or non-industrial accident, the cash benefit may be reduced or, in especially serious cases, denied if the insured person has caused the accident while unintentionally committing a crime or offence (Article 37, paragraph 1, UVG).
- Moreover, in the case of non-industrial accidents, the daily allowance can be reduced during the first two years after the accident if the accident is the result of gross negligence (Article 37, paragraph 2, UVG).
- The Swiss Federal Council is permitted to define the unusual dangers and risks that can lead to the denial of benefits or to a reduction of cash benefits in the case of a non-industrial accident (Article 39, UVG). The Federal Council has issued a relevant rule declaring that benefits are to be denied if the non-industrial accident occurs during military service in a foreign army or if the person participates in acts of war or terrorism or organized crime (Article 49, paragraph 1, UVV). Cash benefits are reduced for non-industrial accidents if the victim has taken part in fistfights, brawls or riots or has exposed himself to danger by severely provoking others (Article 49, paragraph 2, UVV).
- If an insured person resists or refuses reasonable treatment or occupational integration efforts, or does not make a reasonable contribution to such measures, benefits may be reduced or denied temporarily or permanently. But he must be warned beforehand in writing and informed of the legal consequences of his lack of cooperation (Article 21, paragraph 4, ATSG).

758. The pricing of premiums for industrial accident insurance is based on a system in which companies are assigned to tariff categories according to their business type and operational conditions. The most important criteria include the degree of risk and the state of accident prevention. If a company does not follow the regulations on accident prevention and occupational diseases, it can be placed in a higher risk category at any time, even retrospectively.

II. Under Military Insurance

759. In principle, the military insurance scheme also provides benefits irrespective of the insured person's fault. But there are a number of exceptions to this rule:

- Cash benefits may be reduced temporarily or permanently or even denied if the insured person has caused the insured event deliberately or while deliberately committing a crime or offence (Article 21, paragraph 1, ATSG).
- Cash benefits for a family member or survivor can only be reduced or denied if the family member or survivor has caused the insured event deliberately or while deliberately committing a crime or offence (Article 21, paragraph 2, ATSG).
- If an insured person refuses or resists reasonable treatment or occupational integration efforts, or does not make a reasonable contribution to such measures, his

benefits may be reduced or denied temporarily or permanently. But he must be warned beforehand in writing and informed of the legal consequences of his lack of cooperation (Article 21, paragraph 4, ATSG).

760. When determining whether to reduce or deny benefits, the authorities must consider all the circumstances related to the individual case, particularly the degree of the beneficiary's fault and his economic situation (Article 65, paragraph 3, MVG).

§10. Civil Liability

761. According to Article 328 of the OR, the employer is required to respect and protect the employee's inherent rights in the employer-employee relationship and to show due consideration for his health. The employer must take all measures that experience has shown to be necessary to protect the employee's life, health and personal integrity; that can be employed given the current state of technology; and that are suited to conditions at the company or in the household. He must fulfil these duties to the extent that it can be expected of him, taking into account the individual employer-employee relationship and the nature of the work.

762. If the employer culpably violates these duties, the employee may sue him and demand damages for contractual violations, irrespective of any possible benefits from the accident insurance scheme. If the necessary conditions are met, the employee may also sue the employer for damages due to a tortious act. It is of course also possible for the accident victim to take civil action against a third party who is responsible for the accident and sue for damages.

763. If the employer has deliberately or negligently violated his duty to exercise due care, he can in certain circumstances be prosecuted and sentenced under criminal law in addition to being sued under civil law. Punishment is also possible on the basis of the UVG. If an employer deliberately or negligently acts in violation of the regulations on the prevention of accidents and occupational diseases and thereby puts others in grave danger, he may be sanctioned with a fine – provided he has not committed a graver crime or offence that is subject to more severe punishment under the penal code (Article 112, UVG).

§11. Accumulation Rules

764. In some cases, an insured person who has had an accident may have claims against the accident and military insurance schemes as well as against third parties. At the same time, though, both social insurance law and liability law prohibit excessive compensation or enrichment. This means that an injured person may never receive compensation in excess of the damages he has actually suffered. As a result, coordination efforts are often necessary: not only intersystem coordination of the benefits from the accident and military insurance schemes, but also extra-system coordination of the benefits from the social insurance programmes and liable third parties.

765. It must be emphasized that only congruent benefits need be coordinated – i.e., benefits that are provided to the same person and that are similar in terms of their function, the period they are awarded and their link to the insured event. Only in such cases is there a danger of excessive compensation.

766. Articles 63 et seq. of the ATSG contain provisions on the coordination of benefits. A number of additional coordination rules can be found in the individual laws to which the different insurance providers are subject. The following rules apply to intersystem coordination between the accident and military insurance schemes:

- Medical treatment is subject to the principle of absolute priority (Article 64, ATSG). This means that even if there are several claims for benefits, only one branch of social insurance is required to provide the benefits. Medical treatment is mainly covered by military insurance, with accident insurance having secondary liability.
- Additional in-kind benefits (e.g., technical aids and integration measures), as well as daily allowances, are provided by the military insurance scheme if, due to an illness or an accident during the period of insurance, this scheme is directly liable for benefits under the MVG (Article 65, ATSG in conjunction with Article 71, paragraph 2, MVG). The insurer who is directly liable for benefits is the one who must then provide benefits for the current worsening of the damage to a person's health (Article 126, paragraph 1, UVV; Article 31, paragraph 1, MVV).
- Both the accident and military insurance schemes are required to provide insured people with pensions, compensation for damage to integrity, attendance allowances and funeral benefits in proportion to their share in the total damage to their health (Article 103, UVG; Article 76, MVG).

767. For the coordination rules for disability pensions the reader is referred to paragraphs 611 et seq.

768. If an insured event results in claims for social insurance benefits, but it is unclear which social insurance scheme must provide the benefits, the insured person may demand provision of the benefits in advance. Article 70, paragraph 2c, of the ATSG stipulates that in cases where the provision of benefits by the accident or military insurance schemes is disputed, the accident insurance scheme is liable to provide the benefits in advance. If it turns out afterward that military insurance is liable, this scheme must reimburse the accident insurance scheme for the advance benefits within the scope of its legal obligation to provide benefits (Article 71, ATSG).

769. If the insured person has claims against a social insurance programme and a liable third party, in most cases the social insurance programme provides the benefits first. The reason is that it often takes time to enforce the claims under liability law. Under Articles 72 et seq. of the ATSG, the extra-system coordination of benefits that is necessary in such cases (between the social insurance schemes and the liable third party) proceeds as follows: At the time of the insured event, the insurer is generally subrogated to the claims that the insured person and his survivors have against the responsible third party up to the amount of the statutory benefits. This means that the insured person and/or his survivors receive the benefits from the responsible social insurance programme and their liability claim against the third party is reduced by the amount by which the social insurance benefits combined with the compensation owed by the third party for the same time period exceeds the corresponding damages. The social insurance programme may demand this share from the third party based on its right to recourse.

770. It must be noted, in particular, that the right to seek recourse from an employer or his employee is limited in the case of an industrial accident and can be enforced only if these parties have caused the insured event deliberately or it resulted from their gross negligence (Article 75, paragraph 2, ATSG).

Part VII. Unemployment

Introduction

771. Article 114 of the BV grants the federal legislators the power to issue regulations on unemployment insurance. The federal legislators have met their responsibilities and established a corresponding insurance programme that is structured in such a way as to provide adequate compensation for the loss of earned income and to support measures for preventing and combating unemployment.

772. The ALV provides different types of benefits. On the one hand, it contributes to efficient career counselling, job placement, labour market measures and other measures specified by the law. On the other hand, it pays various forms of compensation. Unemployment benefits consist primarily of monetary payments but also take the form of in-kind benefits and financial assistance.

773. On the one hand, the insurance scheme is funded by the contributions of the insured people and their employers. Each group pays half of the required premium. On the other hand, it is supported by contributions and loans from the federal government and the cantons. Until the end of 2010, the contributions paid by the insured people and their employers were fixed at 2% of the annual salary up to a limit of CHF 126,000. Contributions were not paid on the portion of the salary above this limit; nor was it insured.

774. The population approved a revised version of the AVIG in 2010. Since 1 January 2016, contributions of 2.2% of the annual salary are paid on the portion of earnings up to CHF 148,200. Furthermore, an additional 'solidarity' percent will be charged on the whole income higher than CHF 148,200. This measure was taken to strengthen the financial situation of the insurance programme.

§1. Field of Application

I. Territorial Field of Application

775. To qualify for unemployment compensation (*Arbeitslosenentschädigung*), the insured person must live in Switzerland. This condition should be interpreted loosely so as to include foreign nationals who do not have an unlimited residence permit (*Niederlassungsbewilligung*) but who work in Switzerland and possess a residence permit (*Aufenthaltsbewilligung*). The term 'living' refers not only to a person's domicile but also to his habitual residence (actually residing in Switzerland, with the intention of remaining in the country, which is seen as the centre of all important relationships in his life). Exceptions to the residence clause can be found in the FZA. For EU and EFTA citizens, the last country in which they were employed is in principle responsible for paying benefits based on its own legal regulations.

776. Cross-border commuters are ineligible for unemployment compensation since the international agreements applicable to them are based on the principle that the regulations of the state of residence apply in connection with benefits law. This principle generally applies within the scope of the FZA.

777. The ALV ban on paying benefits abroad holds for the entire period in which a person receives benefits. The criterion of living in Switzerland must be fulfilled not only at the onset of unemployment, but also for the entire period during which the benefit is paid.

II. Personal Field of Application

778. All employees are compulsorily insured in the ALV. The term 'employee' is based on the definition in the AHVG.

779. The group of insurees can be broken down into two subgroups. The first consists of employees who are liable for contributions and includes all people who are compulsorily insured in the AHV and who must pay contributions on employment income. Neither the nationality nor the residence status of the employee plays a role, which is why cross-border commuters, seasonal workers, refugees and asylum seekers are compulsorily insured. The second subgroup of insurees consists of people who are not required to pay contributions but are nevertheless insured. They include, for example, young employees between the end of compulsory schooling and the start of their contribution period in the AHV.

780. Although legislators could have set up a voluntary ALV for self-employed people, they have so far refrained from doing so. As a result, self-employed people are not compulsorily insured in the ALV and are not allowed to insure themselves voluntarily.

III. Insured Risks

781. The ALV covers various risks. On the one hand, it provides protection against the risk of joblessness, which means unemployment outside an employer-employee relationship. The people exposed to this risk are those that are currently *not* in an employer-employee relationship and are looking for a job.

782. On the other hand, the scheme protects people against the loss of income due to reduced working hours or a weather-related loss of working hours. In both cases a form of unemployment arises within an *existing* employer-employee relationship due to a temporary reduction in working hours, a temporary closing of a plant or a temporary loss of work.

783. The scheme also covers the risk of an employer's bankruptcy. In this case, it provides insurance coverage against the loss of income in the event of the employer's insolvency.

784. Finally, the scheme provides benefits in conjunction with the risk of imminent unemployment.

§2. Insurance Benefits

785. The AVIG contains an exhaustive list of the various types of statutory benefits. In keeping with the legality principle, benefits not mentioned in the law may not be paid.

786. There are restrictively defined periods for receiving benefits. If these periods are not observed, claims to benefits are forfeited. These periods are intended to prevent abuses and to guarantee the possibility of monitoring the beneficiaries.

I. Compensation for Lost Income

787. Compensation for lost income (*Arbeitslosenentschädigung*) is the main type of benefit provided by the ALV. There are different categories for this benefit, which will be described in greater detail in §3.

II. Counselling and Job Placement

788. As part of ALV coverage, people who are affected by a risk are eligible for counselling and job placement, which the ALV supports with financial contributions. The RAV, in particular, are responsible for counselling and job placement services (Article 85b, AVIG).

III. Labour Market Measures

789. The ALV finances labour market measures for the benefit of insured people and for people who are at risk of becoming unemployed (Articles 59 et seq., AVIG).

790. These measures are intended to help integrate people who are very difficult to place in jobs due to labour market reasons. In concrete terms, the measures serve to improve their employability, to promote professional qualifications based on labour market needs, to reduce the risk of long-term unemployment and to offer the opportunity to gain professional experience. Possible measures include retraining; advanced training and integration courses; temporary employment in special programmes; job orientation subsidies; education subsidies; and contributions to commuting expenses.

IV. Additional Measures

791. As part of the additional measures it offers, the ALV can make a financial contribution to promoting research on the labour market (Article 73, AVIG). Its aim here is to contribute to creating a well-balanced labour market.

792. In addition, compensation offices can support temporary pilot projects that deviate from the law (Article 75a, AVIG). The projects require approval, which is granted if they serve to gain experience with new labour market measures, protect existing jobs or reintegrate unemployed people into working life.

§3. Amount of the Benefit

793. The following section examines the most important type of unemployment benefit: compensation for lost income.

I. Unemployment Compensation

794. Insured people are basically eligible for unemployment compensation (*Arbeitslosenentschädigung*) after a waiting period of (generally) five days of monitored unemployment (Article 18, paragraph 1, sentence 1, AVIG).

795. However, for people who are not obliged to support children younger than 25, the waiting periods can last up to twenty days depending on their insured salary (Article 18, paragraph 1, sentence 2, AVIG).

796. To lodge a claim, the insured person must report to an unemployment fund of his choice (Article 20, paragraph 1, AVIG). Unemployment compensation is provided in the form of a daily allowance, with five daily allowances paid per week (Article 21, AVIG).

797. A full daily allowance amounts to 80% of the person's insured salary (Article 22, paragraph 1, AVIG), with the maximum insured salary currently set at CHF 148,200 per year (as of 2018; *see* Article 23, paragraph 1, sentence 2, AVIG in conjunction with Article 22, paragraph 1, UVV). If the eligible person has children, he also receives a bonus equal to the statutory child and education benefits to which he would be entitled if he were employed. This bonus is converted to a daily figure. Nevertheless, the bonus is paid only if the insured person does not receive child benefits during the period of unemployment and no other employed person is eligible for an allowance for the same child.

798. By contrast, insured people 'only' receive a daily allowance of 70% of their insured salary if they are not required to support children under the age of 25, their full daily allowance is more than CHF 140 (as of 2018) and they do not draw a disability pension for a 40% or greater disability (Article 22, paragraph 2, AVIG).

799. Finally, the Swiss Federal Council defines amounts for people who are exempt from the required contribution period or who receive unemployment compensation after an occupational training programme. When doing so, the council is required to consider age, level of training and the circumstances leading to exemption from the required contribution period (Article 23, paragraph 2, AVIG). A sum of CHF 153 is taken as insured income per day for people who have completed a university degree, a higher vocational training programme or an equivalent programme. An allowance on the basis of CHF 127 is awarded to people who have completed an occupational training programme. All other people older than 20 receive unemployment compensation on the basis of CHF 102 per day, and people younger than 20 on the basis of CHF 40 per day (Article 41 of the Unemployment Insurance Ordinance (*Arbeitslosenversicherungsverordnung, AVIV*)).

800. The employee's contributions to disability insurance (*Invalidenversicherung, IV*), the occupational pension fund and non-industrial accident insurance are deducted from the daily allowance (Article 22a, AVIG).

801. Within the time period in which benefits are drawn, a maximum number of daily allowances can be paid based on the insured person's age and contribution time (Article 27, AVIG). An insured person is eligible for:

- a maximum of 260 daily allowances if they can prove they have paid contributions for twelve months;
- a maximum of 400 daily allowances if they can prove they have paid contributions for eighteen months;
- a maximum of 520 daily allowances if they can prove they have paid contributions for twenty-four months and have completed their 55th year or currently receive a disability pension based on a 40% or greater disability;
- a maximum of ninety daily allowances if they are exempt from the contribution period;
- a maximum of 200 daily allowances if they have not yet completed their 25th year and are not responsible for supporting children.

802. An insured person is eligible for an additional 120 daily allowances if he has lost his job within four years of reaching the AHV retirement age and it is difficult or impossible to place him in a new job for general or labour market reasons (Article 27, paragraph 2, AVIG).

803. In the interests of mitigating damage, it is desirable for the insured person to pursue a gainful activity in the interim. Income from employed or self-employed work earned by the insured person during the period of monitored unemployment is referred to as *Zwischenverdienst*, or interim earnings. The insured person has a right to replacement of 70%–80% of his lost earnings, based on the difference between the earned interim income and the insured salary (Article 24, AVIG).

II. Compensation for Reduced Working Hours

804. The term 'reduced working hours' (*Kurzarbeit*) is used when an employer orders a temporary reduction of working hours or a temporary shutdown of his plant for economic reasons and with the agreement of the affected employees. As a result, the employees' salaries are reduced. Compensation for reduced working hours is meant to offset the loss of the employees' income. Its purpose is to prevent possible dismissals and to secure jobs. In contrast to compensation for lost income, this benefit is paid within an existing employer-employee relationship.

805. Compensation for reduced working hours does not require the insured person to meet a minimum contribution period or reside in Switzerland. Within the scope of the FZA, the EFTA-Agreement and bilateral agreements signed by Switzerland and its neighbouring states, compensation for reduced working hours can also be paid abroad. However, the employee must be liable for contributions to the ALV or be younger than the minimum age for contribution requirements to the AHV (Article 31, paragraph 1a, AVIG).

806. Compensation for reduced working hours replaces 80% of the applicable lost income (Article 34, paragraph 1, AVIG). It is paid for a maximum of eighteen months (= accounting periods) within a two-year period (Article 35, AVIG; Article 57b, AVIV). This maximum period applies to the company and not, for example, to the individual employee.

807. The employer must assume responsibility for (at the moment) a one-day waiting period himself, which means he must replace the worker's lost earnings for the first day of the first six accounting periods, for the following accounting periods for two days (Article 50, paragraph 3, AVIV).

808. To secure the compensation for reduced working hours, the employer must report the reduced working hours to the cantonal authorities at least ten days in advance, establish their necessity and, using documents, provide compelling evidence that the conditions are met (Article 36, AVIG). The employer must pay the compensation to his employees in advance on a regular payday (Article 37, letter a, AVIG). He must file his employees' claim for compensation within three months after the end of each accounting period at the office named by him, acting for the company as a whole (Article 38, paragraph 1, AVIG). Compensation is not reimbursed if it is not claimed punctually.

III. Bad Weather Allowance

809. A bad weather allowance is paid to the employees of certain sectors (listed exhaustively in Article 65, AVIV) in order to replace income that is lost directly and solely due to a weather-related reduction of working hours (Articles 42 et seq., AVIG). At issue is a 'meteorological' reduction in working hours, as it were.

810. The bad weather allowance is not paid if the loss of working hours is caused only indirectly by the weather, pertains to seasonal agricultural work or if the employees have not agreed to the work stoppage (Article 43a, AVIG). Furthermore, an employer-employee relationship must exist.

811. The bad weather allowance does not require the insured person to meet a minimum contribution period or reside in Switzerland. Within the scope of the FZA, the EFTA-Agreement and bilateral agreements signed by Switzerland and its neighbouring states, the bad weather allowance can also be paid abroad. However, the employee must be liable for contributions to the ALV or be younger than the minimum age for contribution requirements to the AHV (Article 42, paragraph 1a, AVIG).

812. The rules for determining the bad weather allowance are the same as those for setting the compensation for reduced working hours (Article 44, AVIG). Within a two-year period, the bad weather allowance may be paid for a maximum of six accounting periods (Article 44a, paragraph 1, AVIG).

813. The accounting periods for the compensation for reduced working hours and the bad weather allowance are added together to determine the waiting period and the maximum benefits within the two-year timeframe (Article 44a, paragraph 2, AVIG).

814. The employer must report the weather-related loss of working hours to the cantonal authorities on a prescribed form no later than the fifth day of the following calendar month (Article 69, paragraph 1, AVIV). If the report is filed late without an acceptable excuse, the claim is shifted by the length of the delay (Article 69, paragraph 2, AVIV). The cantonal authorities issue an order specifying the days for which the bad weather allowance is paid (Article 69, paragraph 3, AVIV).

815. The employer pays the bad weather allowance to employees in advance on a regular payday. He asserts his employees' claim for compensation within three months after the end of the accounting period at the office named by him, acting for the company as a whole or for the place of work (Article 46 in conjunction with Article 37, AVIG).

IV. Bankruptcy Compensation

816. Bankruptcy compensation offers protection to employees by safeguarding their right for four months for work they have performed. If employees are liable for contributions and work at companies that are subject to attachment or employ workers in Switzerland, they have a right to bankruptcy compensation provided that one of the following three conditions is met (Article 51, paragraph 1, AVIG):

- Bankruptcy proceedings have been opened against the employer at a point in time when they have salary claims.
- Bankruptcy proceedings have not been opened solely because creditors were not willing to pay the costs in advance due to the employer's excessive debt levels.
- The employees have not applied for attachment against their employer due to salary claims.

817. Concerning the employee's eligibility, it is irrelevant whether an employer-employee relationship still exists or has been terminated.

818. Bankruptcy compensation covers claims to income earned during the last four months of the employer-employee relationship prior to the opening of bankruptcy proceedings (Article 52, paragraph 1, AVIG). It also covers all earnings for work performed afterward. Nevertheless, for each monthly period, this benefit only provides coverage for the monthly portion of the maximum annual amount of CHF 148,200 (as of 2018; *see* Article 3, paragraph 2, AVIG in conjunction with Article 22, paragraph 1, UVV). Furthermore, statutory social security contributions must be deducted from bankruptcy compensation (Article 52, paragraph 2, AVIG).

819. Employees must file their claim no later than sixty days after publication of the bankruptcy in the official Swiss gazette of commerce or after execution of attachment (Article 53, paragraphs 1 and 2, AVIG). They must do so at the responsible public fund in the locality where the collection and bankruptcy office is located. The claim for bankruptcy compensation expires when these sixty days are up (Article 53, paragraph 3, AVIG).

820. If the public fund pays bankruptcy compensation to the affected employees, their claims to earnings are transferred to the fund matching the amount of the compensation and social security contributions the fund has paid (Article 54, AVIG). Their right to preferential treatment in the event of insolvency and their certificates of unpaid debts are also transferred to the fund.

821. Employees are required to do everything in their power during the bankruptcy and attachment proceedings to enforce their claims against their employer until the fund informs them that it has entered into the proceedings in their place. Afterward they are required to support the fund in every appropriate way in its effort to pursue their claims (Article 55, paragraph 1, AVIG).

822. Bankruptcy compensation must be paid back by employees if, during bankruptcy or attachment, their claim to earnings is dismissed or is not covered for reasons that were caused intentionally by them or were the result of their gross negligence. Compensation must also be paid back if their claim to earnings is retroactively met by the employer (Article 55, paragraph 2, AVIG).

§4. Conditions

823. The following section takes a closer look at the eligibility requirements for unemployment compensation, since this is the most important benefit in the ALV. To receive unemployment compensation, seven conditions must be met cumulatively (Article 8, paragraph 1, AVIG).

I. Timeframes

824. Important timeframes pertaining to both the payment of contributions and the receipt of benefits restrict a person's eligibility for unemployment compensation. The timeframe for contributions defines the period in which the claimant must meet his requirement to pay contributions in the sense of a minimum contribution period or is exempt from this requirement. The timeframe for the receipt of benefits restricts eligibility by establishing a period that is used to fix the duration and amount of benefits.

825. The timeframes for the payment of contributions and the receipt of benefits are two years (Article 9, paragraph 1, AVIG). The timeframe for the receipt of benefits begins on the day on which all requirements for a claim are met (Article 9, paragraph 2, AVIG). The timeframe for the contribution period begins two years before this day (Article 9, paragraph 3, AVIG). If the two-year timeframe for the receipt of benefits has expired and the insured person asserts a new claim to benefits, the two-year timeframes again apply to both the receipt of benefits and the payment of contributions (Article 9, paragraph 4, AVIG).

826. The contribution period is met if, within the stipulated timeframe, a job subject to contributions was performed for twelve months (Article 13, AVIG). Exceptions apply to people who, due to schooling, retraining, advanced training, illness, accident, etc., are unable to meet the contribution period (Article 14, AVIG). There are also special provisions for insured people who take up a self-employed activity during the current timeframe for the receipt of benefits without having received support from the ALV for their self-employed activity (Article 9a, AVIG).

827. In addition, under certain circumstances, the timeframe for the receipt of benefits can be extended for people involved in raising their children (Article 9b, AVIG).

II. Involuntary Unemployment

A. Unemployment

828. The term 'unemployment' is not defined in either the AVIG or the ATSG), but the AVIG does distinguish between different types of unemployment (Article 10, AVIG). 'Full unemployment' means that the insured person is not currently in an employer-employee relationship governed by private or public law. This is the objective element of the definition.

829. The subjective component is that the insured person must be looking for full-time employment. As far as 'partial unemployment' goes, there are two possible forms. Either the insured person is not in an employer-employee relationship, but is looking for part-time employment, or he has a part-time job, but wants to work full-time or pursue an additional part-time job.

830. Unemployment ends when the insured person – depending on the job he is looking for – finds a full- or part-time position, takes up a self-employed activity or withdraws his registration from the labour office.

B. Involuntary

831. In order to lodge a claim for unemployment compensation, the insured person must become unemployed through no fault of his own. If unemployment is the person's fault, he has violated his duty to avoid joblessness. In the following cases, unemployment is considered the person's fault (Article 44, AVIV):

- An employer gives notice to the insured person because of his conduct – specifically, because he has violated contractual duties. The insured person's conditional intent is sufficient for him to be at fault – that is, the insured person must have expected or foreseen that his conduct would lead to the termination of his job. Cases in which the insured person gives notice upon request or of his own accord in order to pre-empt dismissal by the employer are seen as equivalent.
- The insured person ends an existing employer-employee relationship of his own accord without having secured another position. However, this manner of ending a job is not considered to be the insured person's fault if he cannot reasonably be expected to remain any longer in the position.
- Unemployment is also considered the insured person's fault if he ends an employer-employee relationship that probably would have lasted longer and has entered into another employer-employee relationship that he must know, or must have known, is only short-term.
- Finally, unemployment is also considered the insured person's fault if he has not accepted a reasonable permanent position and instead has taken a short-term job.

832. If an insured person is at fault for his joblessness, his claim to unemployment compensation can be suspended (Article 30, paragraph 1a, AVIG). The purpose of suspension is to limit the insurance scheme's liability for damages and to ensure that the insured person makes an appropriate contribution to damages that he could have avoided.

833. The length of the suspension period depends on the degree of the person's fault and amounts to sixty days for each reason for suspension (Article 30, paragraph 3, AVIG) – though the principle of proportionality must always be observed. It must be noted that since the length of suspension is based on the degree of fault, the number of suspension days may even be greater than the number of days for which the benefit can be drawn. When determining the number of suspension days, the implementation offices are required to consider the insured person's conduct and all the important facts of the individual case and to impose a sanction that is in line with fault. Suspension tables have been developed for guidance, but they may not be used in any simplistic, schematic manner. The AVIV stipulates that a suspension of one to fifteen days is to be imposed for slight fault, suspension of sixteen to thirty days for moderate fault, and suspension of thirty-one to sixty days for grave fault (Article 43, paragraphs 3 and 4, AVIV).

III. Availability for the Labour Market

834. To receive unemployment compensation, the insured person must be employable. He is considered such if he is willing, able and permitted to accept reasonable work and take part in integration measures (Article 15, paragraph 1, AVIG).

835. If the cantonal authorities have considerable doubts as to the insured person's employability, they may order an examination by a medical officer at their own expense (Article 15, paragraph 3, AVIG). Physically and mentally disabled persons are considered employable if they can be placed in a suitable job in a well-balanced labour market taking their disability into account (Article 15, paragraph 2, AVIG).

836. An insured person is considered able to work if he is physically and mentally fit and available in the given time period. A person who is responsible for caring for children and cannot be deployed in the way that is usually required by employers is – in principle – regarded as unemployable. The reasons for this person's restricted availability are immaterial; the decisive point is that the selection of possible jobs is severely limited and a position is therefore difficult to find. Nevertheless, practice tends to be less severe in this point because indirect discrimination must be avoided.

837. Employability also presupposes that the person is allowed to work. This means that the jobless person may not be prohibited from work by immigration, asylum, occupational safety, health or trade regulations.

838. These objective components are supplemented by a subjective component – namely, that the person is willing to be placed in a new job. Willingness exists if the jobless person is prepared to accept a permanent position suitable to his personal circumstances during the usual working hours. In addition, the person must make himself available to the public job centre, accept any reasonable job offer and look intensively for reasonable employment. All jobs must in principle be assumed to be reasonable. Article 16, paragraph 2, of the AVIG includes an exhaustive list of jobs that are not considered reasonable. They include, for example, positions that do not meet the usual occupational or local conditions, especially the conditions contained in collective agreements or normal employment contracts; positions that would make it difficult for the insured person to be reemployed in his usual profession (assuming there are prospects for him to do so in the near future); and positions that require a commute of more than two hours each way.

839. If the insured person does not make a sufficient effort to find reasonable employment, he can be penalized with suspension days, which are described in greater detail in paragraphs 832 et seq.

IV. No Other Entitlement to Benefit

840. To qualify for unemployment compensation, the employee must be affected by a creditable loss of work. This is deemed to exist if the loss of work results in a loss of earnings and lasts for a minimum of two consecutive full working days (Article 11, paragraph 2, AVIG). But there is no creditable loss of work if the jobless person has salary claims against the employer or has claims to compensation because of a premature termination of the employer-employee relationship (Article 11, paragraph 3, AVIG).

841. There is also no creditable lack of work if the employer, through voluntary payments, covers the loss of earnings caused by the termination of the employer-employee relationship (Article 11a, paragraph 1, AVIG). But these payments are not credited if they do not exceed the maximum limit of the insured salary (Article 11a, paragraph 2, AVIG).

842. If the employee renounces his salary or compensation claims to the detriment of the insurance scheme, he may be penalized with suspension days, which are treated in greater detail in paragraphs 832 et seq.

843. The insured person is ineligible for unemployment compensation during periods in which he is eligible for pensions or daily allowances from the disability, military, accident or health insurance programmes, the occupational pension system, or the compensation scheme for lost income. He is also ineligible during times in which he receives statutory family allowances. If he has already received a daily allowance from the ALV, he is required to return the benefits paid during this period (Article 95, paragraph 1*bis*, AVIG).

844. Old-age pensions from the occupational pension fund are deducted from unemployment compensation (Article 18c, AVIG). The same applies to the daily allowances from the health and accident insurance schemes that are meant to replace lost earnings (Article 28, paragraph 2, AVIG).

V. Living in Switzerland

845. This condition was mentioned above. Since it is essentially prohibited to pay benefits abroad, the only people eligible for unemployment compensation are those living in Switzerland (Article 8, paragraph 1c, AVIG). The reason for this ban is that residence abroad makes it difficult to review and monitor the eligibility criteria.

846. However, this ban does not apply to EU and EFTA citizens. Additional explanations can be found in Part VII, §1, II, 'Personal Field of Application'.

VI. Age Requirements

847. An insured person is only eligible for unemployment compensation if, in addition to meeting all the other requirements, he has completed the compulsory school time and has not reached the AHV retirement age or is not a recipient of an old-age pension from the AHV (i.e., within the scope of the flexible retirement age; Article 8, paragraph 1d, AVIG).

848. Due to these legal standards, it is impossible to say precisely what minimum age is required for receiving unemployment compensation. It depends on the compulsory school time in the individual cantons. As far as the minimum age goes, insurance coverage is not consistent with contribution requirements. In other words, although employed young people are exempt from the requirement to pay contributions until the end of the year in which they turn seventeen (Article 1, paragraph 4a, AHVG), there are some circumstances under which they are insured at an earlier point in time.

849. However, receipt of both unemployment compensation and an AHV pension is ruled out. As soon as the insured person reaches the AHV retirement age, he may no longer draw unemployment compensation, even if he continues to be employed or has applied for a pension deferral. If the insured person draws his AHV pension before the official AHV retirement age (advance pension payment), his claim for unemployment compensation expires in the month in which the prematurely drawn pension is first paid.

VII. Duties and Monitoring of the Unemployed

850. The insuree must report in person to the authorities in the locality in which he lives or to the job centre specified by the canton (Article 17, paragraph 2, AVIG). He must do so as early as possible but no later than the first day for which he claims unemployment compensation. From this point on, he is required to fulfil monitoring regulations. In keeping with the cantonal instructions, he must report in person to the office responsible for counselling and monitoring talks and ensure that he can normally be reached by the responsible office within one day (Article 21, paragraph 1, AVIV). The office makes the appointments for counselling and monitoring talks for each insured person (at least one every two months), records the days on which the required talks take place, and documents the results in minutes (Article 21, paragraphs 2 and 3, and Article 22, paragraph 2, AVIV). The talks are used to review the person's employability and willingness to work. No counselling and monitoring talks are held between 24 December and 2 January (Article 21, paragraph 4, AVIV).

851. In special cases (e.g., taster courses, job interviews abroad, etc.), the office can, upon request, release the insured person for a limited time from his obligation to take part in counselling and monitoring talks (Article 25, AVIV).

852. In order to receive unemployment compensation, the insured person must make every reasonable effort – with the labour office's support – to avoid or shorten the period in which he is unemployed (Article 17, paragraph 1, AVIG). Most importantly, he must look for work and, if necessary, expand his search to include jobs outside his previous profession. He is also required to provide proof of these efforts. The labour office is required to check the insured person's job-search efforts on a monthly basis and usually draws on regular job applications to do so (Article 26, AVIV).

853. After sixty days of monitored unemployment within the timeframe specified above, the insured person has a right to five consecutive days without being monitored (Article 27, paragraph 1, AVIV). He may choose these days himself. During these days he does not need to be reachable, but must meet all the other requirements. The insured person is required to report these free days – which can only be taken in a week-long block – at the responsible office at least fourteen days in advance (Article 27, paragraph 3, AVIV).

854. Upon orders by the responsible authorities, the insured person must take part in labour market measures designed to promote his employability, as well as in counselling talks, information-gathering events and expert counselling sessions (Article 17, paragraph 3, AVIG). He is also required to provide the documents needed to evaluate his employability or the reasonableness of a job.

855. If, due to illness, accident or pregnancy, the insured person is temporarily unable to work or be placed in a job, or can only work or be placed in a job to a limited degree, he is considered unable to fulfil the monitoring rules. But if he nonetheless meets the remaining requirements for unemployment compensation, he is eligible for a full daily allowance until the thirtieth day after the beginning of the period in which he is entirely or partially unable to work (Article 28, paragraph 1, AVIG). Only forty-four daily allowances are permissible within the above-discussed timeframe. If the insured person receives, from the accident or health insurance programmes, daily allowances meant to replace lost earnings, these allowances are deducted from the unemployment compensation (Article 28, paragraph 2, AVIG).

856. The insured person's eligibility is suspended if he fails to obey the monitoring regulations or the orders from the responsible authorities – specifically, if he does not accept a reasonable job offer; fails to participate in or interrupts a labour market measure without an acceptable excuse; or, through his conduct, makes it impossible for the measure to be held, or undermines its purpose (Article 30, paragraph 1d, AVIG). For more details on suspension days, please *see* paragraphs 832 et seq.

§5. Organization

857. The ALV must perform a great variety of tasks. These are assigned either to the implementation bodies or the supervisory bodies.

I. Implementation Bodies

858. The AVIG contains an exhaustive list of the different implementation bodies (Article 76, AVIG):

859. The main implementation bodies are the unemployment agencies (Article 77 et seq., AVIG). A distinction must be drawn between public and private agencies. Each canton runs a public agency by itself or together with other cantons. In addition, national, regional and cantonal trade union and employers' organizations are permitted to set up agencies individually or collectively. The task of these agencies is to clarify claims for benefits, suspend eligibility for claims, pay benefits and administer the money collected from contributions. While it is true that these agencies are not legal entities, they may act in their own name and issue orders and rulings.

860. The cantonal offices also serve as implementation bodies and are integrated into the cantonal administrations (Article 85, AVIG). Among other things, they advise the unemployed, place them in jobs, clarify their eligibility for claims, determine the reasonableness of work and check employability.

861. Additional implementation bodies include the regional job centres (RAVs), which work to quickly reintegrate the unemployed into the labour market (Article 85b, AVIG); the logistics offices that are in charge of labour market measures (Article 85c, AVIG); the tripartite commissions (RAV counselling; Article 85d,

AVIG); the compensation offices (supervising and ensuring legally compliant implementation processes at the unemployment insurance funds and cantonal offices; Articles 83 and 83a, AVIG); the compensation fund of the ALV (Article 84, AVIG); the supervisory commission (supervision of the compensation fund; Article 89, AVIG); the AHV compensation offices (Article 86, AVIG); the AHV central compensation office (Article 87, AVIG); and the employers (e.g., accounting tasks for the social insurance system; Article 88, AVIG).

II. Oversight

862. Oversight is the responsibility of the Swiss Federal Council (Article 76, ATSG), which has delegated this task to the SECO. Oversight of contributions has been assigned to the Federal Social Insurance Office (*Bundesamt für Sozialversicherungen, BSV*). These bodies are permitted to give orders to the implementation bodies.

Part VIII. Pensions

Chapter 1. The Swiss Pension System

§1. The Three-Pillar or Three-Level Pension System

863. The pension system in Switzerland is based on the three-pillar concept that was incorporated into the BV in 1972 (Article 111, BV).

864. The first pillar of the social security system – old-age, survivors' and disability insurance – is meant to adequately cover basic living needs (Article 112, paragraph 2b, BV). The second pillar – the occupational pension system – is supposed to ensure that people can maintain their accustomed standard of living (Article 113, paragraph 2a, BV).

865. The second pillar consists of a compulsory component that is subject to the Federal Law on Old-Age, Survivors' and Disability Pensions (*Bundesgesetz über die berufliche Alters-, Hinterlassenen- und Invalidenvorsorge, BVG*), and a non-compulsory component that in most cases is based on a contractual relationship.

866. The third pillar comprises private pension plans. Here a distinction is made between tax-advantaged private pension plans (pillar 3a) and voluntary pension arrangements with no preferential tax treatment (pillar 3b, *see also* Article 111, paragraphs 1 and 4, BV).

867. Given the goals of pension benefits, it would be more appropriate in terms of imagery to speak of a three-*level* system. The first level (= first pillar) is designed to adequately meet basic living needs; the second level enables people to maintain their accustomed standard of living; and the third and uppermost level provides leeway for private pension plans tailored to individual needs.

§2. The Aim of Benefits

I. Adequate Coverage of Basic Living Needs

868. As set forth in Article 112, paragraph 2b, of the BV, pensions must adequately cover basic living needs. As the history of this provision illustrates, it was phrased to emphasize the idea that first-pillar benefits must be significantly greater than the minimum income needed for existence (i.e., they must exceed welfare benefits, let alone the constitutionally guaranteed right to emergency assistance as per Article 12, BV).

869. Although the scope of the first-pillar benefits has constantly been expanded, in many cases even the maximum monthly pension from the AHV – currently amounting to CHF 2,350 (as of 2018) – is insufficient to achieve this goal. For this reason, a federal law was introduced in 1966 that allowed the federal government to pay contributions to the cantons to finance supplementary benefits as a way of achieving the goals of the pension system.

870. The system of supplementary benefits targets people with insufficient income. Benefits are based on a (highly schematized) calculation of individual needs. The people eligible for benefits are those that live in Switzerland and receive pensions from the old-age and survivors'/IVs. It is primarily elderly people in nursing homes who today require supplementary benefits – along with recipients of disability pensions. In late 2016, 12.5% of all old-age pensioners relied on such benefits. However, depending on the region – and that is to say on the cost of living and housing in the different regions – the total percentage of recipients of supplementary benefits may be considerably higher. In late 2016, it ranged between 7.3% and 18.9% from canton to canton. In urban areas with a high cost of living, it frequently exceeds 20%.

871. Originally planned as an interim solution, this purely tax-financed branch of insurance has become a central pillar of social security, especially with respect to financing care for the elderly. Within the scope of a major constitutional reform (including a new financial equalization system), on 1 January 2008 legislators transferred the relevant responsibilities that had previously been contained in the transitional regulations of the Federal Constitution (Article 196, No. 10, BV) to regular constitutional law (Article 112a, BV).

872. Furthermore, since 2012, the system of supplementary benefits has been expanded into an important subsystem for financing care for the elderly and disabled. As a result, it has also caused sharply rising costs. In other words, it would be impossible for the first pillar of the pension system to fulfil all the goals of benefits without the tax-financed supplementary benefits.

II. Maintaining an Accustomed Standard of Living

873. According to Article 113, paragraph 2a, of the BV, the goal of the occupational pension system – together with first-pillar benefits – is to allow people to maintain their accustomed standard of living in an adequate way. This goal is vague in two respects. Both the 'accustomed standard of living' and the 'adequate way' in which it is to be guaranteed provide legislators with a great deal of leeway.

874. But it can be shown that the framers of the Federal Constitution intended the first two pillars of the pension system to offer a level of benefits covering around 60% of a person's income earned before retirement. The minimum guarantees of the occupational pension system do not achieve this goal, particularly for middle- and higher-income groups.

875. However, the majority of insured people have additional coverage under supplementary occupational pensions that are based on contractual agreements. The law grants the supplementary occupational pensions a privileged status in the sense that premiums can be fully deducted from direct taxes (Article 82, BVG). In the case of insured people who have such plans, the goal of benefits is usually achieved, provided they have paid contributions for the required number of years by the time they retire.

III. Coverage of Individual Needs

876. In order to ensure the fulfilment of individual needs that extend beyond the maintenance of an individual's accustomed standard of living, the Federal Constitution requires legislators to implement measures in the fields of tax and property policy (Article 111, paragraph 4, BV). Such measures are designed to encourage people to save for their pensions. Private pension plans (*gebundene Selbstvorsorge*), in particular, give people the opportunity to make investments, subject to a defined maximum tax-deductible amount, within a pension insurance policy offered by an insurance company or a pension arrangement set up with a banking foundation (Article 82, paragraph 2, BVG and Article 1, paragraph 1, of the Ordinance on tax-deductible Contributions to Accredited Forms of Provision (*Verordnung über die steuerliche Abzugsberechtigung für Beiträge an anerkannte Vorsorgeformen, BVV 3*)). These types of pensions are available to employees and self-employed individuals.

§3. Structure of the Three Pillars

877. The basic principle of the AHV is one of solidarity. First of all, there exists intergenerational solidarity, since current pensions are financed by working people in a pay-as-you-go system (and also by those non-employed people who are required to pay contributions). Second, there is a redistribution of funds from higher to lower income groups, since total work income is subject to contributions, but pensions are bound by both an upper and lower limit (maximum and minimum pension), and the maximum pension may not amount to more than double the minimum pension (*see also* Article 34, paragraphs 3 and 5, AHVG). Therefore, above a defined level of income, currently (2018) set at CHF 84,600 per year, contributions are not paid towards accumulating pension assets (Article 34, paragraph 4, AHVG). Third, the credits awarded for child-rearing and care giving (Article 29*sexies* and Article 29*septies*, AHVG) promote solidarity between childless people and parents as well as between caregivers and non-caregivers. Fourth, as long as the retirement age for women remains lower than that for men, women require fewer contribution years to receive the same pension benefits, which results in a redistribution of funds from men to women. Finally, thanks to the 'splitting' of the creditable income that is earned during a marriage (*see also* Article 29*quinquies*, paragraph 3, AHVG), there is solidarity between spouses in the AHV.

878. The redistribution of funds is not of central importance in the occupational pension system. It has an impact only within the individual pension funds. But resources are redistributed in a number of ways in this second pillar of pension coverage. For example, redistribution occurs in the defined benefits system (*Leistungsprimat*), since the insured people whose salaries do not increase significantly during their careers help finance the benefits of others whose salaries rise towards the end of their working life. In addition, everyone is required to pay the same contributions regardless of marital status, and the same minimum conversion rate is used for both married and single people (Article 14, paragraph 2, BVG). This means that single people contribute to funding the survivors' pensions of married couples. Since the same conversion rate is used to calculate the old-age pensions for women and men, a redistribution takes place between the sexes, since men are older when they begin drawing a pension and their life expectancy is shorter.

879. By contrast, the guiding idea in the third pillar is that of self-provision. In order to ensure that tax-advantaged pension plans are not used for the wrong purpose, money may only be invested in certain pension products (Article 1, paragraph 1, BVV 3). In addition, the payment of benefits from these pension plans is subject to separate taxation (with reduced rates in most cantons) – that is, the benefits are not added together with other earnings, leading to a higher tax rate.

§4. Old-Age and Survivors' Insurance as a Scheme for All People

I. Insurance Coverage

880. The AHV is meant to be an insurance for all members of society. It essentially provides coverage for the entire resident population of Switzerland, though three different categories of people are distinguished:

A. Compulsorily Insured People

881. On the one hand, people are compulsorily insured in the scheme if they live in Switzerland (Article 1a, paragraph 1a, AHVG) – regardless of whether they are employed, self-employed or non-employed. On the other hand, people are compulsorily insured if they work in Switzerland, regardless of their nationality – a rule that also applies to cross-border commuters (Article 1a, paragraph 1b, AHVG). Furthermore, under Article 1a, paragraph 1c, of the AHVG, coverage is compulsory for Swiss citizens who work abroad either for the Swiss government or for a number of defined organizations (Article 1a, paragraph 1c, AHVG).

882. Despite working in Switzerland, people who are members of an old-age and survivors' insurance programme of another state are not insured if coverage under the Swiss insurance scheme would result in an unacceptable double burden (Article 1a, paragraph 2b, AHVG and Article 3, AHVV). Furthermore, in a number of cases that have been more closely defined by regulators, people who meet insurance coverage conditions only temporarily (based on residence or employment) are exempt from compulsory insurance (Article 1a, paragraph 2c, AHVG and Article 2, AHVV).

B. Continuing Coverage, Joining the Compulsory Insurance Scheme

883. People who work abroad for, and are paid by, an employer based in Switzerland and non-employed students younger than thirty who give up residence in Switzerland in order to take part in an educational programme abroad may continue their coverage in the compulsory scheme (Article 1a, paragraph 3, AHVG). To qualify, these people must have been insured for at least five consecutive years before beginning work or their educational programme abroad (Articles 5 and 5g, AHVV).

884. Certain categories of people are allowed to join the compulsory insurance scheme. They include people domiciled in Switzerland who are not insured due to an international agreement (Article 1a, paragraph 4, AHVG).

C. The Voluntarily Insured

885. Swiss nationals and citizens of the Member States of the EU or the EFTA who do not live in a Member State of the EU or EFTA may join the voluntary insurance scheme if they were compulsorily insured for at least five consecutive years just before joining (Article 2, paragraph 1, AHVG).

886. Statistics show that half of all voluntarily insured people pay only the minimum annual contribution for old-age and survivors' insurance and disability insurance. This currently (2018) amounts to CHF 784 per year based on an annual income of CHF 9,400 (*see* Article 2, paragraphs 4 and 5, AHVG and Article 3, IVG). Only 7% of all insured people pay the minimum contribution to the compulsory insurance scheme. As long as well-to-do people are not permitted to join the voluntary insurance scheme, funds will not be redistributed between high- and low-income groups.

II. Financing System

887. The financing system characteristic of the AHV is the pay-as-you-go system. One of its key features is that the benefits required for a period are financed through contributions from the insured people, their employers and public authorities (Article 102, AHVG). Reserves are generally not accumulated – with the exception of a not insubstantial 'fluctuation reserve fund' (*Schwankungsreserve*, or old-age and survivors' insurance fund; Articles 107 et seq., AHVG). In essence, the contributions from working people are redistributed directly to pensioners.

888. The advantage of this system is that the purchasing power of pensions is guaranteed in line with economic developments. A disadvantage is that there is no guarantee that the benefits can be covered by the accumulated capital when people retire. As in all pay-as-you-go systems, demographic developments play a crucial role.

III. Liability for Contributions

889. All insured people are generally liable to pay contributions, regardless of whether they are employed, self-employed or non-employed. But an exception is made in the case of contributions from non-employed young people, who are not required to pay contributions until 31 December of the year in which they turn 20. Employed young people are exempt from the liability for contributions until 31 December of the year in which they turn 17 (Article 3, paragraph 2a, AHVG). Non-employed men and women are not required to pay contributions once they reach the regular retirement age of 64 or 65, respectively (*see* Article 3, paragraph 1, AHVG). People who continue to work after reaching retirement age must still pay contributions, but the basis for contributions is defined in such a way that these people are given a monthly exemption of CHF 1,400 on which no contributions are collected (as of 2018; Article 4, paragraph 2b, AHVG). The portion of their income exceeding this amount is still subject to contributions without limitation. Only under certain circumstances (pension deferral) do their contributions increase the amount of benefits (cf. Article 39, AHVG). In other words, these contributions are actually a kind of solidarity tax.

890. Although the contribution liability for non-employed people is capped by a maximum annual amount (Article 10, AHVG and Article 28, AHVV), the contribution liability for employees and their employers (based on gross salary) and self-employed people (based on taxable earnings) is not limited. In other words, the basis for calculating contributions is not subject to a maximum amount as in other social security systems. Nevertheless, smaller graduated contribution rates apply for self-employed people with low incomes (i.e., less than CHF 56,400 a year as of 2018; Article 8, paragraph 1, AHVG and Article 21, AHVV).

891. It must be noted in this connection that the awarding of a certain social insurance status, which is carried out under the AHVG (i.e., self-employed or employed), is binding for all branches of social insurance. In the case of working people, the system only distinguishes *tertium non datur* between employed people (employees) and the self-employed. There are no intermediary or hybrid forms such as freelancers, newly self-employed or businessmen. This definition is especially important since compulsory coverage in the insurance schemes that are actually meant for employees (occupational pension system, accident insurance, unemployment insurance) is based on the AHVG.

892. The law provides for the possibility of waiving contributions for people who work part-time and earn only negligible income (Article 8, paragraph 2, and Article 14, paragraph 5, AHVG). The negligible income threshold is set at a (very low) CHF 2,300 per year for both self-employed individuals and employees (Articles 19 and 34d, paragraph 1, AHVV). This rather modest exception to the general requirement to pay contributions serves mainly to prevent disproportionately high administrative costs; its intention is not to create 'insurance-free zones'. The sense and purpose of the old-age and survivors' insurance system, which rests on various ideas of solidarity, is to include all types of income under contributions law. To emphasize the point once again, the exception to the rule – jobs yielding negligible earnings – applies only to the liability to pay contributions, not to insurance coverage, which is based on a person having his residence or (primary) place of work in Switzerland.

§5. Flexible Pension Age

I. Regular Pension Age

893. Since the three pillars of the Swiss pension system are based on the AHV, the regular retirement age in this scheme is used for the entire pension system. This age is currently set at 65 for men and 64 for women (Article 21, AHVG). For many years now efforts have been underway to establish 65 as the retirement age for both men and women, but they have not been successful so far.

II. Flexibility in the AHV

894. If a person wishes to prematurely draw an old-age and survivors' insurance pension, he must currently accept a 6.8% actuarial reduction of the prematurely drawn pension per year (Article 56, paragraph 2, AHVV). Premature receipt of the pension is generally only possible two years before the regular retirement age (Article 40, AHVG).

895. It is also possible to defer receipt of an old-age pension. These people do not increase their pension claims, but receive an actuarially calculated bonus due to the deferral. In the case of the maximum pension deferral period of five years, this bonus currently amounts to 31.5% of the deferred old-age pension (Article 55*ter*, AHVV).

896. People older than the regular retirement age who continue to work must also continue to pay old-age and survivors' insurance contributions based on their income. However, a sum of CHF 1,400 per month or CHF 16,800 per year is exempted in the calculation of contributions (Article 4, paragraph 2b, AHVG and Article 6*quater*, AHVV). The contributions do not affect the amount of the old-age pension.

III. Flexibility in the Occupational Pension System

897. Article 1i, paragraph 1, of the BVV 2 stipulates that pension fund regulations must provide for retirement by the age of 58 at the earliest. This age limit applies to both the regular retirement age based on regulations and the earliest possible premature receipt of old-age benefits. In the compulsory scheme, early receipt of a pension is financed by adjusting the conversion rate. In supplementary pensions, other financing models may be considered (advance financing during employment, purchase of more extensive benefits, etc.).

898. If the regulations or statutes permit it, a reduction of workload and the receipt of a partial pension are also possible (partial retirement). In such cases, a new independent pension is paid at each step of partial retirement, with the claim based on the assessment basis valid at the onset of the new step.

899. Similar to early retirement, pension fund regulations may also provide for a pension deferral. But a pension deferral may not occur without the consent of the insured person and requires that the insured person continues to pursue a gainful activity. The deferral increases the applicable conversion rate (Article 13, paragraph 2, BVG). Although in the compulsory scheme additional payments may not go towards increasing retirement assets (Article 15, paragraph 1a, BVG), such increases are possible with supplementary pension plans. The corresponding contributions may be deducted from taxes, provided they meet the applicable conditions. As a result, in their regulations, pension funds are generally free to provide for diverse and flexible solutions for continued work and the deferral of benefits.

900. If assets in the second pillar of pension coverage have been transferred to a vested benefits policy or to a vested benefits account, the resulting pension benefits may be provided no earlier than five years before and no later than five years after the insured person reaches the regular pension age (Article 16, paragraph 1, FZV).

IV. Flexibility in the Third Pillar

901. With just a few special exceptions, benefits from the third pillar of pension coverage may be paid no earlier than five years before a person reaches the regular pension age (Article 3, paragraph 1, BVV 3). The receipt of pension benefits may be deferred no longer than five years after the regular retirement age. Since early 2008, people who continue to pursue gainful work have been able to pay tax-deductible contributions to pillar 3a for an additional five years after reaching the regular retirement age (Article 7, paragraph 3, BVV 3). This means that the individually designed third pillar of pension coverage allows people to retire between the ages of 59/60 and 69/70.

Chapter 2. Pensions for Wage-Earners

§1. Old-Age Pensions from the AHV

I. Beneficiaries

902. Swiss pensioners may apply to have regular old-age, survivors' or disability pensions paid to any country of residence if this is not ruled out by the regulations of that country. The payment is made by the Swiss compensation fund and in some cases by the responsible Swiss mission.

903. If foreign nationals live in Switzerland, they generally have the same rights and duties regarding pensions as Swiss citizens. Foreign nationals who are subject to a social insurance agreement may draw pensions from the Swiss AHV after they return to their home states.

904. Citizens of countries with which Switzerland does not have a social insurance agreement may have their contributions paid back if they leave Switzerland for good. In such cases, an old-age pension is generally not paid abroad.

II. Regular and Extraordinary Old-Age Pensions

905. The AHVG distinguishes between regular pensions (Articles 29 et seq., AHVG) and extraordinary pensions (Article 42, AHVG).

906. People are eligible for a regular old-age pension if they can be credited with income, child-rearing credits or care credits for at least one full year (Article 29, paragraph 1, AHVG).

907. The extraordinary pension does not depend on contributions. Swiss citizens who have their domicile and habitual residence in Switzerland (Article 13, ATSG) are eligible for an extraordinary pension if until the pension claim arises they were insured for the same number of years as their age group but are not entitled to a regular pension because they were not subject to the requirement to pay contributions for the period of one whole year (Article 42, paragraph 1, sentence 1, AHVG).

III. Calculating Pensions in the AHV

908. The amount of the regular pension is based on the contribution period and the average earned income on which contributions were paid. In the case of non-employed people, it is based on the contribution period and the paid contributions.

909. The regular pensions can be divided into full pensions and partial pensions. For insured people who have paid contributions for the entire contribution period, the regular pensions are paid as full pensions. For insured people with incomplete contribution periods, they are paid as partial pensions (Article 29, paragraph 2, AHVG). A partial pension corresponds to an actuarially computed partial amount of the full pension (Article 38, paragraph 1, AHVG).

910. It is only within the categories of the full or partial pensions that the amount of contributions has an effect on the amount of the pension.

911. Up to an average annual income (Article 30, AHVG) of CHF 14,100, which is revalued using the pension index, a minimum full pension of CHF 1,175 is paid per month (or CHF 14,100 per year, as of 2018).

912. For incomes starting at CHF 84,600, people are eligible for a maximum full pension of CHF 2,350 per month (or CHF 28,200 per year, as of 2018).

913. The maximum pension is equal to double the minimum pension (Article 34, AHVG). This principle is contained in the Federal Constitution (Article 112, paragraph 2c, BV).

914. By contrast, the amount of the extraordinary pension is generally equal to the minimum amount of the applicable regular full pension (Article 43, AHVG) – that is to say, CHF 1,175 per month or CHF 14,100 per year (as of 2018).

A. *The Pension Career*

915. The contribution period is deemed complete if the insured person has as many contribution years as his age group (Article 29*ter*, paragraph 1, AHVG). Contribution years are defined not only as periods in which contributions have effectively been paid, but also as periods during which at least double the minimum contribution has been paid by the working spouse of a non-employed or co-working (but unpaid) person (Article 3, paragraph 3, AHVG). Contribution years also include periods in which child-rearing or care credits can be awarded (Article 29*ter*, paragraph 2, AHVG).

B. *Income and Paid Contributions*

916. Individual accounts are maintained for each insured person who is liable for contributions. The data necessary to calculate the regular pensions is recorded in these accounts (Article 30*ter*, paragraph 1, sentence 1, AHVG; Articles 137 et seq., AHVV).

917. Since 1997, child-rearing credits have been awarded to the individual accounts for children younger than 16, and care credits for the care of lineal relatives or siblings.

918. The child-rearing credits are equal to triple the minimum amount of an annual old-age pension at the time the pension claim arises (i.e., CHF 42,300 as of 2018). They are awarded for all the years in which an insured person assumed parental responsibility for one or several children younger than 16. In the event of joint parental responsibility, the credits are divided evenly between the parents (Articles 52e et seq., AHVV).

919. The care credits are equivalent to the child-rearing credits but must be reported annually (Article 29*septies*, AHVG).

920. In order to determine the person's average annual income, the sum of each year's earned income is first revalued using the pension index (Article 33*ter*, AHVG). The Swiss Federal Council has the revaluation factors set annually. Then the sum of the revalued earned income is added to the child-rearing or care credits and divided by the number of contribution years, which yields the average annual income.

C. Pension Formula and Pension Amounts

921. Two factors play a key role in determining the amount of a pension: the contribution period and the average annual income. The contribution period determines which pension scale is used. With the help of the average annual income, the amount of the pension is then set using the applicable pension scale.

922. The ratio of the insured person's contribution years to those of his age group is used to determine the proper pension scale. In the case of a complete contribution period, pension scale forty-four is used; in the case of an incomplete contribution period, scales one to forty-three (Article 52, paragraph 1, AHVV).

923. The insured person's relevant average annual income is used to determine the amount of the pension on the applicable scale (Article 29*quater*, AHVG).

924. The monthly old-age pension consists of both a fraction of the minimum old-age pension (= fixed portion of pension) and a fraction of the relevant average annual income (= variable portion of pension; Article 34, paragraph 1, AHVG).

925. If the relevant average annual income is smaller than or equal to thirty-six times the minimum old-age pension, the fixed portion of the pension amounts to 74/100 of the minimum old-age pension and the variable portion amounts to 13/600 of the relevant average annual income. If the relevant average annual income is greater than thirty-six times the minimum old-age pension, the fixed portion amounts to 104/100 of the minimum old-age pension and the variable portion amounts to 8/600 of the relevant average annual income (Article 34, paragraph 2, AHVG).

926. Up to a relevant average annual income of CHF 14,100, the minimum old-age pension of CHF 14,100 is paid for a complete contribution period; starting at a relevant average annual income of CHF 84,600, the maximum pension of CHF 28,200 (Scale 44) is paid for a complete contribution period (as of 2018). If the contribution period is incomplete, the amount of the pension is reduced accordingly.

927. Considering the income replacement rate of the extreme values, it yields that people whose average earnings were less than CHF 14,100 have a replacement rate of 100% or more, while people with incomes of CHF 84,600 or more have a maximum replacement rate of 33.3%.

D. Family Status

928. The sum of both pensions drawn by a married couple may not exceed 150% of the maximum old-age pension if both spouses are eligible for an old-age pension or if one spouse is eligible for an old-age pension and the other for a pension from the IV (Article 35, paragraph 1, AHVG). If this maximum amount is exceeded, the pensions of both spouses are reduced on a pro rata basis.

929. People who are entitled to an old-age pension are eligible for a children's pension for every child who would be able to claim an orphan's pension in the event of their death. They are ineligible for a children's pension for foster children who were fostered after the claim arose either for an old-age pension or for a previous pension from the IV. An exception applies if these foster children are the children of the other spouse (Article 22*ter*, paragraph 1, AHVG). The children's pension amounts to 40% of the relevant average annual income underlying the old-age pension. In cases where both parents are eligible for a children's pension, the two children's pensions are reduced if, when added together, they exceed 60% of the maximum old-age pension (Article 35*ter*, AHVG).

IV. Cost-of-Living Adjustment

930. Periodical pension adjustments are regulated by law (Article 33*ter*, AHVG). As a rule, the Swiss Federal Council adjusts regular pensions to wage and price developments at the beginning of every second year by recalibrating the pension index at the behest of the Federal Commission for Old-Age, Survivors' and Disability Insurance. The pension index is the arithmetic mean of both the wage index (compiled by the SECO) and the national index of consumer prices. The Federal Council adjusts the regular pensions earlier if the national index of consumer prices increases by more than 4% in one year.

§2. Old-Age Pensions in the Occupational Pension System

I. Beneficiaries

931. Men who have turned 65 and women who have turned 64 are eligible for pension benefits under the BVG (Article 13, paragraph 1, BVG). However, pension fund regulations may stipulate that people become eligible for old-age benefits at the end of their working lives. In this case, the conversion rate (Article 14, BVG) must be adapted accordingly (Article 13, paragraph 2, BVG).

932. If a person who is compulsorily insured in the occupational pension system leaves Switzerland before retirement, he may in principle withdraw all the savings from his pension fund.

933. The savings in the non-compulsory part of the scheme may always be withdrawn, even if the person emigrates to an EU or EFTA state.

934. If a citizen of Switzerland or an EU or EFTA state continues to be insured against the risk of death, disability and old age in an EU or EFTA state, the savings in the compulsory part of the scheme may not be paid out. The money must be transferred to a vested benefits account at a bank or an insurance policy as part of a private pension plan. It may be withdrawn no earlier than five years before regular retirement. The pension acquired in Switzerland at the time of retirement is paid abroad.

935. If a person emigrates after retirement, there can be no changes to the form of pension benefits. If at the time of retirement an insured person decides to draw a pension, this pension continues to be paid in the same way abroad. In the event of a (partial) lump-sum withdrawal, the money is freely available in the same way it would be if the person resided in Switzerland.

II. Calculating Pensions in the Occupational Pension System and the Amount of Pensions

936. With an eye towards the legal regulations, it is possible only to describe how the compulsory part of the occupational pension system is calculated. As far as the supplementary occupational pensions go, the individual pension funds are free to provide regulations that diverge from the compulsory scheme. Nevertheless, the calculation method for supplementary occupational pensions, based on such key factors as retirement assets and the conversion rate, follows similar rules – though these key factors, specifically the conversion rate, may differ considerably.

937. The following touches upon pension benefits, not other forms of old-age benefits (lump-sum payments, cash payments for owner-occupied homes, etc.).

938. The old-age pension is calculated as a percentage (conversion rate) of the retirement assets that an insured person has acquired upon reaching retirement age (Article 14, paragraph 1, BVG). The amount of the old-age pension is determined by two key factors: the amount of the individual savings (retirement assets) and the conversion rate for these savings.

939. With effect from 1 January 2005, the minimum conversion rate was gradually reduced from 7.2% to 6.8% (letter b of the BVG's transitional rules relating to the amendment of 3 October 2003; Article 14, paragraph 2, BVG, *see also* Article 62b and 62c, BVV 2). The minimum conversion rate was reduced to accommodate life expectancies that have increased since the BVG originally went into effect.

940. The pension fund is required to maintain a retirement account for every insured individual that clearly shows the accrued retirement assets defined in Article 15, paragraph 1, of the BVG (*see also* Article 11, paragraph 1, BVV 2). The retirement assets consist of the retirement credits and interest acquired during the period the insured person belonged to the pension fund, as well as the retirement assets and interest that were transferred from the previous funds and credited to the insured person (Article 15, paragraph 1, BVG).

941. If an insured person joins a new pension fund, the previous pension fund must transfer the accumulated vested benefits (*Austrittsleistung*) to this new fund (Article 3, paragraph 1, FZG). As a result, an insured person usually holds all his retirement assets in a single pension fund.

942. The retirement credits are calculated annually as a percentage of the coordinated salary. The rates are laid down in Article 16 of the BVG. Retirement credits increase as people grow older. It must be noted, though, that these rates only represent minimum legal specifications. The regulations of the individual pension funds may provide for different age credits as long as these are not less than the legally stipulated minimum credits.

943. In the compulsory part of the scheme, interest is paid on retirement credits according to a specified minimum rate. The Swiss Federal Council is responsible for setting this minimum interest rate and reviewing it at least once every two years (Article 15, paragraphs 2 and 3, BVG). This minimum interest rate has stood at 1% since 1 January 2017 (Article 12, letter j, BVV 2).

944. For example, if an insured person has accumulated retirement assets of CHF 400,000 by the time of retirement, his future annual old-age pension under the BVG amounts to CHF 27,200 (CHF 400,000 x 6.8%).

III. Cost-of-Living Adjustment

945. In contrast to the pension benefits from the AHVs, those provided by the occupational pension system are not subject to any binding legal provisions governing the adjustment of benefits. Rather, the law stipulates that old-age pensions are to be adapted to price developments within the financial possibilities of the pension fund. Each year the highest body of the pension fund decides whether and to what extent pensions are adapted (Article 36, paragraph 2, BVG).

§3. Survivors' Pensions in the AHV

I. Survivors' Pensions in the AHV

946. The survivors of eligible people who can be credited with income, child-rearing credits or care credits for at least one full year are themselves eligible for a survivor's pension (Article 29, paragraph 1, AHVG). Whereas both Swiss citizens and foreign nationals are eligible for a pension, foreign nationals may in principle only assert a claim as long as they have their domicile or habitual residence in Switzerland (Article 18, paragraphs 1 and 2, AHVG).

A. Widows' and Widowers' Pensions

947. Widows and widowers are eligible for a widows' or widowers' pension if they have children at the time of their spouse's death (Article 23, paragraph 1, AHVG). The children of the deceased spouse, as well as foster children who are eligible for an orphan's pension, have equal status with the widow's or widower's own children, provided they live in a shared household with the widow or widower at the time of the spouse's death or were taken in as foster children for permanent care and upbringing or were adopted (Article 23, paragraph 2, AHVG, in conjunction with Article 25, paragraph 3, AHVG and Article 49, AHVV). At the time of her husband's death, a pregnant woman has the same status as a widow who has a child if the pregnant woman's child is born alive (Article 46, paragraph 1, AHVV). It is assumed that the late husband is the father's child if the child is born within 300 days of the husband's death.

948. Widows (but not widowers!) without children are also eligible for a widow's pension provided they have completed their 45th year and were married for at least five years (Article 24, paragraph 1, AHVG).

949. Under certain conditions, divorced people have the same status as widows and widowers (Article 24a, AHVG). This is the case if they have children and their marriage lasted at least ten years; if the marriage lasted at least ten years and the separation occurred after the divorced person turned 45; if the youngest child turned 18 after the divorced person turned 45 or if and as long as the divorced person has children younger than 18.

950. The claim arises on the first day of the month following the spouse's death or, in the case of the adoption of a foster child, on the first day of the month following the adoption (Article 23, paragraph 3, AHVG). The claim lapses in the event of remarriage or death (Article 23, paragraph 4, AHVG). If the new marriage is dissolved or declared invalid in less than ten years, the claim arises again (Article 23, paragraph 5, AHVG and Article 46, paragraph 3, AHVV). In addition, the widower's claim for a widower's pension expires when his youngest child turns 18 (Article 24, paragraph 2, AHVG).

B. Orphan's Pension

951. Children whose father or mother has died are eligible for an orphan's pension. If both parents have died, they are eligible for two orphan's pensions (Article 25, paragraph 1, AHVG).

952. Foster children are eligible for an orphan's pension upon the death of their foster parents provided they have been taken in for permanent care and upbringing without remuneration. They are ineligible if they are already drawing a regular orphan's pension when the foster parents die (Article 25, paragraph 3, AHVG and Article 49, AHVV).

953. Foundlings are also eligible for an orphan's pension, as are children born after their father's death (Article 25, paragraph 2, AHVG and Article 47, AHVV).

954. The claim for an orphan's pension arises on the first day of the month following the father's or mother's death or following the child's birth. It expires when the orphan turns 18 or dies (Article 25, paragraph 4, AHVG and Article 47, AHVV). Children who are still in an educational or training programme are eligible for a pension until they complete this programme but no later than completion of their 25th year (Article 25, paragraph 5, AHVG). Moreover, in the case of foster children, the claim expires if the foster child returns to a parent or is supported by the parent (Article 49, paragraph 3, AHVV).

II. Calculation

955. The most important factors in calculating the widow's, widower's and orphan's pensions are the contribution period and the average annual income – determined on the basis of the deceased person's unsplit income and child-rearing and care credits (Article 33, paragraph 1, AHVG). If the deceased was not yet 45 at the time of his death, his average earned income is increased by a set percentage when the survivor's pension is calculated (Article 33, paragraph 3, AHVG and Article 54, AHVV).

956. The widow's or widower's pension amounts to 80% of the old-age pension that corresponds to the relevant average annual income (Article 36, AHVG).

957. The orphan's pension amounts to 40% of the old-age pension that corresponds to the relevant average annual income. The orphan's pension paid to children who were in a parent-child relationship only with the deceased person amounts to 60% of this old-age pension (Article 37, paragraph 1, AHVG). Foundlings receive an orphan's pension that is equal to 60% of the maximum old-age pension (Article 37, paragraph 3, AHVG).

958. If both parents die or the child fulfils the requirements for both an orphan's and a children's pension, the pensions are reduced if in total they exceed 60% of the maximum old-age pension, which is currently (2018) set at CHF 1,410 per month or CHF 16,920 per year (Article 37, paragraph 2, and Article 37*bis*, AHVG). Moreover, an orphan's pension is reduced if together with the father's or mother's pension it exceeds 90% of the average annual income upon which this pension is based (Article 41, paragraph 1, AHVG). It is not reduced if together with the father's or mother's pension it does not amount to more than the sum of 150% of the minimum old-age pension and the minimum amounts of three children's or orphan's pensions (CHF 3,173 per month or CHF 38,076 per year as of 2018). Starting with the fourth child, this amount increases for each child by the maximum monthly amount of the old-age pension (Article 54*bis*, paragraph 2, AHVV).

§4. Survivors' Pensions in the Occupational Pension System

I. Eligibility Criteria

959. Under Article 18, letter a, of the BVG, survivors are eligible for benefits only if the deceased person was insured at the time of his death or at the onset of the incapacity to work that led to death. The person's insured status and death therefore give rise to an obligation on the part of the pension fund to provide benefits.

960. A person is considered insured if he was subject to coverage by the occupational pension system at the time of his death or at the onset of an incapacity to work that led to death.

961. Article 10, paragraph 2, of the BVG stipulates that compulsory insurance ends when a person reaches the regular retirement age (paragraph 2a); the employer-employee relationship is terminated (paragraph 2b); remuneration is less than the minimum wage (paragraph 2c); or the person is no longer eligible for a daily allowance from the ALV because the relevant time-frame has lapsed (paragraph 2d). Due to the termination of the employer-employee relationship, the insured person must leave the pension fund – though under Article 10, paragraph 3, of the BVG, coverage against the risk of death and disability remains in effect one month after the end of insurance (post-coverage period). Afterward the insured status ends.

II. Benefits for Surviving Spouses and Divorced People

962. Under Article 19, paragraph 1, of the BVG, surviving spouses are eligible for a spouse's pension if, at the time of their partner's death, they are responsible for supporting at least one child (paragraph 1a) or, alternatively, they are older than 45 and their marriage lasted at least five years (paragraph 1b). Under paragraph 2 of the same article, a surviving spouse who fails to fulfil these conditions is entitled to a one-time payment equal to three annual pensions.

963. From the phrase 'is responsible for' ('*aufkommen muss*') in Article 19, paragraph 1a, of the BVG, it must be concluded that the surviving spouse is subject to a legal or contractual duty to support the child. An ethical or moral obligation is insufficient in such cases. The person must have had a duty to support the child at the time of the insured event and this duty may not have ceased to exist as a result of the insured risk.

964. An individual is considered a 'child' in the sense of Article 19, paragraph 1a, of the BVG if under the law he is in a parent-child relationship with the surviving spouse. In contrast to Article 23, paragraph 2a, of the AHVG, Article 19, paragraph 1a, of the BVG does not explicitly mention foster children, but speaks generally of the 'children' whom the surviving spouse must support. Foster children are considered 'children' in the sense of the provision only if the surviving spouse has entered into a contractual agreement to support them. Stepchildren are also not mentioned in Article 19, paragraph 1a, of the BVG. Up to now, the rulings of the Federal Supreme Court have not answered the question of whether stepchildren must also be subsumed under Article 19, paragraph 1a, of the BVG. Nevertheless, it must be assumed that the duty to pay support triggers benefits only if this duty was laid down in a contract and the relationship is therefore equivalent to that with a foster child.

965. Under Article 19, paragraph 1b, of the BVG, the marriage must have lasted at least five years. The key factor is not the de facto but the legal duration of the marriage, which can be gleaned from the civil register. In contrast to Article 24 of the AHVG, it is impermissible to combine several marriages to reach this minimum duration.

966. Under Article 19, paragraph 3, of the BVG, the Swiss Federal Council is responsible for defining eligibility requirements for survivors' benefits for divorced people. It has done so in Article 20, paragraph 1, of the BVV 2. This article states that a divorced spouse has the same status as the widow or widower upon the former spouse's death, provided the marriage lasted at least ten years (1a) and the divorced spouse was granted a pension or a lump-sum settlement for a lifelong pension in the divorce ruling (1b). If these conditions are met, the compulsory survivors' benefits for the divorced person are calculated in the same ways as those for the widow or widower.

967. If an actively insured person dies, the full disability pension for which he was eligible at the time of his death must be calculated in accordance with Article 25, paragraph 2, of the BVG. Under Article 21, paragraph 1, of the BVG, the widow's or widower's pension is equal to 60% of the full disability pension for which the insured person would have been eligible.

968. If a person who has already drawn an old-age or disability pension dies, the pension is set on the basis of Article 21, paragraph 2, of the BVG. The widow's or widower's pension amounts to 60% of the last old-age or disability pension that was paid.

III. Benefits for Registered Partners (Civil Unions)

969. Under Article 19a of the BVG, same-sex couples who lived in a registered partnership under Articles 3 et seq. of the Part G have equal legal status with widows or widowers in the sense of Article 19 of the BVG. This means that registered partners are entitled to the same level of survivors' benefits under the same conditions as surviving spouses.

970. Article 19a of the BVG is not included in Article 49, paragraph 2, of the BVG or in Article 89*bis*, paragraph 6, of the ZGB. Hence, this rule is not mandatory for supplementary pensions or non-registered employee pension foundations.

971. If a registered partnership is dissolved in court, Article 20, paragraph 1*bis*, of the BVV 2 dictates that the former registered partner has equal status with the widow or widower upon the death of the previous partner – provided the registered partnership lasted at least ten years and the former partner was awarded a pension or lump-sum settlement for a lifelong pension in the divorce ruling. This regulation corresponds to Article 20, paragraph 1, of the BVV 2.

IV. Orphans

972. Under Article 20 of the BVG, the children of the deceased are eligible for an orphan's pension.

973. Under Article 20 of the BVG, foster children are eligible for survivors' benefits only if the deceased was responsible for supporting them. The obligation to support the foster child can be laid down in a support contract. Concerning the support of the foster child it is requested that the deceased paid most of it.

974. Article 20 of the BVG is rather terse and does not state whether a stepchild is also eligible. There are different opinions on this matter in legal literature. The Federal Supreme Court has not settled the question of whether the stepchild has the same status in the compulsory scheme as the foster child in the sense of Article 20 of the BVG.

975. Under Article 21, paragraphs 1 and 2, of the BVG, the orphan's pension amounts to 20% of the last full disability or old-age pension that was paid.

V. Additional Beneficiaries

976. Article 20a, paragraph 1, of the BVG states that, in addition to the beneficiaries described above, the pension fund may allow the people listed in Article 20a, paragraph 1, of the BVG, to be eligible for benefits.

977. On the one hand, all natural persons who received substantial support from the insured person can be made beneficiaries (Article 20a, paragraph 1a, BVG). According to jurisdiction the term 'substantial support' is not open to interpretation: in principle, the supported individual must have been economically dependent on the insured person and, as a result of his death, must suffer considerable losses that prevent him from maintaining his accustomed lifestyle.

978. On the other hand, partners may be made beneficiaries, irrespective of financial support. Under Article 20a, paragraph 1a, of the BVG, the surviving partner must have been in a steady 'life partnership' (*Lebensgemeinschaft*) with the insured person for the last five years up to his death or, alternatively, he must have been responsible for supporting at least one common child. If a common child exists, the life partnership is not subject to any minimum duration requirement.

979. Furthermore, under Article 20a, paragraph 1, letter b, of the BVG, the insured person may name his children who do not fulfil the conditions of Article 20 of the BVG, his parents or his siblings as beneficiaries. This provision expands the group of people eligible for the original benefits. Beneficiaries can also include individuals for whom the insured person is not or is no longer required to provide support or assistance.

980. Finally, under Article 20a, paragraph 1c, of the BVG, the insured person may make his other legal heirs beneficiaries. In quantitative terms, the benefits are limited to the contributions paid or 50% of the pension assets. The contributions include the employee contributions deducted from the employee's salary during the period of insurance and the transferred vested benefits and purchases of benefits. The pension fund must stipulate which solution it has chosen in its regulations.

981. The provisions described above represent a hierarchical system. The beneficiaries listed in paragraph 1b only receive benefits in the absence of the people described in Articles 19, 19a, 20 and 20a, paragraph 1a, of the BVG. The beneficiaries in paragraph 1c only receive benefits in the absence of the people in 1a and 1b. Under Article 20a of the BVG, this system must be implemented through regulations.

§5. Survivor's Pensions in Other Insurance Systems

I. Accident Insurance Scheme

982. If an insured person dies as a result of an accident, his surviving spouse and children are eligible for survivors' pensions (Article 28, UVG).

983. Surviving spouses are eligible for a pension if they have children who are eligible for a pension at the time of their spouse's death; if they live in a shared household with other children who are made eligible for a pension by their spouse's death; or if they are at least two-thirds disabled or become so within two years after their spouse's death.

984. The widow (but not the widower) is eligible for a pension if upon her husband's death she has children who are no longer eligible for a pension or if she has turned 45 (Article 29, paragraph 3, UVG). The survivor's pension paid to the spouse is equal to 40% of the deceased person's insured salary (Article 31, paragraph 1, UVG).

985. The widow (but not the widower) is eligible only for a one-time payment if she does not meet all the conditions for the pension claim (Article 29, paragraph 3, UVG). The payment for the widow or the divorced wife is equal to the annual amount of the pension if the marriage lasted less than one year, to triple the annual amount if the marriage lasted at least one year but no more than five years, and five-fold the annual amount if the marriage lasted more than five years (Article 32, UVG).

986. The divorced spouse has equal status with the widow or widower if the accident victim was required to pay alimony to him or her (Article 29, paragraph 4, UVG). The survivor's pension for the divorced spouse amounts to 20% of the insured salary but no more than the alimony owed (Article 31, paragraph 2, UVG).

987. The children of the deceased insured person are eligible for an orphan's pension. If they have lost one parent, they receive the pension provided for half-orphans; if both parents have died, they receive the pension for full orphans (Article 30, paragraph 1, UVG). Foster children have the same status if at the time of the accident they had already been taken in by the insured person for permanent care and upbringing without remuneration (Article 40, UVV). The survivor's pension for half-orphans is equal to 15% of the insured earnings, for full orphans 25% of the insured earnings (Article 31, paragraph 1, UVG).

988. In the event of several survivors, the pensions combined may not exceed 70% of the insured salary. The pensions are uniformly reduced if necessary (Article 31, paragraphs 1 and 3, UVG).

989. If the survivors' benefits from the accident insurance scheme converge with those from the age and survivors' insurance/IVs, they are paid as complementary pensions. They are equal to the difference between 90% of the insured salary and the pensions from either of these schemes, but may not exceed the usual statutory survivors' benefits from the accident insurance scheme (Article 31, paragraph 4, UVG).

II. Military Insurance

990. The survivors' benefits from the military insurance scheme (Articles 51–56, MVG) are similar to those from the accident insurance scheme, but they are generally more generous, particularly since the maximum insured salary is somewhat higher (CHF 152,276 as of 2018; the maximum insured salary in the accident insurance scheme amounts to CHF 1,148,200 as of 2018).

991. One specific feature worth mentioning is the survivor's pension for the parents of the deceased. If there is no spouse or children who are eligible for a pension or if their claim is no longer valid, the deceased person's parents are eligible if they are needy. The father and mother each may receive a pension of up to 20% of the deceased person's insured annual salary (Article 55, MVG).

Chapter 3. Pensions for the Self-Employed

§1. Compulsory Insurance

992. In the Swiss system, self-employed people are generally insured against the risk of old age and death only in the AHV and under military insurance.

993. In both systems, old-age and survivors' benefits are calculated according to the same rules that have been discussed for employees, and the reader is referred to these explanations.

§2. Additional Pensions for the Self-Employed

994. Self-employed people may voluntarily increase their pension coverage in the social insurance system by participating in the voluntary occupational pension scheme (Articles 4, 44 and 45, BVG) or by taking out voluntary accident insurance (Articles 4 and 5, UVG).

995. In both cases the regulations are in principle similar to those for employees, but there is a certain degree of freedom in adjusting insurance coverage to the needs of the self-employed.

Chapter 4. Guaranteed Income for the Elderly

996. Old-age pensioners who only receive a pension from the AHV would be forced to live below the poverty level if they did not receive additional benefits. For this reason Switzerland has a system of supplementary benefits that guarantees an adequate standard of living for all pensioners (*see* paragraphs 868 et seq.). Thanks to this system, Switzerland has succeeded in practically eliminating old-age poverty in the country. The system is described in greater detail elsewhere (*see* Part X, Minimum Income Benefit).

Part IX. The Handicapped Persons

Introduction

997. In the following, the term 'disabled' is used to refer to people who, due to illness, a congenital condition or an accident, have suffered permanent physical, mental or psychological damage to their health that results in a severe and permanent impairment of their capacity to participate in social and economic life. In Switzerland, the various risks brought on by disability are not covered by any one social insurance programme alone. Diverse social insurance programmes provide a variety of benefits depending on the specific circumstances.

998. Cases in which a disability leads to the incapacity to work, incapacity to earn a living or invalidity have already been discussed in parts V and VI – as have situations in which the disability results from an accident or an occupational illness. Parts V and VI also detail the related benefits. The primary focus of this chapter is to provide an account of the benefits from the disability insurance programme (*Invalidenversicherung, IV*), which is responsible for providing basic benefits in most cases of disability. These benefits can be substituted or supplemented by benefits from other insurance programmes, including the occupational pension system, accident insurance and military insurance.

§1. Beneficiaries

999. The IV is an insurance programme for all members of society. It provides coverage for everyone who is either compulsorily or voluntarily insured in the AHV. Generally, all natural people who reside or work in Switzerland are insured in the IV, but there are various exceptions under the law (Article 1b of the IVG) in conjunction with Articles 1a and 2, AHVG, and Articles 1 et seq. AHVV).

1000. Swiss nationals and EU/EFTA citizens who do not live in a Member State of the EU or EFTA may join the IV voluntarily if they were mandatorily insured in this programme for at least five years in the past (Article 2, paragraph 1, AHVG).

1001. There is an additional exception in conjunction with international agreements: if a social insurance agreement signed by Switzerland stipulates that only one contracting state is obliged to pay benefits, Swiss citizens or nationals of the contracting state cannot claim a disability pension if the periods of coverage in both countries, when combined, establish eligibility for a pension under the law of the other contracting state (Article 6, paragraph 1*bis*, IVG).

1002. Finally, foreign nationals are eligible for a pension only if their domicile or habitual residence is in Switzerland and if, at the onset of their disability, they have paid contributions for at least one full year or have resided in Switzerland for ten years without interruption (Article 6, paragraph 2, IVG). The only exception to these conditions applies to integration measures, but only if the insured person has not completed his 20th year (Article 9, paragraph 3, IVG). Furthermore, benefits are not paid to family members of these persons who are residing abroad (Article 6, paragraph 2, sentence 2, IVG).

§2. Benefits

I. Income-Replacing Benefit

A. Daily Allowance

1003. If an insured person is unable to work or earn a living temporarily, an attempt is made to integrate him into the job market through integration measures. While participating in such measures, he is eligible for a daily allowance from the IV, provided that these measures keep him from working for at least three consecutive days or if he is at least 50% disabled with respect to his usual job (Article 22, paragraph 1, IVG).

1004. This daily allowance is granted no sooner than the first day of the month after the person completes his 18th year. It expires no later than the end of the month in which a pension is drawn or retirement age is reached (Article 22, paragraph 4, IVG). The daily allowance consists of a basic compensation to which all insured people are entitled and a child benefit for insured people with children younger than 18 or with children younger than 25 who are still in an education or training programme (Article 22, paragraphs 2 and 3, IVG).

1005. The basic compensation essentially amounts to 80% of the last salary earned by the insured person before his health was impaired, but may not exceed 80% of the maximum daily earnings insured under the Federal Accident Insurance Law (*Bundesgesetz über die Unfallversicherung, UVG*; Article 23, paragraph 1, in conjunction with Article 24, paragraph 1, IVG). This maximum figure currently amounts to CHF 406 (2018). If, before integration efforts, the insured person was eligible for a daily allowance from the accident insurance programme (*Unfallversicherung, UV*), the daily allowance from the IV is at least equal to the previously received daily allowance from the UV (Article 24, paragraph 4, IVG). For each child, the child benefit amounts to 2% of the maximum daily earnings insured under the UVG (Article 23*bis*, IVG).

1006. A deduction is made from the daily allowance in cases where the IV bears the full costs of accommodation and food, but consideration is given to whether the insured person is required to provide support for others (Article 24*bis*, IVG). In addition, contributions to the IV, the old-age and survivors' insurance (AHV), the income replacement regulations (*Erwerbsersatzordnung, EO*), and unemployment insurance must be paid on the daily allowance (Article 25, IVG). Finally, the daily allowance must be reduced if the insured person is gainfully employed during integration measures and the daily allowance, together with earnings from this work, exceeds the earned income used as a basis for calculating the daily allowance (Article 24, paragraph 2, IVG in conjunction with Article 21*septies* of the IVV).

B. Disability Pension

1007. Insured individuals are eligible for a disability pension from the IV if:

- they are unable to restore, improve or maintain their capacity to earn a living or engage in their field of responsibility after reasonable integration measures;
- they are at least 40% unable to work on average for one year without a noteworthy interruption and after the end of this year they are at least 40% invalid (Article 28, paragraph 1, IVG).

1008. Eligibility for a pension is determined by the insured person's degree of disability. There are currently four categories. People with at least a 40% disability receive one-quarter of a pension; people with at least a 50% disability receive one-half; those with at least a 60% disability receive three-quarters; and those with at least a 70% disability receive a full pension (Article 28, paragraph 2, IVG). This means that people who are less than 40% disabled are not entitled to a pension.

1009. Furthermore, it must be noted that in the case of people who are less than 50% disabled, a pension (i.e., one-quarter of a pension) is paid only if they have their domicile and habitual residence in Switzerland (Article 29, paragraph 4, IVG). The Federal Court has ruled that this exception is not applicable under the regime of the FZA and the EFTA-Agreement. Quarter pensions must be exported according to these agreements.

1010. The degree of disability is determined by a comparison of income or activities or by using a mixed method:

- In the case of working people, the degree of disability is determined by an income comparison. The income that the insured person is able to earn from an activity deemed acceptable in a balanced labour market after the onset of the disability, medical treatment and all possible integration measures is compared with the income that he would be able to earn without the disability (Article 28a, paragraph 1, IVG in conjunction with Article 16, ATSG).
- In the case of non-employed people, the degree of disability is evaluated by means of an activity comparison (Article 28a, paragraph 2, IVG). The basis of

this comparison is the degree to which the non-employed person is able to engage in his field of responsibility. In the case of people who work in the household, the field of responsibility is seen as including the usual household work, the upbringing of children, as well as charitable and artistic activities (Article 27, IVV).

- If the insured person works only part time, the degree of disability is determined by an income comparison. If the person has an additional field of responsibility, the degree of disability is determined for this area by means of an activity comparison. The two degrees of disability must be set in relation to each other according to the share of the employment activity and the share of the work in the person's field of responsibility. The degree of disability as a whole is derived from this evaluation (Article 28a, paragraph 3, IVG).

1011. The insured person is eligible for a pension six months after asserting a claim to benefits, but no earlier than the month following the completion of his 18th year (Article 29, paragraph 1, IVG). As long as the insured person has a claim to a daily allowance, he has no right to a pension (Article 29, paragraph 2, IVG). His right to a pension ends as soon as he is eligible for an old-age pension from the AHV or dies (Article 30, IVG).

1012. The amount of the disability pension from the IV corresponds to that of the old-age pensions from the AHV (Article 37, paragraph 1, IVG). This means that the minimum pension paid for a full disability is CHF 1,175 and the maximum is CHF 2,350 (as of 2018; Article 34, paragraphs 3 and 5, AHVG). If both spouses can claim a pension, the sum of the two pensions may not exceed 150% of the maximum pension limit (CHF 3,525 as of 2018; Article 37, paragraph 1*bis*, IVG in conjunction with Article 35, paragraph 1, AHVG). This ceiling is not applicable if the shared household is declared to be void by a court (Article 35, paragraph 2, AHVG). In addition to the disability pension, the insured person may receive a child pension if his child is not 18 or is younger than 25 and is still in an education or training programme. This pension amounts to 40% of the disability pension that was determined using the applicable average annual income (Article 38, IVG).

1013. If the person who is eligible for a pension has the renewed opportunity to earn or increase existing income, his degree of disability changes. In such situations, his pension is reduced or withdrawn by the authorities, either on their own motion or upon request. However, the IV pension is revised only if the increase in income is more than CHF 1,500 a year. In addition, in the event of a review, only two-thirds of the amount exceeding CHF 1,500 is taken into account (Article 31, IVG).

1014. If a disability results from an accident, the UV pays a pension supplementary to the disability pension, with the result that the disabled person can receive compensation for up to 90% of his insured income (Article 20, paragraph 2, UVG). People who are insured by the second pillar of coverage in Switzerland – the occupational pension system – receive a disability pension from the occupational pension fund even if they draw a disability pension from the IV (Articles 23 et seq. of the Occupational Old-Age, Survivors' and Disability Provision Law (*Bundesgesetz über die berufliche Alters-, Hinterlassenen- und Invalidenvorsorge, BVG*)). Furthermore, they are entitled to a child pension from the occupational pension fund if their child has not completed his 18th year or is younger than 25 and is still in an education or training programme (Article 25 in conjunction with Articles 20 and 22, paragraph 3, BVG). In some cases, the insured person may also be entitled to a disability pension from the military insurance programme (Articles 40 et seq. of the Federal Military Insurance Law. This pension is granted in addition to the disability pension from the IV. The pension from both the occupational pension fund and the military insurance programme can be reduced if their full payment were to result in excessive compensation for the insured person (*see* Articles 66 and 69, ATSG).

II. Integration Benefit

1015. Insured people who, due to an impairment of their health, constantly require the help or personal supervision of a third party for their daily tasks are considered to be in need of assistance (Article 9, ATSG) and are granted an attendance allowance by the IV. With just a few exceptions, though, they must have their domicile and habitual residence in Switzerland (Article 42, paragraph 1, IVG).

1016. Three categories of need have been defined: slight, moderate and severe (Article 42, paragraph 2, IVG; Article 37, IVV). For people who live at home, the monthly allowance in the severe category is 80% of the maximum old-age pension of the AHV (amounting to CHF 2,350 as of 2018). For the moderate category it amounts to 50%, and for the slight category, 20%. If the insured person lives in a nursing home, the allowance is paid at half the above-mentioned rates (Article 42*ter*, paragraphs 1 and 2, IVG).

1017. Like the IV, the accident and military insurance programmes also grant an attendance allowance (Articles 26 et seq., UVG; Articles 48 et seq., MVG). If the insured person fulfils the conditions for an attendance allowance from the accident and/or military insurance programme, these programmes are required to provide the benefit exclusively, and the IV is not obliged to pay (Article 66, paragraph 3, ATSG).

III. Additional Benefits

A. Integration Measures in General

1018. Integration measures are intended to integrate the disabled person into the job market, whether for the first time or after the loss of a job. The insured person is required to actively participate in all reasonable measures that enable him to keep his existing job, integrate him into working life for the first time, or introduce him into a field of responsibility equivalent to working life (Article 7, paragraph 2, IVG).

1019. A measure is deemed reasonable if it serves the insured person's integration, unless it is inappropriate for his health (Article 7a, IVG). If the insured person does not fulfil his duty, his benefits can be reduced or even revoked in certain circumstances (Article 7b, IVG). In addition, the employer is required to make all arrangements deemed reasonable to find an appropriate solution (Article 7c, IVG).

B. Early Intervention Measures

1020. The aim of these measures is either to allow the disabled person to remain in his present job or to integrate him into a new job in or outside his present company (Article 7d, IVG). Possible measures include:

- Adapting the workplace.
- Training courses.
- Job placement.
- Occupational counselling.
- Socio-occupational rehabilitation.
- Employment measures.

1021. The insured person has no legal right to these measures and their cost may not exceed CHF 20,000 per insured person (Article 7d, paragraphs 3 and 4, IVG in conjunction with Article 1*octies*, IVV).

C. Integration Measures

1022. For an insured person to qualify for integration measures, he must be disabled or threatened with disability. The measure must be necessary and suitable for restoring, improving or maintaining the person's capacity to earn a living or engage in his field of responsibility. In addition, the specific requirements of the individual measures must be met (Article 8, paragraph 1, IVG).

1023. Integration measures include (Article 8, paragraph 3, IVG):

- Medical measures. Such measures are provided until the insured person completes his 20th year. They must focus on integrating him into working life or his field of responsibility (Article 12, IVG). An exception applies to insured people who suffer from a birth defect; here it suffices if the measures serve 'only' to treat their condition (Article 13, IVG).
- Measures to prepare for integration into working life. The insured person must be incapacitated for at least six months and at least 50%, and the measures must aim at establishing the conditions necessary for occupational measures (Article 14a, IVG).
- Occupational measures. Such measures include career counselling, the reimbursement of the additional costs incurred as a result of the disability during the

first occupational training programme, retraining, job placement, subsidies for job orientation, as well as financial aid for launching or expanding a self-employed activity (Articles 15 et seq., IVG).

1024. In principle, the integration measures are only performed in Switzerland. Only in special cases can they be offered abroad (Article 9, paragraph 1, IVG; Article 23*bis* and 23*ter* IVV).

D. *Technical Aids*

1025. Technical aids, such as hearing aids for the deaf, can enable a disabled person to completely or partly overcome his disability. For this reason, people insured in the IV have a right to receive the technical aids that help them perform their job or master their field of responsibility; that allow them to maintain or improve their capacity to earn a living; or that are necessary for schooling, training and advanced training or for the purpose of functional adaptation (Article 21, paragraph 1, IVG).

1026. Even so, the IV does not cover the costs of all technical aids. Rather, the individual categories of aids for which a disabled person can apply are defined in a list (Article 14, IVV). The listed categories are exhaustive and leeway exists only within the list in the respective categories. The technical aids are given or loaned to the disabled person (Article 21, paragraph 3, IVG).

E. *Reimbursement for the Costs of Care*

1027. In many cases, non-employed insured people, in particular, care for children, foster children and family members in their homes. If they participate in integration measures, they may have to depend on the assistance of third parties to provide this care during the duration of these measures. If they can demonstrate that they have incurred additional costs for this care, the IV reimburses them for these costs on the condition that they live in a shared household with children who are younger than 16 or with family members who entitle them to receive care credits under the AHVG. A further requirement is that the integration measure must last at least two consecutive days (Article 11a, IVG).

§3. Income and Assets Test

1028. If the people insured in the IV meet all the legal requirements, they have a right to insurance benefits, regardless of their income and assets. This is a consequence of the solidarity principle. However, although well-to-do insured people are required to pay contributions to the IV on their entire income, the daily allowances and pension benefits are capped at a rather low level. For well-to-do insured people, this means that cash benefits from the IV are not in proportion to their contributions. In order to avoid placing even greater strains on the solidarity system, the legislators have therefore decided to provide IV benefits even to people who are not financially dependent on these benefits.

§4. Procedure

1029. The procedure governing the granting of benefits is initiated by registration on an official form (Article 65, IVG). This registration must be submitted to the responsible administrative authorities (responsibility arises from the applicable legal norms; Articles 40 and 67, IVG). Under social insurance law, if the registration is mistakenly submitted to the wrong office, this office must forward it to the proper authorities (Article 30, ATSG).

1030. The administrative authorities clarify the matter of their own motion without being bound to the applicant's request (Article 43, ATSG). This is a consequence of the underlying principle of judicial investigation.

1031. By asserting a claim to benefits from the IV, an insured person authorizes the people and offices named in the registration to provide the IV bodies with all the information and documents necessary to clarify the claim for benefits or for recourse. These people and offices are obliged to provide this information (Article 6a, IVG). Furthermore, the insured person must undergo an examination by a doctor or specialist and take part in all other necessary examinations (Article 42, paragraph 2, ATSG).

1032. As soon as the IV has received the registration, it determines the insurance-related and benefit-specific requirements. For this purpose, the IV offices have established interdisciplinary regional medical services that evaluate the medical basis of the claim. The IV offices are also able to draw on the assistance of experts, medical and occupational examination centres, the services of other social insurance providers, as well as specialists from private organizations that serve disabled people (Article 59, IVG).

1033. If the conditions upon which the benefits are based, change, the insured person is required to inform the insurance programme of these changes (Article 31, ATSG; Article 77, IVV). If he fails to do so, benefits can be retroactively reduced or repealed, or they can be reduced or discontinued for future periods (Article 7b, IVG). If a pension recipient's degree of disability changes, the authorities can increase, reduce or discontinue the pension on their own motion or upon request (Article 17, paragraph 1, ATSG).

1034. The law does not specify a time period after which a review is required. But in most cases the insurer notes a date on which to carry out a review. If the insurer receives knowledge of relevant changes in the beneficiary's circumstances, this review can be carried out at an earlier date.

§5. Accumulation Rules

1035. The ATSG contains a number of rules on coordinating congruent benefits from different social insurance programmes (Articles 63 et seq., ATSG). In addition to coordination within the system, the ATSG includes rules on external coordination between social insurance programmes and a liable third party (Articles 72 et seq., ATSG). The IVG and the IVV also contain a number of coordination rules (e.g., Article 44, IVG; Article 39*bis*, IVV).

1036. In the case of an insured person who is eligible for treatment, the IV provides the necessary benefits if the military or UV is not required to do so (*see* Article 64, ATSG). With respect to technical aids, integration measures and attendance allowances, the IV also only provides benefits in a subsidiary fashion provided the military and UVs do not offer benefits (Article 65, ATSG).

1037. Daily allowances and pensions are a different matter. In this area, benefits from the IV represent basic benefits. Daily allowances and pensions from other insurers, such as the military and UVs, are paid cumulatively subject to the legally defined maximum limits and barring excessive compensation (*see* Articles 66, 68 and 69 ATSG). However, if the insured person is eligible for compensation under the Law on Income Replacement (*Erwerbsersatzgesetz, EOG*), he has no right to a daily allowance from the IV (*see* Article 16g, EOG).

1038. If integration measures are interrupted due to illness, an accident or maternity, the IV continues to pay the daily allowance, provided the person is not entitled to a daily allowance from another compulsory social insurance programme or a daily allowance that is paid by a voluntary daily allowance insurance plan and is at least equal to that of the IV (Article 22, paragraph 6, IVG in conjunction with Article 20*quater*, IVV).

1039. If a third party is responsible for the insured event, the IV, at the time of the event, takes over the claims of the insured person and his survivors up to the amount of the statutory benefits (Article 72, paragraph 1, ATSG). But the claims are only transferred to the extent that the insurance benefits and the compensation owed by the third party for the same period exceed the relevant damages (Article 73, paragraph 1, ATSG). Furthermore, they are only transferred if the benefits are of the same nature, that is, are congruent benefits (Article 74, ATSG).

1040. For the coordination rules for disability pensions the reader is referred to paragraphs 611 et seq.

Part X. Minimum Income Benefit

Introduction

1041. There is no nationwide right to a state-guaranteed minimum income in Switzerland. However, within the scope of the social insurance programmes, certain groups of people are provided with benefits to guarantee coverage of basic living needs. With regard to these benefits, one can indeed speak of a state-guaranteed minimum income in the form of a special assistance scheme. These benefits are supplementary in nature and provided by the cantons on the basis of need.

1042. As for general assistance schemes, Article 12 of the BV guarantees the right to assistance in emergencies. Furthermore, social assistance benefits are generally available if a person cannot earn a living on his own. These benefits are absolutely subsidiary in nature and intended to serve as a safety net if the minimum income needed to survive cannot be secured in any other way. They are not social insurance benefits but public welfare benefits and are also provided by the cantons on the basis of need.

Chapter 1. Special Assistance Scheme (Supplementary Benefits)

§1. Beneficiaries

1043. In order to receive benefits, people must fulfil one of the following requirements (Article 4, ELG)):

- They must be recipients of an old-age pension from the old-age and survivors' insurance programme *AHV* or be eligible for a widow's, widower's or orphan's pension from the AHV.
- They must be eligible for a pension or an attendance allowance from the disability insurance programme (IV) or have received a daily allowance from the IV for at least six months without interruption.
- They must be eligible for an AHV or IV pension, having paid contributions for the minimum period as defined in the applicable legal regulations.

1044. Concerning residence and place of habitual stay, a distinction is made between Swiss citizens, EU/EFTA nationals and the citizens of other states:

- In addition to the eligibility criteria described above, Swiss citizens and EU/EFTA nationals who are subject to agreements on the free movement of people must be domiciled or habitually reside in Switzerland (*see* Article 4, ELG).
- In addition to being domiciled or habitually residing in Switzerland, nationals of other states must fulfil the following condition: they must have resided in Switzerland for ten years without interruption before applying for the supplementary benefit. The waiting period for refugees and stateless people is five years (Article 5, paragraphs 1 and 2, ELG).

1045. It is important to note that the person's domicile and habitual residence must be in Switzerland for him to assert a claim for supplementary benefits. These benefits are never paid abroad. As regards EU and EFTA states, the FZA includes an explicit proviso stating that supplementary benefits are special non-contributory benefits as defined in the coordinating body of European social law. As such, they are not paid abroad.

§2. Amount of the Benefit

1046. There are two kinds of supplementary benefits: the annual supplementary benefit and the reimbursement of the costs associated with illness or disability.

I. Annual Supplementary Benefit

1047. It is impossible to say generally how high the annual supplementary benefit is. It must be determined on a case-by-case basis. The amount of the benefit corresponds to the amount by which recognized expenses exceed applicable income (Article 9, paragraph 1, ELG).

1048. Consideration is given to the specific situation of the person who applies for supplementary benefits. Furthermore, when the recognized expenses and applicable income are calculated, a distinction must be made as to whether the person in question lives at home or is a permanent or long-term resident of a nursing home or hospital (*see* Articles 10 and 11, ELG).

1049. The federal government provides five-eighths of the funding necessary for the annual supplementary benefits and the cantons cover the remaining three-eighths (Article 13, paragraph 2, ELG).

II. Reimbursement of the Costs of Illness or Disability

1050. The law does not specify the extent to which the costs of illness and disability are reimbursed. It merely states that, in concrete cases, reimbursements will be made for the verified, necessary and unavoidable costs incurred for (Article 14, ELG):

- Dental treatment.
- Support, care and assistance at home and in day centres.
- Spa treatments and rest cures prescribed by a doctor.
- Diets.
- Transportation to the closest treatment centres.
- Technical aids.
- Cost sharing under the compulsory health insurance programme.

1051. This is an exhaustive list. The cantons are in charge of reimbursing these costs.

§3. Income and Asset Test

I. Whose Income and Assets?

A. Annual Supplementary Benefits

1052. In certain cases, calculations of the recognized costs and applicable income are not limited to the personal costs and income of the person who receives a pension, attendance allowance or daily allowance. If this person is required to support family members under family law, his income must also cover the basic needs of all these family members. In order to ensure that the supplementary benefits do indeed guarantee the minimum income that the family needs to live on, the calculations take into account both the recognized costs and the applicable income of spouses, people with orphans who are eligible for a pension, and people with children who establish their eligibility for a child's pension from the AHV or IV. Calculations also include orphans who are eligible for a pension and live in the same household (Article 9, paragraph 5a, ELG in conjunction with Articles 1 et seq. of the Ordinance on Supplementary Benefits to the Old-Age, Survivors' and Disability Insurance (*Verordnung über die Ergänzungsleistungen zur Alters-, Hinterlassenen- und Invalidenversicherung, ELV*)).

1053. However, if a spouse or the couple in question live in a nursing home or a hospital, the annual supplementary benefits are calculated separately and each spouse is attributed half of the joint assets (Article 9, paragraph 3, ELG).

1054. The recognized costs include:
In the case of a person living at home (Article 10, paragraph 1, ELG):

- A fixed annual amount for general needs (CHF 19,290 for single people, CHF 28,935 for married couples, 10,080 for the first two pensionable orphans or children eligible for a child's pension from the AHV or IV, a lesser amount for subsequent children (all figures as of 2018)). The fixed amount includes the cost of food, clothes, electricity, water, taxes, etc.
- The rent of an apartment and additional related costs (a maximum of CHF 13,200 per year for single people; a maximum of CHF 15,000 per year for married couples, people who have orphans eligible for a pension and people who have children eligible for a child's pension from the AHV or IV (as of 2018)).

In the case of a person living in a nursing home or a hospital (Article 10, paragraph 2, ELG):

- The daily fee (the cantons have the right to limit the costs that are taken into account).
- An amount set by the canton for personal expenses, such as clothes, taxes, fees, etc.

For all people (it must be noted that this is an exhaustive list; Article 10, paragraph 3, ELG):

- Job-related expenses up to the person's pre-tax income from employment.
- Building maintenance costs and mortgage interests (on a limited scale).
- Contributions to social insurance schemes (except for health insurance premiums).
- A yearly lump sum for mandatory health insurance based on the average cantonal premiums.
- Alimonies paid under family law.

1055. Applicable income is defined as (Article 11, ELG):

- Two-thirds of earned income in cash or in kind if this income exceeds the following annual amounts: CHF 1,000 for single people, CHF 1,500 for married couples, people who have orphans eligible for a pension and people who have children eligible for a child's pension from the AHV or IV (all figures as of 2018).
- Income from movable and immovable property.
- 1/15 (1/10 for pensioners) of net assets if these assets exceed CHF 37,500 for single people, CHF 60,000 for married couples and CHF 15,000 for orphans eligible for a pension and for children eligible for a child's pension from the AHV or IV (=asset depletion). If one of the people considered in the calculations for supplementary benefits owns real estate that is inhabited by at least one of these people, the value of the real estate exceeding CHF 112,500 must be taken into account in determining assets (all figures as of 2018).
- Pensions and other recurring benefits.
- Family allowances.
- Alimonies under family law.
- Benefits from a contract for lifelong support (*Verpfründungsvertrag*), etc.
- Income and assets that have been renounced.

B. Reimbursement of the Costs of Illness and Disability

1056. Concerning this supplementary benefit, no separate check is made of a person's financial circumstances. It is assumed that the person who requests reimbursement is eligible for supplementary benefits and that his financial situation was checked when these benefits were set (cf. Article 14, paragraph 1, ELG).

II. Exemptions

A. The Annual Supplementary Benefit

1057. The following income is *not* considered applicable income (Article 11, paragraph 3, ELG):

- Support provided for relatives in accordance with the ZGB.
- Public social assistance support, since the supplementary benefits take priority over social assistance benefits.
- Public or private benefits clearly geared towards promoting social welfare.
- Attendance allowances from the social insurance programmes.
- Scholarships and other education grants.

1058. These benefits, which are listed exhaustively in the law, are designed to help the recipients cope with a personal emergency. This is why they are seen as subsidiary to the supplementary benefits and are not considered when such benefits are set.

1059. As explained above, the income and assets of the person in question are only partially applied, and there are family status exemptions in both categories that must also be considered.

B. Reimbursement of the Costs of Illness and Disability

1060. The cantons are free to limit reimbursements to those expenses that are deemed necessary to ensure an economical and functional provision of benefits (Article 14, paragraph 2, ELG). Furthermore, they are permitted to define maximum reimbursement amounts for the costs of illness and disability. Nevertheless, these maximum amounts may not be less than the following annual sums (Article 14, paragraph 3, ELG):

For people living at home:

- CHF 25,000 for single people, widows/widowers and the spouses of people living in nursing homes.
- CHF 50,000 for married couples.
- CHF 10,000 for full orphans.

In the case of people living in nursing homes or hospitals, the maximum amount may not be less than CHF 6,000.

1061. Higher amounts apply to people entitled to an attendance allowance (Article 14, paragraphs 4 and 5, ELG).

§4. Conditions

I. Age

1062. There is no minimum age requirement for the receipt of supplementary benefits. The only exception is people who are eligible for attendance allowances. These people are entitled to supplementary benefits only if they have completed their 18th year (Article 6, ELG).

II. No Other Entitlement

1063. Supplementary benefits can be paid only if all other social insurance benefits have been exhausted. If the recipient or one of the persons who is considered in setting supplementary benefits waives social security retirements, pensions or other recurring benefits to which he is legally entitled – whether by not asserting his claim or by not making de facto use of this income – he is seen as renouncing income. Income is also considered renounced if the eligible person does not challenge the rejection of a claim for income. In such cases, when the annual supplementary benefit is set, a hypothetical income is credited to the person in question.

1064. In principle, the costs associated with illness and disability can only be covered by the supplementary benefit programme if they are not assumed by another type of insurance, e.g., health insurance, accident insurance, military insurance, disability insurance or liability insurance.

III. Willingness to Work

1065. Under the law governing supplementary benefits, recipients of old-age pensions are not required to pursue gainful employment.

1066. Recipients of a survivor's pension are subject to a different rule. When a claim to supplementary benefits is processed, a check must be made as to whether it is possible and reasonable for such persons to work. If this is the case, a hypothetical income from employment is attributed to them. Recipients of disability pensions are treated in the same way (*see* Article 9, paragraph 5c, ELG in conjunction with Article 14a and 14b, ELV). In each specific case, it must be checked whether it is possible and reasonable for the person in question to contribute to his basic needs through employment.

1067. When supplementary benefits are set, consideration must also be given to the possible renunciation of earned income by the people who are taken into account in the calculations. These people may include the insured person's spouse or one or several of his children. Since they are also taken into account when determining supplementary benefits, the benefits must ultimately serve to cover their basic needs, too. For this reason, these people are also attributed a hypothetical income from employment if it is possible and reasonable for them to work.

1068. A person can renounce earned income either by not pursuing gainful employment or by working for free or for an excessively low wage.

IV. Additional Requirements

1069. If a person wants to be reimbursed for the costs of illness and disability, he must apply for reimbursement within fifteen months after issuance of the invoice. In addition, the costs must have been incurred during a time in which the person filing the application met the conditions for receiving supplementary benefits (Article 15, ELG).

§5. Claims and Administration

1070. If a person wishes to file a claim for supplementary benefits, he must report to the responsible supplementary benefits office. Since the cantons are in charge of setting and paying supplementary benefits, they have the power to determine which authorities are responsible (Article 21, paragraphs 1 and 2, ELG). In most cases it is the cantonal compensation agencies (*Ausgleichskassen*).

1071. According to the ELG, the cantonal social assistance authorities may not be charged with this task (Article 21, paragraph 2, sentence 2, ELG). Through this restriction, the legislators wanted to emphasize that the benefits paid in supplement to the pensions from the Old Age, Survivors' and Disability Insurance are not welfare benefits.

1072. The cantons are required to provide potentially eligible individuals with adequate information about the supplementary benefits, e.g., through a leaflet (Article 21, paragraph 3, ELG).

1073. Registration is carried out at the responsible authorities using an official form that in many cases can be downloaded from the Internet. This form is then submitted by the eligible person, his representative or a close relative. It contains personal details and information about the income and assets of all the people who are considered in setting the annual supplementary benefits (*see* Article 20, ELV).

1074. If all legal requirements are met, the applicant has a right to the annual supplementary benefit starting in the month in which the registration is submitted (Article 12, paragraph 1, ELG). If the eligible person is in a nursing home or a hospital and the registration is submitted within six months after admission to the facility, the person has a right to benefits beginning in the month in which he entered the home or hospital – provided all other legal conditions are met (Article 12, paragraph 2, ELG). An additional condition for the reimbursement of the costs of illness and disability is that their reimbursement must be applied for within fifteen months after issuance of the invoice (Article 15, ELG).

1075. The eligible person is required to immediately inform the cantonal administrative authorities of all changes in his personal or economic circumstances. The requirement to notify the authorities also pertains to changes in the circumstances of family members who were considered in setting supplementary benefits (Article 24, ELV). If the eligible person fails to notify the authorities, he runs the risk of being forced to return wrongfully received benefits.

1076. The cantonal implementation office (*Durchführungsstelle*) informs the applicant in writing of the decision on supplementary benefits.

§6. Reclaiming Paid Benefits

I. Claims against the Beneficiary

1077. If it turns out, in retrospect, that a person who claimed supplementary benefits had more assets than were known or were indicated when benefits were set, the wrongfully disbursed amount must be paid back, since the foundation for calculating the supplementary benefits has changed (Article 25, ATSG; Article 42, ELV). The original decision may therefore be corrected. This can be necessary, for example, if a person is retroactively granted a higher disability pension than was considered when the supplementary benefits were set.

1078. The right to reclaim benefits can also be asserted against the beneficiary if the original assets of one of his family members considered in setting the benefits were wrongly assessed.

1079. However, if the eligible person's income or assets improve at a later point in time, this improvement has no bearing on the supplementary benefits already paid.

1080. If a claim exists against an eligible person to return benefits, this claim can be debited from any supplementary benefits that are due to the person. It can also be debited from benefits subject to other social insurance laws that allow such debiting (Article 27, ELV).

II. Claims against the Family

1081. Article 30 of the ELG states that Articles 72–75 of the ATSG are not applicable. This means that, within the scope of the ELG, there is no recourse to spouses or relatives who are responsible for the insured event. As a result, the social insurer providing the benefits does not take over the claims of the insured person up to the amount of the statutory benefits. This is why the social insurer has no recourse to the insured person's spouse or relatives for the benefits it has provided.

III. Claims against a Third Party

1082. Since, as explained above, the ELG explicitly rules out the application of the recourse provisions in the ATSG, the social insurer providing the benefits does not have recourse to any third party who is responsible for the insured event.

Chapter 2. General Assistance Schemes (Social Assistance)

1083. Article 115, sentence 1, of the BV establishes the principle that support must be provided for the needy at their place of residence (cantonal social assistance). As a result, Swiss social assistance law is based on twenty-six different sets of cantonal regulations. Some of these regulations differ considerably.

1084. The same provision in Article 115 of the Federal Constitution accords the federation the power to define exceptions to the rule and delegate responsibilities. Drawing on these powers, the federation issued the Federal Law on the Legal Responsibility for the Support of the Needy (*Bundesgesetz über die Zuständigkeit für die Unterstützung Bedürftiger, ZUG*), which determines the cantonal jurisdictions for persons in need. Nevertheless, the power to frame social assistance legislation rests with the cantons, with just a few notable exceptions (*see*, for example, the Federal Law on Social Assistance and Loans to Swiss Nationals Abroad (*Bundesgesetz über Sozialhilfe und Darlehen an Schweizer Staatsangehörige im Ausland, BSDA, SR 852.1*), the Federal Law on Foreign Nationals and Integration (*Bundesgesetz über die Ausländerinnen und Ausländer und über die Integration, AIG, SR 142.20*) and the regulations in the fifth chapter of the Federal Asylum Law (*Asylgesetz, AsylG, SR 142.31*)).

1085. Next to cantonal and federal law, the directives of the Swiss Conference on Social Welfare (*Schweizerische Konferenz für Sozialhilfe, SKOS*) play a crucial role in the harmonization of social assistance law. As the national professional association for social assistance, the SKOS is comprised of all of the cantons, many municipalities, the Principality of Liechtenstein, federal offices and private social service organizations. It works towards a fair and effective social assistance system and combats poverty in Switzerland.

1086. The directives of the SKOS are recommendations without legal force. They are, however, of special importance as all cantons have largely adopted them in their own law or at the very least use them as a reference, though the specifics vary. Aside from the many practical guidelines, their main contribution lies in the assessment of the minimum subsistence level in social assistance.

§1. Beneficiaries

1087. To be eligible for social assistance benefits, a person has to be in need. Need is defined as the incapability to cover one's own basic living costs sufficiently or in a timely manner (Article 2, ZUG).

1088. As assistance is provided by the canton of residence (Article 115, BV), regular social assistance benefits are only granted to persons with residence in Switzerland, meaning Swiss citizens and nationals of other states with permit to stay, including recognized refugees. Swiss nationals abroad are subject to the BSDA, foreign nationals such as asylum seekers and temporarily admitted persons to the AIG and the AsylG. Persons obligated to leave the country (e.g., due to expulsion), on the other hand, only have the right to emergency support (Article 12, BV).

1089. In contrast to regular social assistance, the so-called asylum social assistance in the AsylG is characterized by highly political considerations with regard to migration, society and finances. Its regulations therefore differ from those of regular social assistance in various parts, with benefits being lower and generally being paid out in kind.

§2. Amount of the Benefit

1090. Aside from the emergency support described in Article 12 of the BV, social assistance represents the lowest level of the social safety net. It prevents people or groups of people from being excluded from society. It protects the existence of destitute people, promotes their economic and personal independence, and guarantees social and occupational integration.

1091. The benefits are intended to provide support in a specific current emergency and must be adapted to each individual case (principle of individualization). In other words, in each specific case, they must be tailored to the goals of social assistance in general and to the needs of the person in particular: not covering more than necessary, but also not less (principle of meeting need). Although the cause of the current emergency is immaterial (principle of finality), effective social assistance must always aim to eliminate the causes of a person's need for assistance.

1092. Cantonal law determines how high the social assistance benefits are, but the rates of compensation have in fact become more similar throughout Switzerland due to the directives of the SKOS. Nevertheless, differences still exist. Most importantly, the cantons are permitted to reduce the benefits by differing amounts if a needy person violates his duty to collaborate or does not cooperate sufficiently.

1093. Welfare benefits consist of basic material security (*materielle Grundsicherung*) and situational benefits (*situationsbedingte Leistungen, SIL*), which make up the social minimum subsistence level, and integration allowances (*Integrationszulagen, IZU*) as well as income exemptions (*Einkommensfreibeträge, EFB*). The latter are, of course, not benefits but the income that the beneficiaries can earn without losing their claim to welfare benefits.

1094. The amount of benefits granted as part of the social minimum subsistence level may be undercut or exceeded during a short period of time (up to three months) if there is a realistic chance to restore material independence (A.6, SKOS).

1095. In contrast to most social insurance benefits and similar to the supplementary benefits described above, social welfare benefits are financed through general state funds (i.e., tax revenue).

I. Basic Material Security

1096. Basic material security covers the daily costs of a modest lifestyle and is comprised of:

- Basic livelihood (depending on the size of the household).
- Housing costs (rent).
- Basic health care costs.

1097. The composition and costs of basic livelihood as understood in social assistance are based on statistics of Swiss households with the lowest income, as persons supported by welfare benefits should not enjoy higher living standards than those living in modest conditions without applying for benefits (B.2, SKOS).

1098. Benefits for basic livelihood are granted as a lump sum. In the case of multiperson households with effectively shared living costs, the sum is degressively determined in relation to household size. A household is considered in its entirety namely in the case of support units such as families (i.e., parents with underage children), married couples and registered partners, but also similar living communities that do not form a support unit, such as cohabiting couples and parents with adult children (B.2.3, SKOS).

1099. Housing costs have to take regional differences into account (B.3, SKOS). Welfare benefits have to compensate for excessive housing costs until a reasonable and cheaper solution is found within an appropriate period of time. This particularly applies to the first few months during which a person is granted welfare benefits.

1100. Welfare benefits cover basic health care, including deductibles and copayments (B.5, SKOS). Premiums of the obligatory health insurance are granted to persons in need in the form of full individual premium reductions.

II. Situational Benefits

1101. SIL complement the generalized benefits that make up basic material security by accounting for health-related, familial, economic and personal circumstances of the beneficiary (C.1, SKOS). Beneficiaries have to request them in advance and their benefit has to be in reasonable proportion to their cost.

1102. SIL have a hybrid nature: on the one hand, they cover basic costs that arise and that are not already calculated into basic material security; on the other hand, they support specific goals that are in line with the goals of social assistance. The margin of discretion of the authorities varies accordingly.

1103. Examples of SIL are:

- Work and integration expenses (C.1.1, SKOS).
- Education costs not covered by scholarships or other education grants (C.1.2, SKOS).
- Child care in the case of working parents; social integration measures, especially with regard to children and teenagers; costs related to visitation rights (C.1.3, SKOS).
- Health costs not covered by insurance or basic material security, provided that they are reasonable, beneficial and accounted for (C.1.4, SKOS).
- Costs arising from social, psychological or pedagogic reasons; household and accident insurance; identification papers; household goods and moves; holidays (C.1.5, SKOS).

1104. SIL do not cover (recurring) costs already factored into basic material security (e.g., regular school books, public transport fares).

III. IZU and EFB

1105. IZUs and EFB are forms of performance-based (rather than need-based) assistance that aim to promote and stabilize the economic and social integration of beneficiaries. They honour social and occupational efforts of nonworking beneficiaries financially with a monthly allowance (C.2, SKOS).

1106. EFB are made on a monthly basis for any income earned (E.1.2, SKOS). They are calculated based on the volume of employment and wage level. They function as incentives with the primary aim to facilitate the uptake of employment or the increase of workload, thus improving the chances of integration so that the financial assistance granted by social assistance may be reduced in the long run.

§3. Means Test

I. Whose Means?

1107. After a person is admitted to social assistance, his individual social minimum subsistence level is juxtaposed against the entirety of his own resources, including benefits from and claims against third parties.

1108. In principle, all disposable income is applicable, except for the EFB mentioned above (E.1.1, SKOS). Different guidelines apply to the income of minors.

1109. Assets are applicable if they are actually available or can be realized at short notice (E.2.1, SKOS). They include funds, securities, personal vehicles, claims, valuables, real estate and any commodities the beneficiary has a claim of ownership to. The authorities of social assistance can abstain from the liquidation of assets if:

– that would cause undue hardship to the beneficiary or his dependents;
– the liquidation would be uneconomic;
– the disposal of valuables is unreasonable for other reasons.

1110. Real estate is retained if it is inhabited by the beneficiary and the housing costs are at market price or below (E.2.2, SKOS). It is also retained if a beneficiary is presumably going to rely on benefits for a short period only, if the amount of benefits is low or if insufficient demand would lead to low proceeds.

II. Exemptions

1111. Aside from the aforementioned EFB that serve as an incentive, the following assets are exempt or partially exempt from the means test:

– Personal effects and household goods (E.2.1, SKOS).
– Compensation for damage to integrity up to a certain amount depending on the size of the support unit, in acknowledgement of the material damage (E.2.1, SKOS).
– Assets belonging to minors that fall under Articles 321 and 322 ZGB (E.2.1, SKOS).

1112. Beyond that, asset exemptions may apply at the beginning of the support period or when ongoing support is no longer necessary (E.2.1, SKOS).

§4. Conditions

1113. The duties of beneficiaries are derived from the goals of social assistance and revolve around the subsidiary principle as well as reciprocity (A.5.2, SKOS).

I. Full Cooperation

1114. Applicants are required to prove their need by cooperating with authorities when determining the facts and circumstances of their situation. Any relevant information is to be shared truthfully and completely. Where necessary, access to the respective files has to be granted to the authorities. In the cases of financial or personal changes to their situation, applicants and beneficiaries have a duty to report them to the authorities without delay and of their own accord.

II. Limitation of Damage

1115. Social assistance benefits are subsidiary to the possibility of self-help, the obligations of social insurers and other third parties to provide benefits, and the voluntary services of third parties. The subsidiary principle of social assistance thus demands anyone seeking assistance to first exhaust his own means. This duty to reduce loss and damage is applicable when applying for social assistance as well as for the entire duration that the person is granted benefits.

1116. Reasonable self-help includes measures such as the search for a new job and participation in integration programmes. A job is considered reasonable if it is adequate with regard to the person's age, health condition and personal circumstances. It is also reasonable to demand that a beneficiary look for employment beyond his regular trade.

1117. Where claims against third parties exist, the beneficiary is compelled to assert his claims, such as in the cases of insurance benefits, alimony, contractual claims, grants and claims for damages (F.1, SKOS). If a beneficiary does not assert his third-party claims or waives other benefits to which he is legally entitled, a hypothetical income is credited to the beneficiary.

III. Additional Requirements

1118. Social assistance authorities may impose additional conditions that oblige beneficiaries to compensate for the benefits they are granted. In line with the goals of social assistance and the subsidiary principle, these conditions must aim to assist the beneficiary's occupational and social integration as well as his independence or to limit damage and ensure that welfare benefits are used as intended (A.8.1, SKOS). Any conditions must have a legal basis, be individualized and comply with the principles of proportionality and equality.

1119. In the case that the beneficiary violates his legal duties or ignores imposed conditions, he may be sanctioned with a reduction in benefits (A.8.2, SKOS).

§5. Claims and Administration

1120. Each canton is in charge of its own social assistance legislation, administration and supervision. Most cantons have delegated the execution of individual social assistance to the municipalities, each of which is in turn responsible for a social facility (*Soziale Dienste*), namely for its finances, infrastructure and quality standards.

1121. Those seeking assistance submit their application for welfare benefits to the social facility of their municipalities, where they are informed about their rights and duties and receive appropriate counsel. Some cantons require the application in writing. Some also allow or oblige authorities to initiate social assistance procedures on their own accord, without prior application.

1122. It is the responsibility of the authorities to investigate the relevant facts and circumstances of a case, a duty complemented by the applicant's full cooperation. As welfare benefits are granted based on need, the procedure as a whole is of highly individual and cooperative nature.

1123. Applicants are expected to grant the authorities access to various information and files such as their bank statements, payroll, tax assessments, tenancy agreement, medical certificates, insurance policies and obligations or claims against third parties. Where necessary, the authorities have the right to carry out an inspection or to seek expert assessments.

1124. Due to the nature of cooperative and need-based nature of social assistance procedures, the applicant's right to be heard is of crucial importance.

1125. Once the applicant's need and the extent of assistance have been determined by a social facility, the competent authority issues a decree (A.7, SKOS). Should the applicant disagree with the decision, he may request a written version of the decree including instructions on his right of appeal. The redress procedure follows cantonal law, though minimum standards set by federal law are applicable.

§6. Reclaiming of Benefits Paid

1126. The applicable cantonal law determines in which cases social assistance benefits are to be paid back, differentiating between benefits that were rightfully and wrongfully claimed. The cantons can also make exceptions on refund duties.

I. Rightfully Claimed Benefits

1127. Rightfully claimed benefits are expected to be paid back following a substantial change to a person's financial situation, e.g., due to large inheritance, winnings or income (E.3.1, SKOS). The directives of the SKOS advise against a refund of benefits based on later income as that would run counter to the primary goal of social assistance, the recovery of economic independence. Where a refund is designated by the cantonal law, the guidelines advise to set a generous income threshold and to limit the duration of the time span during which benefits are paid back. Benefits granted to further occupational and social integration are exempt from refunding.

1128. Social assistance also grants benefits for needs sufficiently covered by third parties (such as social insurers or those obligated to pay alimony) if the third-party benefits are not available in time (F.2, SKOS). Welfare benefits granted ahead of time have to be paid back after receiving the expected payout by the third party, provided that the benefits in question pertain to the same period of time.

II. Wrongfully Claimed Benefits

1129. Benefits are wrongfully claimed and must be refunded chiefly in the case that they were granted on the basis of false information or misused (E.3.2, SKOS). The former occurs when beneficiaries violate their duty to inform the authorities truthfully or neglect to report changes to their situation. In the case of misuse, benefits are used for something other than the specific purpose they were granted for (e.g., insurance premiums, rent), causing the same amount to be paid out again in order to avoid a possible financial emergency in the future.

1130. Depending on the canton, exceptions are possible if the beneficiary claimed benefits in good faith and a refund would cause great hardship.

Part XI. Claims and Adjudication

Introduction

1131. The purpose of procedural law is to implement material law. In 2003 the most important procedural rules were set forth in Articles 27–62 of the Federal Law on the General Section of Social Insurance Law (*Bundesgesetz über den Allgemeinen Teil des Sozialversicherungsrechts, ATSG*) and Articles 8–12a of the Ordinance on the General Section of Social Insurance Law (*Verordnung über den Allgemeinen Teil des Sozialversicherungsrechts, ATSV*).

1132. Furthermore, the regulations of the social insurance programmes contain additional procedural norms that are meant to supplement or replace those in the ATSG. If no relevant provision exists in either the ATSG or the applicable individual laws, the VwVG applies.

1133. An exception to this rule is procedure in the occupational pension system, the second pillar of old-age, survivors' and disability provision. Even if there are good arguments for applying parts of procedural law to the occupational pension funds, their procedures are structured differently in a number of key areas: as a rule, enforcement occurs through legal proceedings, not through administrative procedure. This is due to the fact that the law governing this second pillar is heavily influenced by private law, and the pension funds do not have the right to issue orders to insured people.

1134. The following chapter will confine itself to a description of the procedure governing individual social insurance benefits. Other disputes in the area of social security (e.g., disputes between health care providers and insurers in the health insurance system) follow other procedural rules and are subject to other appeal processes.

§1. Claims

I. Introduction of Claims

1135. Benefits from the social insurance programmes are subject to the principle of party disposition. The social insurers do not examine a person's eligibility for claims on their own initiative. This means that a person who wants to claim benefits from a social insurance programme must register with the responsible programme using the required form (Article 29, paragraph 1, ATSG).

1136. The insurers provide forms free of charge for this purpose. These must be filled out accurately and completely by both the claimant and, if necessary, his employer and/or doctor and then submitted to the insurer (Article 29, paragraph 2, ATSG).

1137. The ATSG does not stipulate whether certain deadlines must be met for registration. This issue is left to the applicable individual laws. If a claimant fails to submit the form properly or sends it to the wrong office, the point in time when the claimant posted the form or presented it to the wrong office provides a basis for deciding whether the deadline has been met and is also relevant to any legal effects of registration (Article 29, paragraph 3, ATSG).

1138. The ATSG contains various regulations on procedure in social insurance law:

- The obligation of the social insurance authorities to forward to the correct office any registrations, requests or other documents that have reached them by mistake (Article 30, ATSG).
- The obligation of the beneficiary, his family members and any third parties who receive benefits to report changes in their circumstances (Article 31, ATSG).
- Investigation of the facts of the case by the authorities ex officio (principle of judicial investigation; Article 43, paragraph 1, ATSG).
- The insured person's obligation to cooperate with investigations, to the extent that these investigations are necessary for evaluating the request and deemed reasonable (Article 28, ATSG).
- The insured person's right to be heard (Article 42, ATSG).
- The provision of free legal counsel if circumstances require (Article 37, paragraph 4, ATSG).
- Issuance of written order in the event of substantial benefits or claims or important instructions, or in the event that the person in question does not agree with a decision. The order must be explained and include information on the right to appeal (Article 49, ATSG).
- The possibility of a settlement, at least in court proceedings (Article 50, ATSG).
- An informal procedure if there is no need to issue an order (Article 51, ATSG).

1139. The claimant must make sure to claim outstanding benefits within five years after the end of the month for which the benefit is owed. After this period, the claim expires (Article 24, paragraph 1, ATSG).

1140. With respect to wrongfully received benefits, the claim for repayment expires one year after the insurer received knowledge of the wrongfully drawn benefit, or, at the latest, five years after the benefit was paid (Article 25, paragraph 2, ATSG).

1141. If the insured person fulfils his duty to cooperate, the social insurance programmes must pay interest on arrears for benefits. They are liable to do so twenty-four months after the emergence of the claim, or, at the earliest, twelve months after the claim is asserted (Article 26, paragraph 2, ATSG).

1142. A particularly important requirement is that both the insurers and the implementation bodies of the social insurance programmes brief and advise the population (Article 27, ATSG). In their respective areas of responsibility, they must inform interested parties of their rights and duties. In principle, everyone has a right to a free consultation. Fees can be charged only if they have been stipulated by the Federal Council and costly examinations are necessary. In terms of the principle of good faith, the social insurance authorities that provide advice are required to inform the insured people or their family members of any additional or more extensive benefits that they discover to exist.

1143. Article 32 of the ATSG describes the main points of administrative assistance. It states that, in response to a well-founded written request and free of charge, the administrative and judicial authorities of the federal government, cantons, districts and municipalities must in each individual case provide the bodies of the social insurance programmes with any data they require to perform the following tasks:

- Determine, modify or reclaim benefits.
- Prevent the unfounded receipt of benefits.
- Set contributions and define collecting rules.
- Seek recourse from liable third parties.

II. Protection against Pledge and Transfer

1144. Article 22 of the ATSG stipulates that claims to benefits cannot be transferred or pledged. Any transfer or pledge is invalid. The aim of this regulation is to protect the benefit itself.

1145. However, the payment of back social insurance benefits may be transferred:

- to an employer or a public or private welfare organization that has made advance payment;
- to an insurance provider that has provided benefits in advance.

1146. It must also be noted that Article 22 of the ATSG only addresses pledges under civil law. This article does not cover enforcement, which is regulated by individual laws and by debt collection and bankruptcy law.

1147. Under debt collection and bankruptcy law, a number of items cannot be pledged, including pensions from both the old-age and survivors' insurance programme (AHV) and the disability insurance programme (IV); supplementary benefits; family allowances; and claims to both pension benefits and vested benefits that are made against an occupational pension fund before they come due.

1148. By the same token, pensions, lump-sum settlements and other benefits that a debtor receives as compensation for physical injury, an impairment of his health or the homicide of a family member cannot be pledged if they serve as compensation or reimbursement for the costs of treatment or for the purchase of technical aids. However, if such benefits are intended to replace lost earned income, they are treated like a salary and can be pledged if debt collection officials judge them not to be absolutely necessary for the debtor and his family.

III. Legal Capacity to Receive Benefits

1149. The benefits to which insured people are entitled are essentially paid to them directly, but there are two exceptions:

1150. If the insured person's employer continues to pay his salary, despite his eligibility for a daily allowance, this daily allowance and similar compensation are paid to the employer on the same scale (Article 19, paragraph 2, ATSG).

1151. The benefit may be paid, not to the eligible person, but to a third party or a public authority if such an arrangement is meant to ensure that the benefit is used appropriately (Article 20, ATSG). The requirement for payment to a third party is that this third party or the public authority is legally or morally liable to support the insured person in question or provides care on a permanent basis. Furthermore, it is required that the eligible person does not use the payments for his own support or for the support of the people for whom he is required to provide, which is why he or the people whom he must support are dependent on the help of the public or private welfare organization. Exceptions can be found in the area of military insurance (Article 12, paragraph 2, MVG), in the benefits awarded for the loss of earned income on the part of service providers or in the case of maternity (Article 19, paragraph 1b, ATSG), and in family allowances (Article 9, FamZG) that do not require the recipient to be dependent on welfare.

1152. Child pensions from the AHV and IV are generally paid together with old-age and disability pensions. However, if the child's parents are not or are no longer married, or if they are separated, the child's pension can be paid to the parent who is ineligible for a pension if this parent assumes parental responsibility for and lives with the child (Article 22*ter*, paragraph 2, AHVG in conjunction with Article 71*ter*, AHVV).

1153. The education benefits stipulated in the FamZG can be paid directly to an adult child on the basis of a well-founded request (Article 9, paragraph 2, FamZG).

This mode of payment is deemed justified if there is a troubled relationship between the parents and the child or if the people who are required to support the child fail to do so.

§2. ADJUDICATION

1154. The appeal procedure is divided in two stages. If the claimant is not in agreement with an order from the social insurance provider and raises an objection, he first goes through an internal administrative procedure. If necessary, this is followed by external judicial proceedings.

I. Internal Administrative Procedure

1155. With the introduction of the ATSG in 2003, administrative procedure was uniformly defined for the social insurance programmes that declared the ATSG to be applicable.

1156. The insurance provider issues an order on any substantial benefits or claims or important instructions with which the person in question is not in agreement (Article 49, paragraph 1, ATSG). This order must be well founded and include information on the right to appeal (Article 49, paragraph 3, ATSG).

1157. The insured person may raise an objection to this order at the responsible office within thirty days (Article 52, paragraph 1, ATSG). The office processes the objection and must reach a well-founded decision in an appropriate time. The decision must include information on the right to appeal (Article 52, paragraph 2, ATSG). The objection procedure is free of charge, and attorney's fees are in principle not paid to the winning party (Article 52, paragraph 3, ATSG).

1158. There is an exception to the internal administrative procedure in the area of disability insurance. After the ATSG went into effect, the objection procedure was initially used in the area of disability insurance, but it was abolished in 2006 because of the large number of objections. The preliminary notice procedure practised until 2003 was reintroduced. The preliminary notice procedure is structured as follows: Before an order is issued, the disability insurance office sends a preliminary notice to the insured person to inform him of the planned final decision on his request for benefits or to give notice of the cancelling or reduction of previously awarded benefits (Article 57a, IVG). The insured person has a right to view the relevant files and raise objections at the disability insurance office within thirty days (Article 73*ter*; IVV). Afterward, the office issues the order on the request for benefits or the cancellation or reduction of previously awarded benefits. This final order cannot be objected. The preliminary notice procedure is intended to facilitate an uncomplicated discussion of the matter and to increase acceptance of the decision. At the same time, it gives the insured person the opportunity to be heard.

II. Judicial Procedure

1159. The insured person may lodge a complaint at the cantonal insurance court against a decision concerning an objection or against an order from the disability insurance programme (Articles 56 and 57, ATSG). The cantons are responsible for setting up these courts. Whereas some cantons have established special insurance courts, others have integrated them into the cantonal administrative courts. The insurance court is the only authority at the cantonal level that may rule on complaints in the area of social insurance.

1160. Complaints, which have a suspensive effect, must be filed within thirty days after the decision on the objection or after the order was received (Article 60, ATSG). Since the principle of judicial investigation holds, the court, with the help of the participating parties, is required to evaluate all the important facts and collect the necessary evidence. The court is not bound to the parties' requests but can modify the decision on the objection or the order in a way that is unfavourable for the complainant. However, it can also award more than has been requested. In either case, the court must give the parties the opportunity to express their views and withdraw the complaint beforehand. The winning party has the right to have its fees reimbursed. The proceedings, which are usually public, must be uncomplicated, quick and free of charge for both parties, though if one party conducts itself in a malicious or frivolous manner, judgment and court fees may be levied (cf. Article 61, ATSG). The IVG contains an exception to the rule of free proceedings. If the complaint proceedings address benefits from the disability insurance programme, the costs are set by the cantonal insurance court on the basis of the cost of the proceedings and independent of the claim's value. They range from CHF 200 to CHF 1,000 (Article 69, paragraph 1*bis*, IVG).

1161. As explained at the start of this chapter, the occupational pension system is subject to a different procedure. The pension funds may not issue orders – that is, the insured people must assert their claims through legal action. They must lodge their complaint with a court defined by cantonal law. This court is responsible for all claims against the pension fund, regardless of whether they concern mandatory benefits or those that go beyond the legally required minimum. As a rule, the same insurance court that rules on other disputes in social insurance law is also charged with handling complaints in the field of occupational pensions.

1162. In matters subject to public law, people may lodge a complaint with the Federal Supreme Court against the decision of a cantonal insurance court (Article 62, ATSG). The same holds true for complaints against decisions in the occupational pension system.

1163. As a rule, the complaint has no suspensive effect (Article 103 of the BGG). It must contain a request and explain why the claimant does not accept the disputed decision (*see* Article 42, BGG). In contrast to the cantonal insurance courts, the Federal Supreme Court is bound to the requests of the participating parties (Article 107, paragraph 1, BGG). Furthermore, proceedings before the Federal

Supreme Court are subject to a fee, unlike those at a cantonal level (*see* Articles 62 et seq., BGG). But due to the social component of the proceedings, legislators have created a framework with a low maximum fee. In the case of disputes over benefits, the court fee ranges from CHF 200 to CHF 1,000. This fee can be increased to a maximum of CHF 10,000 to reflect special circumstances. The claim's value does not play a role in setting the fee. The purpose of the fee is to induce the litigants to give careful consideration to lodging a complaint. The winning party is essentially entitled to have its legal fees reimbursed, but the social insurance programmes are excluded from this rule since public authorities and organizations that perform tasks under public law have no right to have their legal fees reimbursed.

Selected Bibliography

Legislation

Gächter, T. (ed.), Studienausgabe Sozialversicherungsrecht 2019, Gesetzesausgabe mit Verweisen und Anmerkungen, Zurich/Basel/Geneva: Schulthess, 7th ed., 2019.

Imhof, T. (ed.), Sozialversicherungsrecht. Gesetzgebung, Basel/Geneva/Munich: Helbing & Lichtenhahn, loose-leave.

Reviews of Court Decisions

Eugster, G., *Bundesgesetz über die Krankenversicherung (KVG)*, Zurich/Basel/Geneva: Schulthess, 2nd ed., 2018.

Kieser, U., *Bundesgesetz über die Alters- und Hinterlassenenversicherung (AHVG)*, Zurich/Basel/Geneva: Schulthess, 3rd ed., 2012.

Kupfer Bucher, B., *Bundesgesetz über die obligatorische Arbeitslosenversicherung und Insolvenzentschädigung (AVIG)*, Zurich/Basel/Geneva: Schulthess, 5th ed., 2019.

Meyer, U./Reichmuth, M., *Bundesgesetz über die Invalidenversicherung (IVG)*, Zurich/Basel/Geneva: Schulthess, 3rd ed., 2014.

Müller, U., *Bundesgesetz über Ergänzungsleistungen zur Alters-, Hinterlassenen- und Invalidenversicherung (ELG)*, Zurich/Basel/Geneva: Schulthess, 3rd ed., 2015.

Rumo-Jungo, A.,/Holzer, A.P., *Bundesgesetz über die Unfallversicherung (UVG)*, Zurich/Basel/Geneva: Schulthess, 4rd ed., 2012.

Stauffer, H.-U., *Die berufliche Vorsorge (BVG/FZG/ZGB/OR/FusG)*, Zurich/Basel/Geneva: Schulthess, 3rd ed., 2013.

Handbooks

Bollier, G.E., Leitfaden des Schweizerischen Sozialversicherungsrechts, Wädenswil: 15th ed., 2018.

Greber, P.-Y./Kahil Wolff, B./Frésard-Fellay, G./Molo, R., Droit suisse de la sécurité social, Volume I, Bern: Staempfli, 2010.

Kieser, U., Sozialversicherungsrecht in a nutshell, Zurich/St. Gallen: Dike, 4th ed., 2017.

Kieser, U., Schweizerisches Sozialversicherungsrecht, Zurich/St. Gallen: Dike, 2nd ed., 2017.

Selected Bibliography

Locher, T./Gächter, T., Grundriss des Sozialversicherungsrechts, Bern: Staempfli, 4th ed., 2014.

Maurer, A., Schweizerisches Sozialversicherungsrecht, Band I: Allgemeiner Teil, Bern: Staempfli, 2nd ed., 1983.

Meyer, U. (ed.), Soziale Sicherheit, in: Schweizerisches Bundesverwaltungsrecht, Basel/Geneva/Munich: Helbing & Lichtenhahn, 3rd ed., 2016.

Perrenoud, S./Kahil-Wolff, B./Frésard-Fellay, G., Droit suisse de la sécurité social, Volume I, Bern: Staempfli, 2015.

Riemer-Kafka, G., Schweizerisches Sozialversicherungsrecht, Bern: Staempfli, 6th ed., 2018.

Scartazzini, G./Hürzeler, M., Bundessozialversicherungsrecht, Basel/Geneva/Munich: Helbing & Lichtenhahn, 5th ed., 2012.

Widmer, D., Die Sozialversicherung in der Schweiz, Zurich: Schulthess, 11th ed., 2017.

Commentaries

Dupont, A.S./Moser-Szeless, M., *Loi sur la partie générale des assurances sociales (LPGA)*, Basel: Helbing & Lichtenhahn, 2018.

Fuchs, M. (ed.), *Kommentar zum Europäischen Sozialrecht,* Baden-Baden: Nomos, 7th ed., 2017.

Gerhards, G., *Kommentar zum Arbeitslosenversicherungsgesetz, Vol. I (Art. 1–58), Vol. II (Art. 59–121),* Bern: Haupt, 1987; *Vol. III (Teilrevision 1990 und Regesten des EVG 1987–1992),* Bern: Haupt, 1993.

Greber, P.-Y./Duc, J.-L./Scartazzini, G., *Commentaire des articles 1 à 16 de la loi fédérale sur l'assurance-vieillesse et survivants (LAVS)*, Basel/Frankfurt a.M.: Helbing & Lichtenhahn, 1997.

Hürzeler, M./Kieser, U., *Kommentar zum Unfallversicherungsgesetz (UVG)*, Bern: Staempfli, 2018.

Kieser, U., *ATSG-Kommentar*, Zurich/Basel/Geneva: Schulthess, 3rd ed., 2009.

Kieser, U./Reichmuth, M., *Bundesgesetz über die Familienzulagen*, Zurich/St. Gallen: Dike, 2010.

Maeschi, J., *Kommentar zum Bundesgesetz über die Militärversicherung (MVG) vom 19. Juni 1992*, Bern: Staempfli, 2000.

Rubin, B., *Commentaire de la loi sur l'assurance-chômage*, Zurich: Schulthess, 2014.

Schneider, J.-A./Geiser, T,/Gächter, T. (ed.), *Kommentar BVG/FZG*, Bern: Staempfli, 2nd ed., 2019.

Valterio, M., *Commentaire de la loi fédérale sur les prestations complémentaires à l'AVS / AI (LPC)*, Zurich: Schulthess, 2015.

Monographs

Bucher, S., Eingliederungsrecht der Invalidenversicherung, Bern: Staempfli, 2011.

Müller, U., Das Verwaltungsverfahren in der Invalidenversicherung, Bern: Staempfli, 2010.

Schaer, R., Grundzüge des Zusammenwirkens von Schadenausgleichsystemen, Basel/Frankfurt a.M.: Helbing & Lichtenhahn, 1984.

Stauffer, H.-U., Berufliche Vorsorge, Zurich/Basel/Geneva: Schulthess, 2nd ed., 2012.

Periodicals

Cahiers genevoises et romands de sécurité sociale, Geneva: University of Geneva (until 2016).
Haftpflicht und Versicherung, Zurich/Basel/Geneva: Schulthess.
Pflegerecht, Bern: Staempfli.
Schweizerische Zeitschrift für Sozialversicherung und berufliche Vorsorge, Bern: Staempfli.

Selected Bibliography

Index

The numbers here refer to paragraph numbers.

Index

Index

Made in the USA
Monee, IL
18 October 2026

66037597R10155